Parenting with Dignity

The Early Years

TEACH KIDS TO

LAUGH?

Mac Bl—

The ideas in our heads
do rule our worlds—
Barbara Bledsoe

Parenting with Dignity

Dignity

The Early Years

Mac Bledsoe

ALPHA

A member of Penguin Group (USA) Inc.

ALPHA BOOKS

Published by the Penguin Group

Penguin Group (USA) Inc., 375 Hudson Street, New York, New York 10014, U.S.A.

Penguin Group (Canada), 10 Alcorn Avenue, Toronto, Ontario, Canada M4V 3B2 (a division of Pearson Penguin Canada Inc.)

Penguin Books Ltd, 80 Strand, London WC2R 0RL, England

Penguin Ireland, 25 St Stephen's Green, Dublin 2, Ireland (a division of Penguin Books Ltd)

Penguin Group (Australia), 250 Camberwell Road, Camberwell, Victoria 3124, Australia (a division of Pearson Australia Group Pty Ltd)

Penguin Books India Pvt Ltd, 11 Community Centre, Panchsheel Park, New Delhi—110 017, India

Penguin Group (NZ), cnr Airborne and Rosedale Roads, Albany, Auckland 1310, New Zealand (a division of Pearson New Zealand Ltd)

Penguin Books (South Africa) (Pty) Ltd, 24 Sturdee Avenue, Rosebank, Johannesburg 2196, South Africa

Penguin Books Ltd, Registered Offices: 80 Strand, London WC2R 0RL, England

International Standard Book Number: 1-59257-291-X
Library of Congress Catalog Card Number: 2004113215

06   05   04   8   7   6   5   4   3   2   1

Interpretation of the printing code: The rightmost number of the first series of numbers is the year of the book's printing; the rightmost number of the second series of numbers is the number of the book's printing. For example, a printing code of 04-1 shows that the first printing occurred in 2004.

Printed in the United States of America

Note: This publication contains the opinions and ideas of its author. It is intended to provide helpful and informative material on the subject matter covered. It is sold with the understanding that the author and publisher are not engaged in rendering professional services in the book. If the reader requires personal assistance or advice, a competent professional should be consulted.

The author and publisher specifically disclaim any responsibility for any liability, loss, or risk, personal or otherwise, which is incurred as a consequence, directly or indirectly, of the use and application of any of the contents of this book.

Most Alpha books are available at special quantity discounts for bulk purchases for sales promotions, premiums, fund-raising, or educational use. Special books, or book excerpts, can also be created to fit specific needs.

For details, write: Special Markets, Alpha Books, 375 Hudson Street, New York, NY 10014.

Contents at a Glance

Foreword

My Bledsoe family shares a common belief that the ills plaguing our nation and specifically our young people should be and can be cured at home by parents armed with effective parenting tools. Because I saw firsthand the effectiveness of the commonsense parent education curriculum my parents created through their experience as public school teachers and as parents, I decided to throw the spotlight the NFL affords me into supporting this curriculum, Parenting with Dignity.

I feel blessed and fortunate to have been given some natural abilities that allow me to play football, a game I truly enjoy. I was further blessed with two wise and loving parents and a family environment that provided me with strong basic values and a support system where I could grow, develop, and pursue my goals with their full support and unconditional love. When I entered the NFL, I was asked for money and for my time and I was happy to contribute, especially when making the world a better place for kids. After three years, though, I decided I wanted to dedicate myself to something I believed in with all my heart. What I believed with all my heart was that my parents had some commonsense information that could give parents tools to teach their children how to make good decisions. The outgrowth of these tools is that parents have a plan for how they will parent and what they will teach, rather than parent in the "crisis management" mode.

Parenting with Dignity is the curriculum developed by my parents, which is now available as a 9-week course on videotape or DVD with the further enhancement of a Spanish translation option. Now this book, *Parenting with Dignity: The Early Years*, makes the same curriculum more specific to the world of young children.

This curriculum is based on two simple premises: 1) your children will make *all* of their big decisions, not some, but all of them, and you will not be present, therefore 2) the way to help ensure good decisions is to teach that child how to make decisions based on your own family values and beliefs, and in most cases by anticipating the decisions that they will face and teaching them *before* they face the decision.

Once this initial curriculum was fully up and running, my life changed. My wife Maura and I became the parents of four children under the age of 6! It is interesting for me to note that in 16 years of formal schooling, I was taught not one thing about the most important job any of us will ever undertake—being an effective parent. Nowhere in school was I prepared for the most intimidating experience of my life—the 20-minute ride home from the hospital with my wife and our first son. After taking that trip four times, Maura and I encouraged my dad to write another book, this time aimed at life with toddlers. The Five Rules for Parents still guide our interactions with our children, but with this book filled with advice for those parenting toddlers, our tool chest of information to use in being more effective parents has been filled with many specific ideas about potty training, sibling rivalry, manners, and the whole gamut of Life With A Toddler. With the support of our families, their strong basic values, their unconditional love, and the Parenting with Dignity principles, we are teaching our children how to make decisions and determine their behavior in their interactions with us as a family and with the growing world outside the boundaries of our own house.

I invite and encourage you to learn and use the commonsense tools in this book to create a home filled with dignity, love, and children who know how to make good decisions.

I give you my sincere appreciation for your endeavor to be effective, dignified parents of small-size people.

Drew Bledsoe

Introduction

Set Yourself Free From Crisis Management

I detest the term "Terrible Twos." This book aims to eradicate the idea that raising kids who are near the age of two is somehow difficult or torturous. Those developmental years constitute the most exciting period in the lives of young children, and it's a real fallacy to view them as terrible. Join me in this book as I erase forever any frustration you might feel in raising kids under school age. Hopefully, you will begin to experience the unparalleled joy of watching your toddlers discover their amazing identity in this big, wonderful world!

Ever since my wife and I began developing our Parenting with Dignity curriculum, we have confronted the frustrations of new parents of all ages raising young children. When we started out, we were convinced, like many others, that there was just a period in child development when children became contrary, defiant—in a word, difficult.

I operated from the mistaken assumption shared by almost everyone I met or read, that "It is just a stage that children go through." I know you've heard it. Your parents have probably told you stories about how you passed through this phase yourself. People will offer personal stories and anecdotes to support the idea that children go through a stage that is just unavoidable.

But hold onto your hats, because I'm here to tell you anyone telling you that is mistaken! As we worked with more and more parents and watched this phenomenon more carefully and intelligently, we discovered some families who had somehow been blessed with children who did not seem to fall into this dreaded "Terrible Twos" pattern. These parents just seemed to dodge the bullet and were able to negotiate this period causing other families so much stress without sharing the frustration. Their kids had been vaccinated against the "Terrible Twos"! Barbara and I discovered the problem was not the children or their developmental stage at all; the problem was the parents!

Lack of a Plan

As I observed children posing problems for their parents when their young personalities began to develop, it became increasingly obvious that the tail was wagging the dog—the parents were caught in a never-ending loop of crisis management, and the children's budding development was running the show. The more that I looked, the more I saw parents trying to raise their children without a plan!

To me, the problem isn't the "Terrible Twos," it's parenting without a plan! I saw that there was an obvious difference in the approach of those parents whose children seemed immune to the "Terrible Twos": *They all had a plan!* And they followed it!

Rather than *reacting* to a child who had just discovered that screaming in a restaurant could attract the attention of everyone in the place, they anticipated that the restaurant posed a new and threatening situation—and they prepared their children by outlining some desired behaviors *before* they got there.

These parents didn't wait for their children to throw a fit at bedtime. They realized that bedtime was an unwelcome interruption of their child's exciting day, though certainly a necessary one, so they laid out a plan for bedtime well ahead and gave their children an expectation of an equally exciting time that was approaching … bedtime!

The awakening of the young spirit in every child can be a time of great turmoil if the journey is unguided. I like to explain it like this. As a young child is developing, it's like they're moving into a wonderful new house. The house is huge, and every day brings the discovery of a new room or two. This can be frightening, especially if the rooms are dark and mysterious. But it can also be very exciting if each new room is viewed from outside with the lights on, and preceded by a little explanation.

Make no mistake; I am *not* saying that you should solve all problems for your children. I am saying that you must prepare your children for what is coming. Give them some idea of how to negotiate new situations.

As your child goes on his first visit to the grocery store, he is entering "a brand new room" with new furniture and tons of new things to see and touch. The *appropriate* behavior for this "new room" is not intuitive! The *intuitive* behavior is to run to the first brightly colored item within reach and grab it! Think about this for a minute. Your child goes into a grocery store unrestrained by a baby seat for the first time, and right there is a whole shelf full of candy bars! What do you think is going to happen? How silly is it for us to say the cause of this is the "Terrible Twos"? What happens is the result of a simple lack of advance planning and instruction on the part of the parents.

The vaccination for the "Terrible Twos" is planning and foresight! This book will challenge you to stop and think in *advance* of the situations you can very easily predict. This book will challenge you to develop a plan for your actions in guiding and teaching your children through the most exciting period in their lives!

I will grant you that it is difficult to anticipate every situation where your child will encounter something new, exciting, and tempting, but stop and think about it. Most situations that trigger "Terrible Two" behaviors are easy to predict. If you, as the parent, do just a little thinking ahead and prepare your children for just some of these situations, there will be a lot less turmoil and inappropriate behavior.

This book proposes five simple rules you can apply over and over in all kinds of situations. The rules are easily mastered and easily adapted to a wide variety of situations, but there is nothing magic about them. If one of them does not work for you, don't use it. However, if you choose to discard one of the rules, I challenge you to create one to replace it. Think! This book is really all about challenging you to think about what you're doing.

T-I-M-E

One other fallacy seems to accompany the fallacy of the "Terrible Twos," and that is the mistaken idea that there is a shortcut to teaching children. Many people hope that a parenting book will explain some magic and simple formula for teaching and managing children's behavior. There is no short cut! The techniques outlined in this book are going to involve an investment of your time. If you're not willing to spend T-I-M-E, then this book is not for you.

However, the investment of time you make today will decrease the amount of time—time yelling, time disciplining—you will have to spend in the future. Granted, for some behaviors you wait a long time to recoup the time you have spent.

It takes a lot more time to get ready to go to the grocery store if you have to plan and practice the appropriate behavior three times before you go. It may take six repetitions before your child masters it and is able to follow it without your careful guidance and patient reminding. But once she's mastered it, the effort will pay off with time saved on every trip to the grocery store!

Building the routine of anticipation and positive excitement for bedtime in a young child may take a while, but once the routine of excitement is established, the time gained back will far outweigh any investment in the beginning.

Like I said, there is no shortcut! If you have a behavior that you wish to teach your child, you must invest the time to teach it. There is no other way.

Attitude Shift

The attitude shift that must take place is not in your child, it's in you! To implement the techniques proposed in this book, you will have to begin to view yourself as a *teacher*, to view your job as a parent as that of the guide for life. You must become the calming influence in your children's lives, the one who always anticipates and understands the bumps in the road and calmly guides your children over them with reliably good advice and direction.

Develop this attitude about your role in your child's life: You do not build smooth roads, you teach them to negotiate rough terrain.

You must change from simply reacting to what your children do. You must become proactive. You must become the one with the plan. If you want your child to share toys, you must teach them how. If you want your children to know what behavior is acceptable in a restaurant, you must teach them. Children aren't born knowing how to eat a balanced diet! They can learn, but *you must be their teacher!* Not only must you teach the desired behavior, you must teach your children that their own world improves when they do as you say.

This is a radical attitude shift for many parents raised by parents who only reacted to them. The most common questions I receive from parents begin, "What do you do when...?" and my answer always begins, "Well, what did you teach them to do in that situation *before* they were actually in it?"

A mom writes, "What should I do when my son hits his brother?" If she always waits until her son hits, he is dictating the terms of the action. She is always caught in the mode of crisis manager and is rarely ever the teacher.

This book will attempt to teach you a new way of thinking that is no longer reactive. Think and anticipate, then develop a lesson plan.

In this book you will read letters from people just like you, facing problems you've either already encountered or can count on facing in the future. When you read their letters, try to visualize your own situation and think about the responses I give. Use the letters to anticipate situations and develop strategies before you confront problems.

Rule #5: Send a Message of Love

As you read this book I hope and pray that you do not just go to one problem, read for a solution to that problem, and stop there. I hope you will read the book from cover to cover! However, even if you don't, I have one suggestion before you begin. In every chapter I will suggest the application of one or more of our Five Rules for Parents. I will apply Rule #1 here, Rule #3 there, Rule #2 and Rule #4 there, and so on.

But Rule #5 should be applied in every situation. It's the most important rule. I may not mention it in every situation, as my assumption is that you will be applying it constantly as an everyday habit. You will be sending a message of love to each of your kids all day, every day.

Kids who are confident that they are loved unconditionally are ten times easier to teach! Children who know that they are loved are more easily convinced that your advice is given to help them. Children who are loved and know it can more readily accept new and strange situations. They can meet new challenges with excitement.

Use Rule #5 in almost every situation. Make desired behaviors into games. Write instructions down. (For children who cannot read, draw them.) Make the words, "I love you" a part of most instruction in some way. Let your children see the love in your eyes when you catch them mastering skills and behaviors.

What Do You Want?

It is my belief that it is *your* job to teach what you believe to your children. I believe that you have the obligation to decide what you believe and to teach that to your children. I try to avoid giving advice about *what* you should teach your children, and I try to stick to teaching you *how* to teach *whatever you want* to teach your children. This is not always possible, but I try. At times my feelings and values show; please ignore them if they conflict with yours. This book is not written to promote any moral, ethical, religious, political, or personal agenda.

The first step in any teaching process must be to answer the question, "What do I wish the end result to look like?" You must always decide and be able to articulate precisely what it is you are trying to do. You would never go to an airport and ask for a ticket without specifying a destination! As a matter of fact, you would probably never buy a ticket without asking for a time of departure and arrival!

Be just as demanding of yourself when you begin to teach your children. Decide precisely where it is you are going, when you are going to start, and when you expect to get there. Be flexible enough to adjust the itinerary for problems along the way, but be precise in your planning.

It is my hope that you will make very careful choices of what to teach your children. When you make those monumental decisions, I hope that you will turn to these pages for help in building the skills to teach what you have chosen to your children.

Laugh Every Day!

Finally, please enjoy this book! Don't take the job of parenting too seriously. It's the most important job you will ever have, but you must do it with a smile and a ready laugh—even if it means laughing out loud at yourself!

When I travel, I'm often asked to autograph books. I always write some short phrase or idea along with my name, and the saying I most often write is, "Teach your children to laugh by laughing with them *daily!*"

Please do that. Make it a habit to laugh with your children at least ten times a day! Just let your hair down and laugh with your kids. If nothing else, you'll be a whole lot happier and your kids will see a happy parent every day. And along with that, your children will learn how to create their own happiness.

Happiness is an attitude you can choose! Your children need to know that, and it's your job to teach them. Actually, children are born knowing joy and laughter, but you still must keep that spirit alive. There's no better way to do it than to laugh with them.

Please enjoy this book. Laugh at it and learn from it!

Chapter 1

Five Rules for Parents

It's hard to start a car without the key. We need to discuss a couple of keys to our Parenting with Dignity curriculum before we can start with the task of dealing with situations specific to toddlers and preschoolers. The situations and concepts we discuss in this book are of little use without an understanding of our Parenting with Dignity philosophy. So here goes ...

It all starts with one basic concept:

The Ideas in Your Head Will Rule Your World

It does not matter where the ideas come from, and it doesn't matter whether they are right or wrong, once an idea is in your head, it will rule your world.

Only a few months ago I gave a keynote address to 3,000 people at a regional parenting conference. In the talk, I mentioned the difficulties parents face with their children abusing drugs. During the question-and-answer period following my talk, a clergyman stood and offered, "I think we need to decriminalize drugs because drug use is a victimless crime." He was offering this as a counterpoint to my comments in my address about how damaging drugs are to American youth.

My first reaction to this man's comment was sheer astonishment. I couldn't believe this man was willing to stand in front of all these people and say that! Then I realized that he had an idea that was ruling his world. Not only did I disagree with him, but I also have a very different idea that rules my world.

I replied, "I disagree! I do not believe that drug use is a victimless crime! In my 29 years of teaching, 46 kids who sat in my classroom are now dead."

Continuing to address the fellow, I said, "Now, sir, please listen carefully to how those 46 young people died. Three of them died of causes that might not have been preventable. One boy died of a disease; one girl died when a car airbag exploded in her face during a slow-moving accident in a parking lot; and the third died in a private airplane crash while flying with his father.

"But, sir, hold onto your seat and ask yourself if you still can consider drug use a victimless crime when I tell you that *the other 43 kids were either stoned, high, or drunk at the time that they died!* Those kids were all victims of drug use! And that figure is just the tip of the iceberg. Every member of those kids' families, their friends, their teachers, their coaches, their pastors, and the other people who loved them were hurt by their drug use and were all victims, too!"

That clergyman had an idea that was ruling his world: He was willing to stake his personal reputation in front of 3,000 people on the idea that illicit drug use is victimless. *That idea was ruling his world!* It did not matter to him what I had just said. The idea in his head was so powerful that he did not even listen to what I said, instead choosing to form a smart retort. I don't know where his idea came from and I am pretty sure his idea is wrong, but nonetheless, it is ruling his world.

Ideas are powerful. They are more powerful than laws. We have laws against discrimination on the basis of race, gender, sexual orientation, and physical disabilities. However, we can still point to demographic evidence that discrimination still occurs—at work, in education, in health care, and in housing. Even though the 19th Amendment was added to the Constitution of the United States of America in 1920 to give women the right to vote, we still have discrimination against women in the workforce, in hiring practices, and in unequal pay for equal jobs. These negative, prejudicial ideas are more powerful than the law!

Ideas have such control over our thoughts and actions that we can't even see some of the most damaging of them. I often hear people say, "I don't have time to do that!" or "I will do it as soon as I find more time!" The truth is that T-I-M-E is the great equalizer of all mankind. A rich man cannot buy more, a wise man cannot invent more, and a lazy bum cannot waste more than 24 hours in a day!

The truth is that we all have just 24 hours to do what we believe is most important, but most people still cling to the idea that they will somehow find more! People can and do use their time on what they choose, but nobody has ever found extra time. Despite the fact that spare time can never be found, people still cling to the idea that they will do something when they find the time! I'm even more shocked when I ask those time-starved people how many hours they watch television. They are too busy to play with their children, but they find time to watch 15 hours of television each week.

Until Columbus came along, people believed the earth was flat. And we still celebrate Columbus Day, marking the day when that great visionary "discovered" America. Does it not strike you as odd that we still teach kids that Columbus *discovered* America when there were very civilized people there to meet his boat? That idea still rules our world even though we know the truth!

Your kids can get equally powerful ideas in their heads about their world and their actions. They have ideas that rule their worlds just like we do. Often they can't even put those ideas into words yet, but they use them regularly to get what they want. They use the ideas to govern their actions. Do any of these ideas sound familiar?

If I cry and throw a fit, somebody will meet my needs.

If I need to eat, all I need to do is scream!

If I want a toy another kid is playing with, all I have to do is hit and grab!

Wow, wouldn't it be neat if our toddlers expressed the need for food by doing something less irritating, something other than crying? If we let a child randomly go through their natural assortment of actions (crying, waving arms, making faces, kicking their feet) and reward the most annoying behaviors with food or attention, we have taught them an idea that will rule their world. They couldn't put the idea in words, but nonetheless it does rule their world: Crying gets food! Screaming gets attention! We must acknowledge that the ideas in our kids' heads will rule their world because they are humans, too!

I am *not* saying that you should neglect your child when he or she cries. Rather, what I am saying is that, with a little thought, we can probably give a reasoned response to their crying and fussing in many situations and thus teach our toddler some other forms of expressing discomfort.

Many parents think that the best parent is the one who meets their child's every need. It is a fallacy that the best parents are the doting moms and dads who anticipate every situation that might make their child uncomfortable and remove the discomfort before the child runs into it. I am trying to teach you *how* to teach your children, from the earliest ages, to meet their own needs, solve their own problems, and make their own decisions, in acceptable and appropriate ways. It is possible to begin teaching your children these reasoning behaviors from the moment that they are born.

The Five Rules for Parents are aimed at teaching you how to teach children to think for themselves and solve many of their own problems rather than being just the "on-call problem solver" for children. Using these rules, you will create the idea in the child's head that she can participate successfully with her environment rather than being controlled by it. This may not seem to be much of a difference to you right now, but jump ahead a few years and the difference for your child will be monumental. The child who was raised by parents who solved every problem for her is now fourteen and out with some friends. "Mom and Dad Problem-Solvers" stayed home. Now the young lady is faced with a decision. She has no experience in decision-making and she has no ideas in her head about how to confront a problem and make a decision. A real problem rears its ugly head and the child makes a terrible decision.

On the other hand, take a look at a child raised by parents who allowed him to make decisions at an early age, giving him guidance in making decisions rather than making them all for him—in other words, planted some ideas in his head about how to make good decisions. This results in a much different picture. This child will most likely make a good decision in the same situation. He has been allowed to make decisions and has a head full of good ideas on making them.

So many parents are deluded into thinking that the ideas in their own heads will somehow protect their children. This is not true. Your children will only act on the ideas in their own heads! Your kids will make *all* the big decisions in their lives because, when those decisions are made, you will not be there to make the decision for them! The ideas that you have taught them will rule their world. The ideas you have taught them will be what they use to make those big decisions.

But I'm getting ahead of myself here. For now, just know Parenting with Dignity principle number one: *The ideas in your children's heads will rule their world*. If you're going to be successful in getting your toddler to behave in a desired manner, you must teach them *ideas* that will result in positive and desirable actions.

Five Rules for Parents

We started building Parenting with Dignity by developing Five Rules for Parents. Following our own guidance for teaching, these rules are *behaviorally* described actions that parents can use to implant desired

5

ideas in the heads of their children. As I've traveled the country in recent years, I have become even more committed to using these five simple rules. As a matter of fact, since writing my first book I've found that these rules are amazingly useful to parents of all ages with kids of all ages. Here is why these rules work.

The biggest mistake parents make in raising their children is that they try to do it without any plan. They are simply managing from crisis to crisis. What they are doing may not necessarily be wrong, but without a plan to their action, *the action is usually too late!* Most of the techniques I propose are intended to be used *before* there is a problem. If parents wait until a child has hit his sister to teach him how to get along, it may not be too late, but it is far more difficult to teach the desired behavior. If parents wait until they are in the grocery store and the kids are running around and grabbing toys and candy, it's more difficult and stressful to teach the appropriate behavior.

If we approach raising kids with no plan—if *crisis management* is our only plan—then we can find ourselves out-matched by a toddler. In both of the preceding cases, the idea behind the undesired behavior is already in place! The wiser plan would be to teach the kids the desired behavior *before* they hit their siblings or *before* they get to the grocery store!

The Five Rules are your positive plan of action for teaching ideas to kids *before* the problems crop up. With little ones, teaching desired behaviors in advance is going to require lots of foresight, role-playing, demonstrating, modeling, and practicing.

I also want to stress something very important: Your plan for the early years must include many nonverbal lessons. Most of what you teach a very young person will be nonverbal. They will watch you and others and imitate, trying out various behaviors and seeing what responses they get. Ideas can be conveyed without words. A very young child can watch another person hold a spoon and form an idea about how to hold and use a spoon without a word. As the child becomes increasingly verbal you'll be able to use more words, but you won't be able to completely rely upon them.

So let's take a look at the Five Rules and understand how they work. (You'll be repeatedly applying each of these rules to specific situations as you go through the rest of the book, so this section ought to become dog-eared from constant use!)

Rule 1: Tell Your Kids What You Want Them to *Do!*

Rule Number 1 is *End any criticism with a positive statement of expected behavior*, or, simply put: Tell your kids what you want them to do! I know, this sounds too simple. You're saying to yourself, "This fool thinks I can get my kids to do what I want just by *telling them?* I don't think so!"

Stay with me for just a little bit. This probably sounds so fundamental that you wonder why I would include it here. "Tell my kids what I want them to do? I do that all the time!" But experience has taught me that the more active your kids are (and the more you have), the greater are your chances of getting caught in the trap of telling your kids what *not* to do: *"Stop that! Don't hit! Quit yelling!"*

Before you can communicate to your children precisely what you want them to do, you must decide and be able to show and articulate, usually in more than one way, exactly what it is that you want them *to do*. You must explain the expected behavior in specific terms your child can understand. What does the behavior look like? Feel like? Sound like? Your toddler's vocabulary is developing rapidly but is by no means equal to yours, so this will take much thought. Remember, just because you said something does not mean your children heard it, understood it, and can translate what you said into productive action. You'll have to use some advanced acting and demonstration skills to communicate the desired behavior. Even verbal toddlers rarely can translate verbal instructions into actions.

For example, asking a two-year-old to hold onto your finger while going to the grocery store might not be effectively communicated with words. You might need to take the child's hand and wrap it around your finger to communicate that desired behavior. Then, as you enter the store, you might have to repeat it several times before it becomes a regular and practiced behavior. As we put this rule to work in specific situations described in this book, you will develop your skills at communicating desired ideas to your toddler to rule his world.

As you practice clarifying in your mind what behaviors you want from your toddler, you will get better at creating strategies for communicating them. It also helps if you have a sales pitch explaining why the desired behavior will bring about positive and rewarding outcomes for your child. I will outline suggestions for you as you read this book, but keep in mind that they are your kids. You know them, you love them, and most important, you know better than anyone what you want them to do. Develop your own ideas and techniques!

Look at what I'm saying from a kid's point of view. Let me try giving you a command to see what happens in your mind. My command is: *Do not kick elephants.* What did your mind do with that? It found the "not" in the sentence and crossed it out. And what are you picturing? *"Hmm, am I going to stand under the trunk or to the right of the tail to get a kick in?"* The thing is, it's impossible to picture *not kicking* an elephant without picturing *kicking an elephant!* Would you even have thought of kicking an elephant if I hadn't told you *not* to? Notice also that saying "Do not kick elephants" gives you no idea what I want you to do instead. Even if you obey, you still have received no *positive* direction!

Your kids are no different. When you tell kids, "Do not spill your milk," you have helped to create a possibility in their minds. Spilled milk! "How do I manage a glass full of liquids at a table?" These expectations are too vague and technical for the toddler mind. "What do you want, Dad?!"

Try something like this—and how you demonstrate it is much more important than the words. Sitting at the table next to your child, tell him, "When you have a cup without a lid, do this ...." Then, hold your cup in your hand with your arm straight in front of you, lean forward so your chest hits the table, set the glass on the table, and sit back in your chair. Demonstrate this action, then have the child do it three times.

Now give them the sales pitch: the reason behind the idea, showing how things will be better for the child if he or she does what you have said. *"If you put your glass there like we just practiced, you can wave your arms all around and you will still have milk in your glass!"*

We have watched this technique used with our grandchildren, and it is something to watch them all with their cups of juice, water, or milk at meals. All of the cups are placed an arm's reach away, and beverages are never spilled! An occasional reminder might be necessary, but there's no pushback or argument.

It does make sense to use cups with lids, at least until your kids are able to sit at the table with the rest of the family. Reserve teaching until it is really necessary. Cups with lids also make lots of sense when toddlers are drinking away from the table.

Many times it's so easy to do things for small children, rather than teach them how to do them, that we often miss opportunities to teach good problem-solving skills. Let's look at one more application of Rule #1 before we move on.

One simple but time-consuming task that jumps to mind is putting on shoes. It can be a big help to have little ones capable of putting on their own shoes. And they can do it! (I must note that children's shoes with Velcro fasteners are really cool. Kids can operate those with great success.)

A great time to start is when your children start walking. Like I said, I know it's much faster to just put the shoes on your children rather than wait for them to do it themselves, and when you're in a hurry it's fine to just put the shoes on and get going. But on days when you have time, let the child try doing it with some assistance.

Sit down on the floor and have one of your shoes there for demonstration purposes. Lay the shoes out in front of her. Show her how to hold the tongue in one hand and the heel of the shoe in the other, then put her toe in the shoe. Demonstrate this a few times with your shoe. Then help her get her shoe in her hands in the same manner. Guide her to put her foot in her shoe a couple of times, then leave her to try on her own. If she gets them on, great! If she doesn't, just let it go for another try later.

Always let your child try on her own, with no pressure from you and no timeframe for finishing. Keep repeating this process for days. One day your child will suddenly amaze you with her ability to get her shoes on herself! The minute she's successful in putting on her own shoes, make it part of her daily routine. Simply put her shoes there with her as she is getting dressed and leave her with the task. If she has shoes with laces, teach her to put the shoes on and then come to you to get them tied. Leave the tying for when you feel that her finger dexterity is advanced enough.

Once she learns to put on her own shoes, the time savings will begin to add up every day—and it *really* adds up when you have two or three children! The small amount of time you invest in teaching will pay off many times over.

Teach children to become self-sufficient as early as possible. Once you have this rule firmly in mind, you will find lots of applications for it. I will apply this rule to teaching your toddler what you *do* want in many more situations in this book. You will find it helpful in a wide variety of situations.

Rule 2: Criticize the Performance, Not the Person

Hey, I'm not delusional! I know there will be times when you couldn't have anticipated your toddler's actions. It is not even desirable to antic- ipate everything for your children. You won't be able to give guidance in every situation before they do something wrong. So when your tod- dler does something unacceptable and you have not given guidance ahead of time, naturally it may be necessary to criticize or correct his or her actions.

I am fully aware that sometimes you have to demand that a child stop doing something—especially if they're endangering themselves or another child. Just remember that telling them to stop doing something doesn't teach them anything other than to stop. It must remain just that ... *instruction to stop.*

When criticism becomes necessary, focus what you say on your toddler's actions, not on them. "Bad boy" and "bad girl" should be stricken from your vocabulary! That's not an idea you want to rule their worlds. Remember, you are trying to construct clear ideas in the child's mind about desired behaviors. Criticism of behavior doesn't mean they're a bad person; you're just criticizing the undesirable behavior. Word it that way. *"That is the wrong thing to do. You are a good kid and you are smart. Here is what you should do the next time."*

This seems like such a small distinction, but it is so critical to differentiate, with your words and actions, your children's behavior from their self-worth. I believe that parents' failure to make this distinction is the reason why the concept of self-esteem has been so misunderstood in recent years. People have confused self-esteem with performance; parents have been led to believe that scolding or correcting a child will damage the child's self-esteem.

Nothing could be further from the truth. Correction is necessary to guide and shape appropriate behavior, but it must be criticism of performance and not criticism of the person.

The distinction to be made here is that the kid's behavior need not establish self-worth. As a matter of fact, most of the time you can even give your child a compliment while you are correcting her behavior!

This sounds easy, but it takes great care and planning to do it. Plan ahead and practice focusing on the behavior to be corrected. Here is an example: Your toddler is crashing his toy trucks into each other so violently that you are worried he will ruin the trucks or hurt himself or another child. As you prepare to intervene, avoid the natural urge to scold him or take the trucks away. Instead say, "Billy, you are always so careful with your toys. Let's play with them the way you were yesterday. Remember when you were running them down the ramp you built with some books? Remember the way you were doing it?" (As you talk to him, reconstruct yesterday's play, calling to mind his positive image of himself.)

If the rough play continues, it may be best to simply remove the toys (or the kid) from the room. Those actions need no explanation. You are simply acting to see that nothing destructive or dangerous is taking place. There need be no comments about the action of the child. Your actions will speak louder than any words.

No matter what you do, don't be misguided into thinking that, by removing the toy, you've taught the child anything about your expectations for future behavior. All you've done is stop the undesired behavior for the moment. There's also no call for incriminating or negative statements about Billy! But you do still need to teach him the positive lesson of what you want him *to do*.

(Note also that, if Billy learns that the only time you sit and play trucks is when he crashes them, guess what? He'll keep crashing them to get your attention! Make sure you take time to sit and play trucks when he is trucking gently!)

Rather than saying, "You little brat, you make me so mad when you make messes!"—which might be the truth when your daughter pulls all the magazines off the table—say, "Sally, you're such a curious little lady, and I'm glad you want to read magazines, but you don't need to pull all the magazines off the table to see the one you want. Just do it like this …."

This may seem insignificant, but it really is an important distinction. With the first response, you plant in your daughter's head a very negative idea about herself. With the second response, you encourage your daughter to continue to be curious and give her an appropriate action to replace her previous action. Neither statement permits the messy behavior, but the latter gives positive instruction without making a negative comment about the child.

You will see many applications of this rule as we move on through the book.

Rule 3: Don't Assume They Learned It: *Repeat It!*

Repetition is fundamental to all learning. Rarely do we learn anything on first exposure, and our children are no different. Kids are people, too!

Also, when you teach desired behaviors, you are actually attempting to establish habits, and habits require repetition. Remember that when you set out to teach your child something, and accept that you will likely have to repeat it a couple times—maybe *many* times. *Keep the anger out!* So often I witness parents following this rule and repeating things to their children, but they become angry because they are repeating it. Accept repetition as a reality of learning and simply repeat things for your children.

If you have repeated or demonstrated something a number of times and your kids are still not doing it, then you need to find another way to say it. Take time to think before you begin attempting to teach your toddler something. Come up with at least three ways to say or show the same thing. With little ones, at least one and maybe all of the methods should *not* involve words!

Let's say you're teaching a little one to use a fork. You might first hold the fork yourself and demonstrate to the child how you hold it. Next, put the fork in the child's hand, actually shaping her hand into the right grip. Then you eat with your fork, and have your child take a bite using her fork. If she's having difficulty getting the right grip, simply put the fork and her hand back in the proper grip. (If you're keeping score, that would be *one* repetition!) This will probably go on for many meals and many days before she internalizes the desired behavior, but keep repeating the lesson until she masters it.

Try to avoid teaching a child something before she is ready for the lesson. It can be difficult to tell, but pay attention. Kids will begin to show by their actions when they are ready for certain lessons. Put a fork and spoon on her tray at dinnertime, then watch. When she starts to pick up the fork and play with it on the plate, she's most likely saying, "I'm ready to learn how to use this thing!"

Repetition is key in instilling appropriate behavior. Kids rarely master table manners in one showing! Be relentless and creative, and give them many opportunities to see and demonstrate the desired behavior. Play games that give repetitions. Set a small table and sit down together. Take turns asking for things and saying "please" and "thank you." Don't respond to requests that aren't preceded by "please!" Then do the same thing at dinnertime. Take turns asking for each food at dinner, rather than just loading up a plate.

While watching TV, point out people who are using "please" and "thank you" and people who are not! When a storybook has a passage about eating, insert "please" and "thank you" as you read. (You know, of course, that as a parent you have the divine right to alter and edit stories to fit the lessons you are currently teaching, right?)

Let your child hear you praising their new skills to a friend or family member. That is another repetition. Take them to a restaurant and, without the child hearing, ask the waiter to stop by and compliment the manners being demonstrated at your table. That is another repetition.

Of course, the strongest way to reinforce this behavior is to always respond immediately to any appropriate use of "please" and "thank you"! That's a powerful repetition that works!

Repeat and repeat an idea until it becomes an idea that rules your child's world. You will know the idea has been repeated often enough when the behavior has become as natural to your child as breathing and blinking!

Rule 4: What They Say to Themselves Is What Counts

Self-motivation is the only true motivation. No matter how much you would like to motivate and control your children, the controlling force in their lives will be what they tell themselves.

It doesn't matter what I say to you if you're repeating in your head, "Boy, he doesn't know what he's talking about." The controlling idea would be what you're thinking, not the validity of anything I was saying. Shoot, just listen to any heated discussion of politics between two opinionated adults. An argument by person A does not change person B's mind, because person B is not really listening. Person B is arguing in their head with what person A is saying. Kids are no different!

The techniques we use with our children must always be aimed at guiding our children to make their own positive statements to themselves. It isn't our words that direct their actions, it is their words.

Don't be mistaken. I'm not saying that you simply bombard your child with positives. That doesn't work! With toddlers it may seem harder to determine what they're saying to themselves, but it actually isn't. If you give a task to a toddler and he tries to do it and then quits, listen and watch. Whether he says to himself "I can" or "I can't," I guarantee one thing: he will be right! If you give your toddler a fork to use and he throws it down, he is telling you he doesn't think he can use it. It might be best to let it go for the moment, and then later get him to, say, use a little shovel in a sandbox. As he successfully manipulates the shovel, get a spoon for him to use in the sandbox in the same way. You won't have to say anything—he'll be saying it for himself with his actions: "I see how to use this thing! I'm doing it!" (He might not be using words, but the skill is nonetheless being stored as an "I can do this" statement.)

Help kids phrase "I can" statements. It may be annoying as the child grabs things away shouting, "Me do it!" But that *is* the goal! Let them try. It might be difficult to sit patiently and watch a child mess up some simple task you could have completed in half the time, but let them do it. Encourage them to take on tasks. Is your goal to do it for them forever, or for them to master skills for themselves? Celebrate their newly acquired skills!

Give a kid meaningful things to do around home and offer encouragement and feedback that affirms his belief in himself and his ability to take on tasks. *"Would you please help me set the table? Would you put one of these spoons on each placemat? Thank you!"* This isn't the time to correct the kid. Getting the spoon in the proper place can come later. *"Would you put this paper in the recycle bin. It is the red one. Would you please open the door for me so that I can take the suitcase to the car?"*

Rather than simply offering "Good job!" types of feedback, follow these requests with *self-reward* statements. By this I mean something like, "Doesn't it feel good to really help Mommy?" Better yet, ask her to tell you how she feels about helping.

That is the goal: getting the child to verbalize for herself the feeling of accomplishment in doing something significant. That then becomes a very good habit!

When your children master a task, ask them to tell you and others about their success. Guide them to share their *feelings* of accomplishment with you. This is almost as important as the actual accomplishment. Saying it *affirms* the accomplishment.

Be careful to model positive statements for them. Attempting to be modest, we adults often develop a habit of responding to a compliment with a negative or self-deprecating statement. When someone says, "Gee, you did a wonderful job speaking at the banquet last night," we seem compelled to say something like, "Oh, I thought that I sounded terrible," when what we should say is a simple, "Thank you!"

Kids pick up on that. I hear kids mimicking negative statements about themselves that they have heard adults use repeatedly. As a teacher, I felt like I always had to correct this self-deprecation by telling them, "That was a compliment. When someone offers you a compliment you should either say 'Thank you,' or, 'Thank you, would you say that again?'!"

Guide your children to affirm their own accomplishments with positive statements about themselves and their performance.

Rule 5: Send a Constant Message of *Love*

All humans learn to speak the language they are exposed to. That is key, because love is a language! If we wish to have our children speak the language of love, then we must make sure *we expose them to the language of love on a continuous basis.*

There are two important corollaries to sending a message of love to our kids:

First, love is not just something you say, it's something you *do*. You can fake that you care but you can't fake being there. To send a message of love to your children you must show up. Love is not a spectator sport. Our kids need to have love expressed to them daily. With the little ones, it's pretty simple. We need to hug them often. We need to get down on the floor with them and play with toys. We need to sit down and read with them on a regular basis. We need to go in and lie down with them occasionally at naptime. We *must not* allow ourselves to be too busy to spend *time* with them—lots of it.

Toddlers, especially, need actions more than words to give them a feeling of being loved and valued. I know the temptation, when they're playing quietly and nicely, to run into the kitchen or office to do something you need to do. But, sometimes, just put your work and chores aside and get down on the floor and join in. That action says loudly and clearly to your child, "You are important to me and I noticed you!" Find regular activities to do with your children. Make it a routine to get dressed together in the morning. The shared time says "I love you" better than any words ever could.

Listen carefully to your kids. Stop what you are doing, get down eye-to-eye, and just listen. First, you will hear some fun and funny things! Also, you will send a message to your child. Listening affirms that he is important to you and you love him! Think how much better you feel when your partner stops folding the laundry or mutes the TV to listen to you. Your children are no different.

The time kids most need to hear the message of love is the time you feel least able to say it. When you're stressed to the point of sending your child out to live in the street, that's probably the time when their heart is most open to receive your message.

Now here are ten simple ways to communicate love to your children. These are simple and involve action on your part. They will take some time, but they are very workable.

Kids spell love T-I-M-E! Parents must give freely and lovingly of their time.

Say It

Kids must hear us say "I love you" to them! It should be the first thing they hear every morning and the last thing they hear every night. They should hear it in the middle or at the end of arguments, on the phone, and at unexpected times. No matter what, you must say the words, "I love you!" If you don't say the words, it's likely that all your other attempts at expressing love will fail. Without the words, your kids just might miss the message completely!

I was 36 years old before I heard my dad say the words "I love you" to me. He was a loving man and he had expressed his love to me in many ways, but he had not said the words. From that I had gotten the mistaken idea that my dad did not love me. I respected him, it was important to me to please him, I looked up to him and admired him as much as any man I had ever known, but I just wasn't sure that he loved me.

This is not a risk we can take. We cannot risk any misunderstanding when it comes to love: We must say the words! Once we have done that, we can focus on the other ways to communicate our love to our children. If we fail to tell them regularly that we unconditionally love them, they may miss the message when we send it in other important ways. If we say it first, they will understand that the other messages we send—concerns, expectations, disappointments—are also messages of love. My dad told me that he loved me in every other way, but because he did not say the words, I missed the message.

Make sure that your children get the message daily. Start saying the words before they can understand them and never stop!

Write It

Writing is a magical form of human communication. There are a number of tangible reasons that writing is a wonderful, unique, and effective method of communicating.

First, what you write to someone is more permanent. It delivers your message today, tomorrow, next year, even 10 years from now. If you write something to someone, it will last as long as they keep it. If you would like to have a degree of immortality with your children and with future generations, just write to your kids. It doesn't have to be mushy or lovey-dovey. Write often, write from the heart, and be sure to touch on many subjects. Write about your kids and write to them.

Many might think I'm crazy for even talking about writing to toddlers who cannot yet read, but I'm not. Put down your thoughts to your children in writing daily. It will be a wonderful journal for them to read someday. My wife, Barbara, started writing to our children the day each one came home from the hospital, and she has kept it up. She has written down their actions and antics. She has written what she was attempting to teach them at various stages in their development, and she has written down her feelings at important times like first birthdays and first steps. Those are very important moments to save, and written words are really different from pictures. Sometimes she would read her words to our children just like they were bedtime stories. The kids loved to hear her read her observations about them!

Some very important things happen when you write to your kids. Writing says you thought about your kids while you were not with them. Do you think about *un*-important people when they are not around? Writing says that you think about your kids often. Write them often, even if it's brief and spontaneous. Many times the best form of writing is on pieces of paper that tell your kids where you were when you wrote. Write on pieces of paper from work. Write on office stationary, write on envelopes, write on the back of discarded invoices!

Write letters to your children and mail them to them. Let them go to the mailbox and find a letter from you with a postmark on it. When they open the letter, read your words to them. Sure, they live in your house, but a letter is unique and important. It will get their attention in a way that a talk in the kitchen simply won't! A letter says, "This is something that I want you to know with some formality." Save those letters for them to read when they get older.

When you write, you can word your thoughts and ideas very carefully and precisely. Everyone has had the experience of saying something in the heat of the moment that they didn't really mean. Writing prevents that; when you write, you can get it just right. One of the most loving things parents can do for their children is to write to them about what they believe: about honesty, integrity, compassion, courage, love, family, and so on. Write about what your family means to you. Write down bits of wisdom and advice about various aspects of life, to help your kids make big decisions. They may not have a use for the advice right now, but someday they will, and they can turn to it when they need it. Write about things that are important to you, like ethical and moral issues that you feel are important, or values and spiritual issues that are close to your heart. Write down your precise spiritual beliefs. Write about your beliefs about freedom, America, and democracy. Don't write as if you are telling your kids what to think. Tell your kids that these are important ideas to you, and that you simply want them to know what you think about them. Give those writings to your kids on a regular basis. Read them aloud and then let your kids see that you are saving them in an important place. Don't be surprised if your children request that you read from "Their Book" occasionally at bedtime.

When you write to your kids, it becomes permanent. It says the same thing today that it says tomorrow, next week, next year, and 10 years from now—as long as the writing is kept! We can ensure that our kids keep the writing we give them by showing them what we do with things that have been written to us. Let them see that when we receive special cards, we keep them in a special place. Let them see that we occasionally go back to those cards and read them. Help them select a place where they can keep special written messages—a locking box, leather-bound notebook, or scrapbook. Show them how to keep the important things that have been written to them over the years. Model it for them! Save the important things that have been written to you and let them see that you keep what they write to you.

If you have written to your children about important ideas over an extended period of time, your ideas will have a much greater chance of becoming the ideas that rule the world of your kids. Another advantage of writing to your children in the early years will be having something to turn to yourself when your children reach the teen years and begin to develop independence and naturally begin to challenge you. Many parents find these years painful, but parents who have written down some of the fond memories find them helpful in maintaining perspective later on.

Write to your kids! Write often, write well, write from the heart—just write.

Make It

Making something for a child is a great way to show her you love her. Make doll clothes or toy cars for your little ones. Dads can make stuff for dolls and moms can make stuff for cars. It doesn't have to be something huge or complicated. Making simple things is often the best way to communicate your love!

If your young one has had a particularly disappointing day, make his favorite meal. So often we get things backwards, and only make their favorite meal on kids' birthdays, or when something great happens, but we forget to offer rewards and encouragement when things aren't going so well. Making a favorite meal is proof positive that you're on their side, and available to help. It just might be the confirmation of love that the child needs!

You can also make tapes or CDs for them. When they're little ones, we can read their storybooks onto audiotapes for them to listen to while traveling or as they play in their rooms. (Barbara even put our kids into some of the stories.) We can sing songs onto tape for them. We can record them simply talking while they're young, then let them listen to their own words a few years later, to show them how much they have grown, matured, and changed.

Videotape works great for this, too. Make videos of them playing or talking, then watch them together as they grow. Have a tape or CD playing in the background while you're taping, to remind them of their past tastes in music. You might even use this as a way to influence their taste in music, by pairing music you might choose for them with pleasant experiences on video that they'll play over and over. Who knows? When they become teens, they may already have a taste for positive music!

You can also make tapes or CDs of music for them to listen to while playing. We hear from so many parents expressing frustration about the quality of music available for children. With just a little bit of effort, parents can influence the music our kids listen to by recording music that our kids like and that meets our own standards. Listen to your recordings in the car or during playtime in the house or the yard.

Another key to making things as an act of love for our kids lies in making things with them. When they're young, we can make cakes with them, or make cards with them. As they grow older, the things we make can suit their age and interests. Collections can work in the same way. Collecting trading cards or little cars can allow a mom to have an interaction with a young boy whose interests are in sports or cars without Mom having to play the game or get dirty working on motors. Parents can interact with their kids by adding to the collection and finding ways to store and categorize the items. Pay attention to your child's interests and let that guide what you collect. (Beware of collections driven by television. Those are often artificially created interests, and the collections are very limited and manipulate your kids for financial gain.)

As you're making things with your children and for your children, always be watchful for opportunities to build relationships around the things that you build.

Play It

Seek opportunities to play with your children. This is critical during the early years. Develop a habit of playing with your toddlers and it will be a lifetime relationship.

That is what people do when they love each other: They play! All too often we find parents who take the job of parenting too seriously. They seem to think that every conversation or activity has to be loaded with guidance and advice. That's not true. Play and laughter is a great way to build a relationship with a child. It's also a great way to extend your own childhood! Let your hair down and play with your kids, if for no other reason than to have some fun.

My gosh, sometimes dinner can wait—especially if it's snowing! In the life of a three-year-old, snow is brand new! You'll find it's fun for parents, too. Turn off the stove and go make a snowman! Dinner can wait. As a matter of fact, a late dinner might also be fun for the whole family. Eat by candlelight in front of the fire after coming in from building snowmen.

Don't wait until your kids say that there is nothing to do in your hometown and then try to argue with them ... you will lose that argument. Just have an activity planned for your family every weekend. Go on a picnic. Play a game in the yard. Play simple card games before dinner. Play Chutes and Ladders or Go Fish and keep score over weeks and months. Play for a penny a point or a dime a game. It will be a reason to continue playing. (You can even lose on purpose to bait the game into "extra innings.") Play tricks on your kids and let it be known that you are fair game for tricks as well. Put surprise toys in their shoes, put blocks of wood in their sandwiches, and get ready for some fun tricks to be played on you. (It might be necessary to establish some rules and guidelines, though, so things don't get out of hand.) Don't be surprised if you try to get up from Thanksgiving dinner and find that someone has been under the table and tied your shoelaces together.

In all the shared laughter, you'll find you've established a relationship of joy and fun in your family. Play is magic for building lasting relationships. Remember that the people we laugh with are usually the people we seek out in times of difficulty. If you have built a tradition of laughter with your kids, they'll feel much more comfortable coming to you in times of need or trouble.

I sincerely believe that kids will be much more secure and capable of making big decisions for themselves if parents simply play more with their kids. If parents drove older cars, lived in smaller and less pretentious homes, had fewer fancy and expensive toys, and spent more time playing with their kids, kids would be more secure in their belief that they are important, valued people. If parents played more games with their kids, they might not find it so difficult to talk with their kids about important things, because they will have built comfortable relationships with their kids through years of play and laughter!

Play with your kids. It's an excuse to enjoy life and be young forever, and a chance to build a fun and lasting bond with your kids.

Look at Them

Let your children know that you love them by looking at them. Everyone knows the feeling of being spotted from across the room by someone who loves us. We all know the unspoken delight of catching someone looking at us and knowing that person loves us. Let your kids feel that glow of affection often.

Go to the school play or church Christmas pageant and let your child catch you looking at him while he stands to the side in a critical scene in which he has no speaking part. Let your child catch you watching her in the parade while everyone else is watching the float in front of the band. It will be clear proof to your children that you came to watch them—not the play or the parade!

Let your kids see themselves just the way that you see them. Take a video camera along and take pictures of them just the way you see them. Zoom in on your kid during the critical scene so all that can be seen is your child! That's the way you see him, so let him see it on the tape. Take pictures of your children when there is something exciting going on like the Fourth of July fireworks display. That will let them know that you are watching them with a love that transcends fireworks.

Remember also that the video camera has a microphone on it! Make some loving comments to your kids while shooting. It's like allowing your kids to overhear you saying nice things about them to others. The only thing to remember about your comments is that they're rather permanent and they will definitely be repeated. Be careful of what you say!

What you tell your kids by being there and watching them is, "No matter what is happening around you, I am watching you because I love you!"

Listen to Them

Stop what you are doing and listen to your children. Resist the urge to say it for them. Resist the urge to jump in and criticize or even formulate criticism in your head. Democracy teaches self-worth because one of the basic tenets of democracy is that everyone must participate for it to work! Another tenet of democracy is that every person must have the chance to be heard. Your children deserve to be heard. Our children cannot be heard if we are always talking! Push things aside and give your kids your undivided attention. Stop mixing ingredients in the kitchen. Turn off the TV. Put down the paper. Turn away from your desk, look them in the eye, and listen!

Parents are constantly telling us that their kids won't talk to them. In almost every case, the problem is not that the kids don't want to talk. The problem is that the parents don't often listen. Kids learn quickly, and all it takes to dry up conversation is a couple statements like, "Can't you see I'm busy?" or "Not now, I'm reading the paper." If you never listen to them, don't be surprised if in time your kids never talk to you. We've finally learned that listening is often all kids want from us. We started asking, "Do you want advice or do you just want me to listen?" Nine out of ten times, all they want is for us to listen.

As a schoolteacher, I did some of my best teaching between classes or during the quiet time in the mornings before school and in the afternoons after school. Kids would drop by to talk. Notice that I didn't say they stopped by to listen! That's a key distinction. I learned six very good "listening words" from a counselor and I used them at times like that: "Oh!" "Really!" "Wow!" "Ummm!" "I didn't know you felt like that!" and "Tell me more!" While the kids would talk, I would fill pauses in their talking with one of those six words or phrases. Those words and phrases let kids know that you hear what they're saying, and they are nonevaluative in nature. They encourage the speaker to continue, but they offer nothing approving or disapproving.

Very young children are just like my students were. They need to be listened to regularly. They will learn to work their own way through a problem by talking to you about it. Small children can be hard to listen to because they take a long time to form their ideas into words, but *give them time*. Your listening gives kids a chance to work out their decisions before they act. If they know you will listen, they can work their way through a tough decision by trying out their ideas on you first.

People who love you will listen to you. If you love someone you will listen to them, so listen to your children. You love them!

Touch Them

Sometimes a hug is the only way to reach another human being. Always have one available for your young kids. Little ones need to be hugged often. It will fix a world of hurt for them. Many times a pat on the back is worth a thousand words of praise. A pat on the back, an arm over the shoulder, or a hug can often be the only way to express love. Use them all. Walking by a youngster working on a drawing or playing independently with a toy and stopping just long enough to pat her on the head or on the back is often all the reward she'll need to keep on with the productive behavior. That touch of approval can convey so much, so take the time to reach out and do it.

Keep It Positive

Develop a habit of always having something good to say, so that your kids always hear you talking about what is right rather than what is wrong. Remember, the ideas in your kids' heads will rule their world. You may think you're talking about how things ought to be, but often the idea that kids pick up is that everything is wrong and nothing is right. If you spend time talking about what's wrong with the world, the "wrong" is winning! Talk about what is right!

That is how wrong ideas work. Somebody does something hurtful or hateful and then we read about it, talk about it, and the wrong idea begins to occupy our thinking. We must take control of that in our homes. We need to talk about good things and positive ideas! We shouldn't be surprised if our kids have a negative outlook on life if all they hear is their parents talking about how bad things are at work and how nobody ever does anything right. If you want your kids to have a positive outlook, you need to talk about good and uplifting things!

Make a bulletin board at your house dedicated to local heroes. Clip out articles from the paper about good things that are happening in town. Always have ideas for fun things to do on the calendar in the kitchen. Clip out articles about upcoming concerts and live theater, then go to them. With your young kids you might need to read the announcements to your children. Invite a local hero to dinner. Head on down to the skateboard park and watch the kids show their stuff. Join the walk for the food bank. Join a Habitat for Humanity building project and take your kids along. Clean out some closets for Goodwill. Take a meal over to a shut-in elderly couple and bring some joy into their life; let your three-year-old hand the dish to them. Take a Christmas dinner to a needy family during the week before Christmas and let your children sit down with them and share dinner.

The biggest tragedy in all of the negative stuff on TV is that it is the only voice in the room. Speak up about all of the good stuff that you see. Talk back to the TV. Turn it off and talk about something happy or uplifting.

If you want your kids to see the good side of human nature, you must show it to them! Let your kids see you giving an extra thank-you or an extra tip to an especially cheerful waitress or service technician at the auto shop. Write thank-you letters to unsung heroes in your community and ask your kids to sign them along with you. A scrawled signature of a three-year-old will give your letter more impact to the one receiving it, too!

Sound off to your kids about what you believe and why you believe it. Don't think that you can just sit back and wait for the world to bring a positive outlook to your door—the world won't do it. You must stand up and create their positive outlook for them.

Define It

Mom, Dad, home, family, friend, honesty, *love*. Your actions will define these and many more words in the lives of your toddlers. What are your actions saying? Your children's definition of "Mom" and "Dad" will forever and always be what you were and what you did. Ask yourself, "How do I want my kids to define family?" Then let your actions define it that way! Your kids won't remember much of what you say, but they will remember forever exactly how you acted!

Look at the word "family." What do you want the definition of "family" to be? Whatever happens in your home will forever be the definition of family for your kids. Are you living that definition? If not, your kids will have in their heads what you are living and not what you want them to have. If what happens in your house is arguing and shouting, then their definition of family will be just that! You cannot just harp on the negative things and expect your kids to place high value on family!

I suggest that every family sit down and write the definitions of some key words: family, mom, dad, honesty, togetherness, happiness, security, love, and so on. I have read definitions written by families in our parenting classes, and some of the most wonderful definitions were created by kids under five and then written down by the parents. "A family is a place where we all laugh and cry together." After you write the definitions, ask everyone, "How can we live out those definitions?"

Teach It

Give your children this list! With little ones you could make the list into pictures and tell them stories about each picture on the list. Actively teach them how to be loving to family, friends, grandparents, people less fortunate, their parents, or their pets! Continually look for opportunities to model love for your children.

Teach them that if they want to have a friend, they must be a friend. Start them off at age two telling their friends that they care for them (say it!). Help your kids make cards for each other; as they get older, have them write their own cards (write it!). Help kids develop habits of games and activities with other kids and grandparents (play it!). Help kids make things with other kids and make things for others (make it!). Teach children of all ages to ask questions—and then listen to the answers (listen to them!). Show your kids how to hug others at times of need or times of hurt (touch them!). Teach your children to speak up for good things that they see in others (keep it positive!). And finally, teach your children to teach others to do all of the above (teach it!).

Your children will lead very fulfilled and connected lives if they develop behaviors and habits that connect them to others in loving and caring ways. By teaching your children these steps, you will be preparing them for amazing happiness. If your children go out into the world able to care for and express themselves, they will live fulfilled and meaningful lives!

Chapter 2

Acting Out

"What do I do with my child who screams and cries about everything?"

Children try out their available behaviors and they'll repeat the ones that work; the ones that don't work will disappear. Sometimes they act out by screaming and crying. Sometimes they act out by ignoring you. Sometimes the acting out can be seen as they lash out at other children.

As I talk to parents nationwide, this is one of the most common questions or problems: kids who get angry, frustrated, rambunctious, jealous, tired, or otherwise agitated and then simply erupt in a fit of screaming, crying, stomping, hitting, breaking things, or all of the above. Others describe kids who seem to go into a shell and ignore everything their parents say. "I'm pulling my hair out ... I can't take any more of this. My child is Dr. Jeckyl and Mr. Hyde! Sometimes he can be so adorable and then there are times when I feel like we have a Tasmanian devil living with us!"

If you ever feel this way, this chapter will try to give you hope. First, if you are feeling this kind of frustration, let me put your mind at ease: *You are not alone!* If you also find that your child behaves mildly when others are around and erupts only when you are there, you have lots of company, and it is not time to give up!

First, let's examine some common dynamics of this prevalent problem.

Kids Use What Works!

When kids enter the world they have a limited repertoire of behaviors at their disposal for expressing themselves. A baby uses the most simple and natural human method of expressing discomfort, the most obvious is crying! It is a universal human response, and babies use it indiscriminately at first. They cry when they're tired. They cry when they're hungry. They cry when they have wet their britches. They cry when they have messed their pants. They cry when they're cold. They cry when they're hot. They cry when something hurts. They even cry when they need to be held or hugged. It's universal, and it almost always works!

As a matter of fact, most parents soon learn to recognize different cries for different causes. My wife Barbara's ability to recognize the cry of pain in one of our sons saved his life. She knew by the way that he was crying that he was not just wet, hungry, or needing comfort. He was in pain and his cry was as effective at communicating as the words "I am in dire, life-threatening pain!"

Kids Learn Even If You Do Not Intend to Teach Them!

As babies grow, they learn more and more about what works and what doesn't. They can't verbalize their thoughts, but rest assured they are learning. A certain action results in a predictable response. Just because you're not *consciously* teaching something to your children does not mean that no teaching is taking place. *Teaching something to a child does not require intent to teach on your part. You're teaching by your actions every minute you're with your kids!* If your child cries every time she's uncomfortable, and you pick her up every time she cries, that action is teaching your child to cry at the drop of a hat.

Don't misunderstand what I'm saying here. I'm not saying you should never comfort a crying baby. You *should* comfort crying babies! I'm saying you can learn to recognize there are different cries for different reasons. Learn to spot the differences and comfort the cries that need comforting, and try to anticipate cries of frustration and head them off by spotting the frustration and alleviating it. Teach your child more effective ways of communicating and dealing with problems they encounter.

Teach your child how to make decisions and solve problems by seeking help from you and other adults and other people like siblings. If a child is crying to get up on a chair, just lifting them onto the chair teaches a child that their cry got them onto the chair. Rather than solving the problem for the child, a better technique might be showing the child how to push a box over to the chair and climb on it, rather than just lifting the child. The idea is to teach the child to interact effectively with his or her environment rather than solving problems for them.

I believe that many parents are deceived into thinking that their role with children is to always provide comfort for the child, to always smooth the road. I think that the wise parent teaches the child how to negotiate steep and winding roads on their own! The wise parent is the one who is ready to comfort, encourage, and console a child, but at the same time encourages them to try again, perhaps in a different manner. The wise parent picks up a child who has fallen from a bicycle, dries her tears, and then puts her back on the bike with encouragement and a steadying hand to try again—with the handlebars firmly held in her own small hands!

When I was a young boy, my father was amazing at doing this with all four of us kids. He did not become annoyed with our mistakes. He just methodically showed us how to think in situations in the future. This process can begin with very young children. Cries of frustration should be met with methods for solving future problems rather than having problems solved by parents.

I watch our daughter-in-law, Maura, do this constantly with our grandchildren. She is so intuitive that she makes it look natural, but it is not. However, it can be learned rather easily. For example, the other day I watched her with one of our grandchildren who was having a problem eating with a spoon. The little guy was just beginning to use utensils and was ineffectively chasing peas around his tray and screaming with anger. Rather than reaching over and feeding him, she put his hand on the table and showed him how to load the peas by pushing the spoon and peas against his hand on the table. For the next ten or fifteen minutes, I watched him squeal with joy as he pushed peas across the tray into his hand and load them on his spoon.

The easy thing would have been to have fed him. Her method was to teach him to solve the problem himself. If she had simply comforted him by feeding him or by picking him up, she would have taught him that the way to solve eating problems was by crying!

As you will learn many times in this book, many things can be taught long before a level of frustration results in crying or other annoying and unacceptable, but natural, kinds of actions.

Consider this letter I found, attributed to an anonymous author. It's a message (written by a former child) that every adult should read, because children are watching you and doing as you do, not as you say!

When You Thought I Wasn't Looking ...

When you thought I wasn't looking, I saw you hang my first painting on the refrigerator and I immediately wanted to paint another one.

When you thought I wasn't looking, I saw you feed a stray cat, and I learned that it was good to be kind to animals.

When you thought I wasn't looking, I saw you make my favorite cake and I learned that the little things can be the special things in life.

When you thought I wasn't looking, I heard you say a prayer, and I knew there is a God I could always talk to and I learned to trust in God.

When you thought I wasn't looking, I saw you make a meal and take it to a friend who was sick, and I learned that we all have to help take care of each other.

When you thought I wasn't looking, I saw you give of your time and money to help people who had nothing and I learned that those who have something should give to those who don't.

When you thought I wasn't looking, I saw you take care of our house and everyone in it and I learned we have to take care of what we are given.

When you thought I wasn't looking, I saw how you handled your responsibilities, even when you didn't feel good and I learned that I would have to be responsible when I grow up.

When you thought I wasn't looking, I saw tears come from your eyes and I learned that sometimes things hurt, but it's alright to cry.

When you thought I wasn't looking, I saw that you cared and I wanted to be everything that I could be.

When you thought I wasn't looking, I learned most of life's lessons that I need to know to be a good and productive person when I grow up.

When you thought I wasn't looking, I looked at you and wanted to say, "Thanks for all the things I saw when you thought I wasn't looking."

Start a habit of displaying meaningful ways of reacting to the world and be ever mindful of the obligation to always teach to a higher level of action. Your young child will shape much of his behavior by watching and imitating you and your actions.

I wish that you could read the number of e-mails I answer daily to people who seem to have a higher standard for the behavior of their children than they do for themselves. People write about "extreme frustration" with a child's lack of patience. Well, my gosh, where do you think that the child learned to be impatient? From a frustrated parent? I think so.

Grandmothers have long told us that children learn behaviors from their mothers while they are still in the womb. I think that perhaps we should listen to them. We should model desired behaviors around children long before they are capable of verbalizing them or understanding our words.

Parents Can Teach Desired Behaviors to Very Young Kids!

If you never try to teach your kids other methods of expression, those instinctual methods will linger for a long time. Sure, many of the annoying behaviors will go away naturally, but an attentive parent can ease and speed the learning exponentially. Waiting for the cruel world to teach can be a very hit-or-miss proposition—and it often teaches lessons we would rather went unlearned.

If you notice your child getting frustrated with a toy (this is not hard to spot), rather than waiting and then comforting the frustrated, crying child, sit down with her and help her solve the problem with the toy. Your actions teach the child that she can look to you for assistance in solving a problem, which will lead to a feeling of mastery. More important, she has found a way to express that feeling other than crying. As your child becomes verbal, it is possible—and satisfying for both of you—to teach them that simple words like "Help!" and "please" work better than crying to get adult assistance.

Of course, none of this works if you're not *present* (there's that time issue again) and *attentive*, able to recognize the frustration before the crying erupts. In the long run, though, you will have taught the desired behavior and be free from years of tantrums and crying! Invest a little time and observation with a plan now and reap a lifetime of desirable behavior later! Or, let the crying appear, reward it, and watch the crying continue for years … your choice.

Let me point out that it's difficult to implement our program of face-to-face parenting if the bulk of your child's waking hours are spent in childcare. I am not attempting to lay a guilt trip on working parents here. I am simply laying out the very real factors you need to consider.

If you have deemed childcare a must, then you have the obligation to your children to select the childcare provider carefully to ensure they will be your partners in teaching your child. Spend careful time investigating providers and select one that does more than just keep the kids. Find one that is interested in helping you to teach appropriate behaviors.

When you're at home together, you must not spend your child's remaining waking hours doing other things. I feel strongly that you must spend your limited time together in close contact with your child.

I know these are strong words, and many parents will be arguing with me in their head at this point. I am bitterly aware that for many parents it is extremely difficult to make ends meet any other way, but I also know that children must be a priority if you are to raise them successfully. Think long and hard any time you find yourself saying, "I am doing this because I am too busy to spend time with my kids."

Now let's get specific with some actual examples from real parents with kids at various stages of development under age six. I hope you will find situations similar enough to some you are experiencing to give you some practical help.

(The situations throughout this book are real, related to me by parents either in person, on the phone, or via e-mail. This book is not a work of fiction!)

Kids Learn by Watching Us

Dear Mac,

My wife and I have two boys, almost six and barely three. Our oldest started school last August. We recently purchased your book after your appearance on the Today *show. We have read through the first three chapters over the past couple of weeks or so. There are so many things we, as parents, seem to be doing wrong. We have tried a couple of your suggestions and they seem to help.*

One thing that continues to be an issue is our oldest not listening. Sometimes it takes three and four times and the raising of the voice (okay, close to yelling) for our son to do what he is asked. It is hard to follow your suggestions when the "not listening" seems to equally set me and my wife off. We both grew up in very disciplined homes, yet neither one of us has ill feelings toward our parents. That harsh approach used on us does not sit well with us, but we feel that we are failing our son, because nothing else we are doing seems to work, either. We feel he lacks confidence and self-esteem because of us. He is a super-sweet boy with a huge heart and I want to be a better parent!

We will continue to read the book but in the meantime, help!

First of all, these parents are doing the right thing in beginning to read and search for skills that will help them be better parents. If you are doing likewise, keep it up—there is so much information out there to help you. Also, please consider getting together with other parents and going through a parenting curriculum together. Our Parenting with Dignity course on DVD or videotape would work well. Believe me, you will learn more from the other parents as you discuss common problems than you will learn from any curriculum.

But let's get down to the nuts and bolts of the situation they're in with their son.

I am going to say something that, at first, may seem to place the responsibility for change in the wrong place: on the parents rather than their inattentive son! But I sincerely hope you will see what I'm saying is accurate and will help their relationship.

I must suggest it might be a good idea to get your child's hearing tested to see if he can actually hear you. Here is a very practical hearing test. Sometime when you are giving him instructions to do something, instead of saying, "Son, will you please go and make your bed?" insert another phrase for your hearing test. Say (in a quiet voice), "Son, would you like a chocolate bar?" If he answers with an immediate "Oh boy! Yeah!" his hearing is probably okay. (Don't betray your child's trust: Have a small piece of chocolate for him if he does hear you!) If he ignores the offer of a chocolate bar just like he has been ignoring your commands, I recommend a professional hearing test administered by a trained pediatrician or health care professional at school.

These parents need to accept a simple fact: They have taught their son to *not listen!* That's right! *They* have *taught* their son to not listen. If he doesn't listen, and it works, then he will repeat that behavior. Like I said, teaching something does not require the intent to teach! Their actions have taught their son to ignore them until they shout. He has learned that if he ignores quietly spoken directions he can continue to play and get away with it. This kind of interaction can creep up on you without you even being aware of it.

They may not have set out to teach that ignoring behavior, but their actions taught it. He has learned a bad habit, but they can teach him a different one. They need to teach him that they mean what they say the first time they say it. They must teach him that a direction in a conversational tone is to be obeyed.

How do you do that? You give directions in a conversational tone of voice—and then see to it that they are followed! They say that they were both brought up in disciplined homes. I do not know exactly what they are referring to with this statement but I am going to assume that they mean that as they were growing up, punishment was used regularly. Well, I will not suggest that parents use punishment, but I will suggest that you *insist* that requests be followed.

Let me explain what has pretty obviously happened to these parents and their son. If you tell your child to go and pick up his toys and he doesn't do it and you let it go, he just learned something: He doesn't have to pick up his toys when you *quietly* say to do it! All he has to do is ignore you and life goes on, he can keep doing what he was doing. Now, consider the fact that he has lived six years of his life ignoring their quiet instructions, and it's not too hard to see why he *seems* to not listen to what they say. And if they generally repeat something three and four times with him not responding, then he's going to think, "This stalling works for me!" When they finally yell, he responds. He heard them all along, but he has learned that they don't really mean it until they shout.

By the way, it's highly unlikely that he does not listen or that he does not hear them. He does hear them! However, he has learned to simply *disregard* their early commands. He has learned to be a *selective listener*—just like his parents!

Oh, yes, we're all selective listeners. Let me demonstrate. Imagine that you are in a room full of people talking. Your mind is hearing almost everything in the room, but you've learned to filter out unimportant noise. You can carry on a conversation with all kinds of noise and conversation going on around you. However, to demonstrate that you truly were hearing everything being said but filtering out the unimportant, just imagine for a moment that if someone in the room says your name, that immediately gets through to your conscious brain, and you pay attention to what that person is saying to or about you. Psychologists even have a name for that very useful filter: they call that your Reticular Activating System.

To demonstrate that your Reticular Activating System is working right now, just be very quiet where you are sitting and listen. Invariably there is some noise to be heard wherever you are, but while you were reading, you did not consciously "hear" it because your Reticular Activating System filtered it out. However, the minute I asked you to listen, you started consciously "hearing" the background noise loud and clear. Psychologists will contend you were hearing everything all along, but experience has taught you how to ignore sounds that are not critical or important. Your child uses his Reticular Activating System to filter out your quiet directions. You simply need to retrain his filter to respond!

Parents' Action

Begin by telling your child that what you've been doing hasn't been working, and you, his parents, are going to do something different. You won't be yelling, but he *will* be responding to you. Explain the following procedure to him. And then do it.

From now on, when you ask your son to do something, take the time to stand directly in front of him and ask him to stop what he is doing and look at you. When you have his attention, explain, in a friendly but firm way precisely what you want him to do.

This doesn't ensure that he is actually listening. His Reticular Activating System can even filter you out while he is looking at you! It has been trained for six years to ignore directions that aren't yelled!

At this point, apply Parenting Rule #1: Describe the desired action in behavioral terms he can understand. Say, "I want you to listen to me carefully because I am going to ask you to repeat back to me what I want you to do." When you've explained what you want him to do, ask, "Okay, now what did I just ask you to do?"

You are applying Rule #3 here, ensuring an accurate repetition of your instructions. He must understand them to repeat them to you. You're also applying Rule #4: getting him to say this command for himself. This process of repeating your words back to you will ensure that he consciously and carefully listens, because now he has to repeat it! Odds are that the first time you do this, he may have difficulty telling you what you just asked him to do. After all, he's had all that experience tuning you out! If he can't repeat what you said, say, "Okay, listen one more time and this time I want you to be able to tell me what I asked you to do." Repeat the instructions. Ask him again to repeat them.

When he successfully repeats the instructions, calmly say, "Okay. Now, look at my face: I'm smiling, I'm using a pleasant tone of voice, and I said 'please,' but I meant what I said, so I'm going to stand here until you start. So let's go!"

Do not make threats about what you're going to do if he doesn't get up and do it. Simply tell him that you will stand there until he starts. If he's watching TV, turn off the TV; if he's playing with something, take it out of his hand; if he's looking at a book, take the book away. Don't threaten or get angry. Feel calm. Just stand there and wait for him to get started. Believe me—when he believes you're not going anywhere until he starts, he will start! By waiting for him, rather than yelling at him to start, you are empowering him by letting this be a choice.

When he begins, give him a sincere "thank you" and leave. Stop back in a few minutes to see how he is progressing. If he has stopped before he has finished, *do not* repeat your instructions. Ask *him* to repeat them to you. (Rule #4 again!)

Now, both parents must be on the same page. Make a pact that you will both follow this process. (Please remember that I was answering a couple in this letter. If you're a single parent, make a pledge to yourself!) Plan ahead for the time and place of your next instructions to your child. Practice your words and your tone of voice. Plan to spend the time to wait for him to both repeat your instructions and get started on what you asked—whether it takes 15 minutes or half an hour! Then, with a smile on your face and joy in your heart, patiently give your *behaviorally described* instructions. Also, promise each other that *you will not yell under any circumstances*. Yelling only teaches your child that you do not mean what you say until you yell. (There is a whole chapter on this later in the book.)

Finally, make sure you tell him "Thanks!" when he has finished. You are applying Rule #5 here, really letting him know you love him by showing that you respect him and value his efforts. The whole process also helps him learn how good it feels to do what is asked of him and how it feels to be asked in a dignified tone of voice. Show him that whether he does it cheerfully or angrily, he still has to do it—so ask him, "Why not do it first time, cheerfully?"

Don't worry about his sense of self-esteem. Feeling positively about himself will come naturally from having his parents speak respectfully to him and from doing what he is asked! His actions will create his positive self-esteem. Your expressions of pride in his abilities is yet another application of Rule #5.

Start slowly. Give him only three directions or requests in this manner each day for one week. If things seem to be getting better, gradually increase the frequency. Eventually, you should be able to tell him that he's so good at following instructions that you trust him and he doesn't need to repeat them.

After a while, you'll be able to give him instructions and, rather than wait for him to do them immediately, give him timeframes and deadlines and allow him to learn to budget his own time and choose when to do his chores. Now you're teaching him how to make his own decisions!

Now let's talk about what I mentioned earlier about their son only ignoring them and listening to others. Hey, does that tell you anything about his learned behavior? He has learned that *they* do not mean what they say the first time but others are to be listened to. This speaks very loudly about learned behavior and how selective it can be. Do not interpret a child's actions as any sign of respecting others and disrespecting you. He has just learned to differentiate between people who mean what they say and people who don't! He is a bright and perceptive person; I would like him to work for me when he is old enough!

> You don't need to attach artificial consequences or punishments to requests in order to convince children that you mean what you say. In fact, I sincerely believe that in most cases punishment diverts kids' attention away from the request and focuses it on the punishment and how unfair it is or how mad they are at you. Do not allow yourself to be diverted into discussions when you give directions. Just stay there and ensure that the request for action is followed by action!

Grocery Store Tantrums

Dear Mr. Bledsoe,

We have two girls under the age of five (four and a half and two). We are so frustrated when we take them to the grocery store! They run all over the place and grab things. They scream and yell with excitement and pull toys and candies, etc. off of shelves and generally embarrass us with their loud and obnoxious behavior. What can we do? We have tried punishment but it has no effect!

Frustrated in the Shopping Mall

These girls sound like some adults I know! Have you ever been to a sale at Wal-Mart?

All kidding aside, let's get one thing straight. Parents are up against the greatest marketing minds in the modern world, whose sole purpose is to determine how to get people, especially kids, to act just that way! These creative marketers are constantly searching for new ways to attract customers' attention and to get them to pull products off shelves because they feel that they *must* have them. When you take your kids into any store, you're matching wits with the best. (As a matter of fact, I think marketing agencies direct their best efforts at creating needs in kids!)

However, there is hope, because you have one of the most powerful forces in the world on your side: you're a parent and you love your kids! I believe you're up to the task because you have more at stake than any marketer—you're trying to do the best for your kids.

Parents' Action

Now, with all of that out of the way, let's plan a trip to the grocery store for your family. You're going to apply Rule #1 and Rule #3 here. What are they? "Tell your kids what you want them *to do*," and "Don't assume they learned it: repeat it!" You will precisely describe the behavior you want from your children, and you will "repeat" it in the most powerful of ways: you're going to practice the desired behavior before you get to the grocery store! Then you are going to give them more repetitions (Rule #3) of that same desired behavior. Okay, here we go.

Sit down at home with your kids and lay out the plan for a trip to the grocery store. First, have them help you make out your shopping list. Even your two-year-old will be able to offer some suggestions for the list. Let her add a couple of her favorite things. Next, divide up the list among the whole family, giving your kids some fun items to find and put in the shopping cart. Kids who can't read can get their items verbally from you in the store—or some creative parents take labels and empty packages and make "visual" grocery lists from used packages and labels. (Man, would marketers love to see me encouraging you to develop "label loyalty" like that in your kids!)

Once the lists are made and divided up, you're ready to practice the desired shopping behavior at home. Using a toy grocery cart, wagon, or box, have your kids each hold onto the grocery cart with one hand as you walk around the house and pretend you're in the grocery store. Place samples of the products on their list around the house and let them practice walking in an orderly manner to pick out their products and put them in the cart. Please remember one thing here. These are kids, and getting their items will be exciting and fun. Have fun with them and let them be a little excited! When you see something on your list, let them help you to get your items in the cart.

When you go on the actual shopping trip, try to have both Mom and Dad go along. (Single parents may be able to find a grandparent or friend to go along the first time. After all, if they've been listening to your frustrations, they'll probably be glad to help!) If you go alone with two kids, they'll force you to abandon the "man-to-man" defense and go to the "zone," which is really hard to use with kids.

On the way to the store, have the kids look at their grocery lists or quiz them on what they're going to get at the store. (This is Rule #3 and Rule #4: repeating it and saying the desired behavior for themselves!) What are they going to do with the grocery cart? "Hold onto the cart with one hand until we spot one of our items!"

As soon as you arrive at the store, let them pick out the cart you will use. Have them grab the cart with one hand and, with their list in the other, boldly venture into the battle zone. Keep the cart moving quickly to each kid's products, helping them spot what they are looking for. You will not believe how this will "blind" them to other attractive products. They're getting to buy products they want and they are *focused on that purposeful task and thus are nowhere as easily distracted by marketing ploys!* And the shopping trip will be *fun!*

I would strongly suggest that you take your first couple of shopping trips at a time when you're not in a hurry or under stress. Why? Well, I hate to seem like I'm preparing for failure rather than success, but let's talk briefly about what to do if the kids revert to their old ways of running wildly to attractively packaged and placed items. Let's say you go into the store and, after picking out three items from her list, your daughter runs off to a display of dolls. Very quickly, pick her up, walk quietly out to the car, and go home. Be cheerful but firm. She may cry, she may throw a fit, but don't let it change your demeanor. Remain cheerful but firm. Absolutely do not try to give any verbal instructions at this time! That would be as unwise as me trying to teach you how to program your VCR while you're in a fight with your spouse. You can't learn at a time of stress like that, and neither can your daughter. Your actions will speak louder than words could. This is not a punishment, nor is it an artificially created consequence. It is simply what will happen every time your family goes to the store and someone doesn't follow the plan and the shopping list!

Use those initial trips exclusively as a teaching time. A little time invested now will result in years of relaxed shopping in the future. Think about it. If you can teach your kids to each handle a third of the items on every shopping trip, in the next 10 years you will save yourself countless hours. In fact, if you commit to this approach, when your kids can drive you'll be able to send them to do your shopping, because they'll be trained to handle the task!

As a parting thought here, I would like to point out that you are teaching your children how to make intelligent choices while shopping. Make a list and stick to it. Avoid impulse buying by being purposeful and discriminating in all purchases. As soon as you deem it possible, start to include your children in the money side of purchases. Have them select items within a budget.

Attention Is a Reward — Be Careful How You Use It

When we began Parenting with Dignity, we had the greatest young lady, Marcela Orozco, working for us. She was a creative, effective, energetic employee, and she was instrumental in setting up our whole operation. At the time she had three wonderful sons ages four, five, and six. (She remains a close family friend today and even more wonderful parent to her family.)

Childcare was an issue for Marcela, so I told her to bring the boys to our office at the end of each school day. We had tables and even a toy room where they could play. I felt that having her kids around gave our office—which was dedicated to parenting, after all—a nice feel, and underscored our belief that kids learn by watching us, and that kids need to see their parents working. They need models. I knew Marcela and I knew that this arrangement would allow her to work more effectively than if she were having to leave to take her boys from school to childcare. The youngest was in an early preschool and the other two had different schedules. Plus, our kids were grown and I just liked having the boys around! I enjoyed leaving my desk to play and spend time with them. They were a welcome diversion from the hassles and responsibilities of a taxing schedule.

One school holiday, I told Marcela to bring the boys in for the whole day. I had a day of writing ahead of me so I was in my office, which was separate from Marcela's office but had a big window with a clear view of Marcela and the boys. This turned out to be a very instructive day for me! I could observe the dynamics of the interaction in the other room without being a participant.

Marcela was an industrious worker and she had planned to take care of some important correspondence at her computer while the kids played. She had arrived half an hour early and the boys were dressed in their best play clothes, all "scrubbed and polished" for a day at the office! Marcela had laid out great plans for the boys to do some coloring, and had each boy outfitted with his own backpack full of coloring and craft materials and snacks for the morning break. She was using Rule #1 by first deciding on the desired behavior and then rehearsing before the situation. However, even with all that preparation, there was still a problem.

The boys were with Mom and they wanted her attention—and like all kids, they were going to get it one way or another. So here is what

I observed happening. The minute the kids would start to color, Marcela would hurry to her desk and begin to work on her correspondence. Soon after that the boys would start to create a ruckus. They would yell for her to come and look at their work or they would begin to roughhouse or argue. Nothing serious, but still a commotion.

Marcela would go to the boys and help them to get back on task, then she would go back to her desk. The minute they felt that unconscious need for attention (and it was a totally unconscious need, not a diabolical scheme or anything like that), they would again start doing something other than what they were supposed to be doing. Marcela was caught in a vicious cycle but she could not see it. *The boys were misbehaving to get her attention, and was it ever working!*

Finally, I called Marcela on the intercom and asked her to come in my office for a second. I briefly explained what I had observed, then told her she had my permission to use the office and the rest of the workday as an "experimental lab." I didn't care if she got any correspondence done at all!

"Just try this," I said. "When they're coloring, go look at what they are doing, compliment them, and maybe even sit down and color with them. The minute they start to bicker and create a problem, leave and go back to your writing and ignore them."

She went back in the room with the boys and started doing just that. She rewarded the boys' appropriate behavior with attention and praise, and she responded to negative behavior by leaving. It took about three instances of each before the kids got the idea. She did not need any words! Good coloring and attention to the desired task got lots of confirmation. Inappropriate behavior got them nothing. (Remember that negative attention is almost the same as positive attention in a kid's eye. The boys would not have been able to articulate this, but it's true.)

Children have a human need to be noticed. If they fail to get noticed for positive actions, they will resort to negative actions. I hear this from kids in juvenile court when they say, "The only way that I can get my dad's attention is to screw up."

I watched the same dynamic in my classroom repeated a thousand times over my 29 years of teaching. A child unable to attract positive attention will most certainly resort to getting negative attention.

This book is not aimed at boring you with results of research, but many research studies and research institutes are finding similar if not identical brain wave patterns in the brains of children receiving positive attention and children receiving negative attention. The logical explanation seems to be that a human being needs to be recognized or acknowledged. Lacking that recognition in a positive form, a human will seek it in negative ways.

Now let's look more closely at Marcela's actions and the dynamics of this interaction with her sons. The technique of going to the kids when they were doing what they were supposed to and ignoring them when they were not was an application of Rule #4. She was creating a circumstance where her boys began to understand something very positive for themselves. I doubt that they could have put it into words, but they were speaking with their actions! Good behavior works; bad behavior doesn't!

Later I suggested that Marcela help the boys verbalize what they were saying with their actions. "When they're coloring quietly as you have instructed them to do, ask them how it feels to be doing such a good job of being on task. Try to get them to verbalize that it feels good to be doing exactly what Mom asked them to. In doing this you will be helping them to make appropriate behavior self-rewarding!"

Self-rewarding behavior is the longest lasting behavior. For Marcela, spending extra time teaching *now* gave her hours of time later.

Who Is the Adult in Your Relationship with Your Child?

I was watching Dr. Phil on TV the other day; since he has an opportunity to be a worldwide authority on parenting and so many people follow his teachings, I want to know what many parents use as a parenting model. He was dealing with three families who were having various problems with their kids acting out. The parents were all having almost identical problems. Unfortunately, I felt that Dr. Phil was compounding their problems, because all of the techniques he was advocating were reactive in nature.

He was counseling the parents only to react to the child's negative behavior—with escalating levels of punishment in response to the kids' undesirable actions. One father said, "So you advocate removing everything from our daughter's room and feeding her with a straw through the keyhole?" That dad was perceptive about the advice he was receiving. If all the parents did was react to the child's negative behavior with escalating levels of punishment, then the only limit on how far this cycle would go was how far the kid chose to push it! Many kids will push parents far beyond any punishment the parents are willing to dole out. This father understood!

I was dismayed that not once was there any discussion of the *desired* behavior. One little girl was over-dramatic and threw fits all the time, and all I heard the adults talk about was her negative behavior and the parents' punishment response to it. The poor little girl! How was she supposed to know what behavior to use instead? No one was giving her any ideas for new, appropriate behaviors! If the adults had ideas about what they wanted the poor kid to do, I didn't hear them, and I doubt seriously that the child had heard any other ideas about how to behave! Dr. Phil did not offer any suggestions of teaching the desired behavior; he was only advocating raising the artificial consequences of the negative behavior.

If we wait until a child is exhibiting the negative behavior and simply react to it over and over, we are caught in a vicious cycle. The way to break that cycle is to teach the desired behavior *before* the dysfunctional or wrong behavior appears. Don't try to teach it while you're shouting and she's crying about the negative behavior. Nobody can learn during a time of agitation or frustration—especially not kids! Like I said earlier, that's about as wise as me waiting until there's a show on TV that you have to record to keep your job and then attempting to teach you to program your VCR by slapping your hand when you touch a wrong button!

Wouldn't it be more reasonable and make more sense for me to sit down with you and the operator's manual the day before the show and go through the steps a few times? Wouldn't you learn better if you had some time to practice the steps, make some mistakes, and correct them? Practicing the steps would help you store them away in your head before the critical event.

The same is true for kids. A much more reasonable approach to parenting this girl would be to demonstrate and help her practice some ways of getting adult attention in an appropriate manner *before* she is in the situation. Use Rule #1. Devise some specific behaviors to demonstrate and practice with the young girl.

You might decide that you would like your child to say words like "Would you please help me?" Or "Help!" or "Daddy" or "Mommy." You might try giving your child a secret family word that means "I need your attention right now." (We did it and we used the word more than they did to get their attention.)

Now here is the key: if you tell your child that they must use certain words or phrases or even a secret word to get your attention, then when they use the word or phrase, *you must give them your attention immediately!*

If you tell your child how to get your attention in a positive manner, then you must demonstrate by your actions that it works. It drives me crazy to listen to parents tell children to say "please" when they want something and then watch the child say "please" and hear the parent answer, "Not now, can't you see I'm busy?"

Lying—the Ultimate Form of Acting Out

Dr. Phil also talked to the parents of another girl who had begun to lie to her parents about everything. Her parents said the lying had begun before the age of three and had been escalating for over 10 years! The daughter was now 13 and they said that they had tried every punishment in the book: time-out, grounding, withholding privileges, spanking, restricting the use of the phone and TV, limiting her choices of clothing, and so on. I would say they have a couple of slow learners in their family—but the daughter is not one of them! They had 10 years of proof that punishment doesn't work!

Can you tell this was a frustrating program for me to watch? Not one time on the program was the word "truth" uttered. The young girl, the parents, Dr. Phil—no one spoke of what they expected the child *to do!* All they talked about was the lying and the escalating levels of punishment. How is that poor girl supposed to learn what to do instead? Nobody has made one attempt to teach her how to tell the truth, and nobody was teaching her the wonderful benefits (the sales pitch from Rule #1) of being honest! That may seem obvious to you and me, but it is no more obvious to a child than programming a VCR is to someone who doesn't already know how to do it!

Children need to be constantly exposed to stories about the benefits of honesty. Read about "George Washington and the Cherry Tree." Read about Pinocchio and then propose other ways that he might have resolved his difficulties by telling the truth. Ask children questions and reward honest answers with hugs. Give children tasks and ask them to tell you honestly how they performed. Reward honest answers with more lavish praise than answers that claim outstanding performance.

If you want your children to tell the truth, you had better not let them watch you telling the grandparents that you have a commitment when they know you just don't want to spend the weekend with them. They'd better not hear you calling in sick when you're not. When the cashier at the grocery store gives you too much change, your children had better see you take the money back just because it is the honest thing to do.

I hope you will use Rule #1 with your kids long before they are 13. I hope you will identify ways of teaching your kids *desired* behaviors long before *negative* behaviors are habits, ingrained as deeply as lying was for this young girl.

When the girl is being punished (no matter what the punishment), I doubt that she is sitting in her room saying, "Oh! *Now* I get it! I'm going to tell the truth!" I am positive that as she sits in her room while grounded she is saying, "I hate my parents and I will never get caught lying again. I will cover my story better next time!"

You will all most certainly catch your little ones in some fib. All children will try out altering the truth to protect themselves. "Did you eat all of your dinner?" you'll ask, and with half a plate full of food in front of her, your daughter will say, "Yes!" as though she thinks you can't see. These are "teachable moments." Stop and give her the opportunity to tell the accurate story. Be patient and let her get the facts straight, then help her to experience the sense of self-worth that comes from telling the truth by rewarding her with hugs and positive attention. This is certainly not the time to scold her with a "bad girl" admonition.

Putting It All Together

Acting out is a natural way that kids tell you they are confused about how to deal with their world. Teach them more effective ways of dealing with their world and the acting out will disappear quite rapidly— simply because it doesn't work very well!

Parenting with Dignity is about a different way of thinking and a different way of teaching. *Teach kids what you want them to do before they are in the situation!* Don't just react. Decide what the desired behavior is and figure out a way to teach it. Create a plan. They are your kids and you know them. Use words if you must, but also demonstrate and *practice* the desired behaviors. Model the positive behavior for them.

Let your toddlers experience you getting their attention in a calm voice. Let them experience you telling the truth. Then do not assume that you have taught them until your kids actually do what you set out to teach on a repeated basis!

All the while, you, the parent, are teaching them.

Never assume that you have taught a thing until your kids actually do what you set out to teach! They must do it on a repeated basis! Their actions will show you that they are learning.

Chapter 3
Bedtime

"Will our children ever go to bed without a fight? Will we ever be able to get our son to sleep in his own bed?"

Bedtime *can* be the most enjoyable and rewarding time of day for both parents and kids. Who is going to be the adult who takes charge and creates an enjoyable bedtime experience in your household?

Parents who have gotten into bedtime hassles with a child or two or three may be inclined to argue about that. However, if you're one of those (many) parents battling with their kids at bedtime, read on. I sincerely believe you'll find that bedtime can change at your house fairly simply.

The question is simple: Who is going to be the adult who takes charge and creates an enjoyable bedtime experience? First, let's take a look at the dynamics at bedtime. Life is exciting for young children. Not just kind of exciting, *really* exciting! They're experiencing new and wonderful things every minute. They haven't yet learned to recognize when they are tired, and even if they do, they're certainly not willing to give in to it. There are toys to play with, discoveries to make, "mountains" to climb, and running and shouting to do! "Yahooee! Who wants to go to bed?"

Let's take a page out of Lola Whitner's book. Lola was a master teacher who taught in the classroom next door to me in Walla Walla, Washington. She hasn't actually written a book about teaching, but she should! She used what she called her "sit in the bleachers" technique to figure out how to deal with students she was having trouble with. She would simply wait until the kids had gone home, then she would sit in the seat of the student she was having difficulty with and try to visualize the situation from the kid's point of view. Lola told me that when she did that, she would usually realize what had gone wrong— and it was usually some mistake she had made.

So let's sit in the bleachers with your toddler at bedtime and see if we can find some enlightenment. Look at your relationship with your kids at bedtime to see if some of the dynamics we'll discuss in this chapter might be at work.

> Careful observation of life through your children's eyes can help guide you in devising plans for working effectively with them.

Crying at Bedtime

Dear Mr. Bledsoe,

At bedtime we always have an endless battle with our 3-year-old daughter. The minute we put her in bed and leave the room, she begins to scream. We have tried everything and she will keep it up until we give in and go to her. Some nights we are up after midnight with this routine. We cannot get anything done in the evenings. We are completely at our daughter's mercy. We go to bed in a frazzle and our marriage is being tested because we have no time for us. Help!

Sincerely,
Frazzled Parents

First, if the volume of my e-mail is any indicator, this is a very common situation. In fact, many parents are in a much *worse* situation at bedtime than these parents. Another couple wrote to tell me that not only did their son create a similar situation, he adds a little something extra to the nighttime fight: after about three minutes of hysterical crying, he throws up! So count your blessings! Of course, I'm not trying to trivialize the frustration parents in this situation feel. The big thing I wish to tell parents is there is hope! As a matter of fact, I will propose that you and your kids may soon view bedtime as the most enjoyable part of every day! Don't doubt it, just read on, try my proposals, and see what happens. Even if bedtime does not become your favorite time of day, at least you will no longer *dread* it.

To begin with, let's look at this situation from your child's point of view.

Fact #1: Kids are people, too! They don't respond any better than adults do to being surprised with sudden commands. In fact, they're less capable of being surprised with unexpected commands than we are.

Fact #2: Life is exciting for kids! At every moment what they are doing has totally captivated their attention, and they'll have difficulty breaking that kind of rewarding concentration.

Sit in her seat for a second. Do you give her any kind of an advance warning about bedtime? Or do you simply surprise her by announcing, "It's bedtime!" How would you like it if I came to your house when you were halfway through your favorite TV program, shut off the TV with no warning, and said, "Go to bed, right now"? You probably wouldn't react very positively, so it's reasonable to think your child won't, either.

Think about this a little further from her viewpoint. Of course, for you, watching a TV program is enjoyable, but you could probably pull yourself away from it if you needed to. With kids, what they're doing *right now* is the most captivating and exciting thing in the world. A TV show for children is much more engrossing and exciting than it is for you. Kids have the ability to turn themselves over completely to their current activity. "Right now" is the most important moment—in some ways the *only* moment—in their life, and certainly more important than anything you could suggest. They need to have some warning and some preparation for disengagement.

Parent's Action

Begin preparing your toddler for bedtime hours *before* bedtime. Talk during dinner about what is going to happen at bedtime. Say things like, "Tonight at bedtime we'll read your favorite book," or, "Tonight at bedtime you get to wear your favorite pajamas." If your child isn't old enough yet to understand the words, you can still create the same anticipation of bedtime by holding up the favorite book or the pajamas. Take your child into the bedroom and lay them out by the child's crib or bed. They'll get the picture: bedtime is coming! Help your child prepare for it and anticipate it in a positive way.

You may be thinking, "Gee, I don't have that much time. I'm too busy with housework to lay out books and pajamas hours ahead of time!" Well, you can spend a little time now, or you can spend hours fighting at bedtime—your choice! If you teach them well at two, from then on you'll have years of savings every night at bedtime. Like money in the bank, it will return great dividends in the long run.

As bedtime approaches, give small reminders about the fun that's coming. You might even be able to take some small steps toward the actual act of getting in bed. At some point well before bedtime—a half-hour, an hour—go into your daughter's bedroom with her and make a game of getting into pajamas, then play with her for a few minutes—or longer! Putting on pajamas then becomes paired in your child's mind with a fun time with you. Many parents even put on their own PJs with their kids. Try it. You might find it fun to play around and relax in your pajamas for the last few hours of the day!

Later, give another alert by setting a timer and telling your daughter that when the timer goes off, you both are going to go in the bathroom and brush teeth and wash hands in preparation for bed. Try to set the timer to ring at the same time as the end of a video or the end of a game. Let her have the timer near her so that she can see it. Even kids who can't yet recognize numbers or tell time can get the picture that when the timer goes off, it's time to head for the bathroom.

Some parents tell me that they like to set the timer and then when it goes off, they set it for an additional five-minute reprieve. It's a double reminder of winding down play and gradually moving ever closer to bedtime. It also makes kids think they got a bonus! They rapidly learn that when the timer first goes off, it's a warning and they know that there's a very short time to play before it will ring again and action will follow.

As you're giving these "alerts," it always helps if you stop what you're doing and join your kids for a brief moment. Help them learn that bedtime is not an unpleasant time of separation from play and contact with Mom and Dad, but rather a very pleasant time of progressive interaction. When you lay out the PJs, go in and lay out your nightclothes, too. When your kids brush their teeth, get out your toothbrush and brush your teeth, too. (You're going to brush your teeth anyway, why not do it with them?) They learn more from your actions and example than they do from your words. You are brushing your teeth, so it is natural for them to do it, too.

Routine is a key word here. By establishing a very pleasant routine, you are building a positive idea in your daughter's head that will repeat almost every evening. More important, keep in mind that *these times of interaction with your kids are fun!* Let yourself in on them. Time flies, and it won't be long before your kids are too old for some of these warm interactions.

Enjoy bedtime with your kids! Your enjoyment will be contagious. *The ideas in your head will rule your world.* If you say to yourself, "Bedtime is a nightmare!" then it will be. On the other hand, if you say to yourself, "I love bedtime with my kids!" that will become your reality. Do not be fooled—your children understand your feelings long before they understand your words. When they can't understand your words, they must react to your actions, body language, tone of voice, and your facial expressions. If your one-year-old looks at you and you look angry, he doesn't need words to know that this is not a pleasant time of day. Imagine what you look like to your kids and ask yourself, "Would I view this picture as a pleasant time of day? Would I like to get ready for bed with this person as my guide?"

If you're acting frustrated or angry at bedtime, don't be surprised if your child is! Kids will imitate you. Your actions will speak much louder than your words … especially to a pre-verbal child. My gosh, like I just said, they can't understand your words so they must react to your actions, body language, tone of voice, and your facial expressions.

You might even try standing in front of a mirror as you pretend to announce bedtime. Look at your face honestly and ask yourself how you look. Make your face look inviting and loving. Get a real smile on your face. The only way to do that is to think of something truly happy.

What's Next If the Crying Persists?

What do we do if the buildup goes great, but everything still falls apart at the critical moment of getting into bed? I'll assume that you've spent a few nights building positive anticipation of bedtime, giving the little one a ton of time and attention, but when it's actually time for bed, he still puts up a fight.

Well, unfortunately, lots of kids do cry and even scream at bedtime. It can be a reasonable reaction, if you look at it from his point of view. He's anticipating a time of separation and loneliness. After all, he's gone to bed before—he knows what that's all about! He's thinking, "That's when the room gets dark and Mommy and Daddy leave me alone! I know what's coming and I don't like it!" (They may not be able to form this in words, but the feeling is just as real!)

Parent's Action

First, make this a time of close physical contact. Kids are very tactile, and they like to be hugged and cuddled. It's comforting and reassuring for him to feel physically close to you. Have a chair in his room to snuggle together in, or, if he's made the move to a big-boy bed, get into bed with him and read the book he picked out earlier. Make bedtime a warm, reassuring, and above all *relaxing* time, the time when he gets to be the closest to you. Accepting this as a regular feeling of security may take time, but keep at it and Rule #3 will take effect. Repetition of the pleasant experience will replace past discomfort.

Singing also works well at the end of the day. Pick a few peaceful songs and build them into the bedtime ritual, singing softly to your kids and helping them relax. Music recaptures past emotions and feelings for all of us—singing a few common songs at bedtime will pair that music with the relaxing feelings of a welcome bed and the secure feeling of Mom and Dad's quiet company at bedtime. I have sung songs at bedtime with our grandkids, and when they stay with us, they almost always ask me to sing those songs! They like that feeling of comfort that comes from singing a familiar song.

Do not be fooled into thinking that the only one who needs to change at bedtime is your child. *Prepare to change yourself, too.* The change that will bring the best results with your kids is the change in your own attitude! *The ideas in your head will rule your world.* If you allow yourself to think, "I am so busy, I don't have time to spend an hour just getting my kid in bed every night," rest assured your child will make sure you spend more time than that!

Commit to this as a very important and pleasing time in your day. Build positive anticipation of bedtime in your own mind and your child will sense it and imitate your happiness and peace! Let yourself enjoy the physical closeness, too.

Pay attention. While cuddling with your child, you will actually feel the tension leave her body. You will feel her body temperature rise slightly as she relaxes. You will notice her breathing become smoother, slower, and more rhythmic. Look for those cues and let them lead you to "feel" the right time to leave her alone to go to sleep. Sleep will be very welcome to a tired child. Allowing children to go to bed while agitated or excited will almost always result in difficulty in sleeping. My gosh, look at yourself! Try laying down to go to sleep after a vigorous workout or an exciting or inspirational movie. It's very difficult to relax and bring on sleep. Multiply that with a child's more complete involvement in his exciting day and you can see very clearly the help they need relaxing, getting comfortable, and turning loose the day's excitement.

Barbara and I encounter many, many kids in our travels. Almost universally, kids will tell us that Grandma and Grandpa are the ones who always make them feel loved. Almost as often, kids will tell us how Grandma and Grandpa are the only people who will slow down enough to just spend quiet time with them at bedtime. Be like Grandma or Grandpa! Watch them with kids and imitate them.

I've Tried Everything—Now What?

So you've tried all of the strategies above and bedtime continues to go poorly! You give plenty of "alerts." You lay out books and PJs. You brush your teeth together. You get into bed and cuddle and comfort. You sing familiar songs. But when you tuck her in and begin to leave, she erupts into tears and starts another bout of unpleasantness. You're at your wits' end! Now what?

Parents' Action

Be calm. Your repetition of these relaxation strategies will eventually work! Give it time. Rule #3 will take over. Remember, your child may have had a couple years—a *big* portion of her life—to get used to this hassle at bedtime. It may take weeks to establish a new routine. But if in the immediate present she's crying and you just can't stand it—okay, just to break the old habits, here's an effective technique to use as your daughter gets used to the new bedtime ritual.

Go to the store and get a small rechargeable flashlight. You could even take her with you and let her pick one. You might even find one in the shape of Winnie the Pooh or Tigger. Now add another step to getting ready for bed. Tell your little one to put two toys and a couple of books in her bed before you go there to read. Then tell her,

"Tonight after we finish reading, you get to have this cool flashlight in bed with you and you can play with the toys and books that you put in your bed. You may not get out of bed, but you can play in bed as long as you wish. The only light will come from your cool new flashlight."

You are establishing that going to bed is non-negotiable, but going to sleep is up to your child. You are practicing Rule #3: You're saying that bedtime is coming and the time has not changed, you're just "saying" it in a different way.

It will amaze you how fast this will result in sleep. If your daughter gets out of bed, don't try to reason with her at this time. Simply pick her up and put her back in bed. And leave. Do not bend on that. Bedtime has been established well ahead of time; it has been made a comfortable time; and the toys and the flashlight have given her something fun to do until sleep comes, so it is now time to establish that getting out of bed is unacceptable.

Words will be very counter-productive. Words said now will tell her that this is a time to negotiate, argue, and fuss. Your actions must establish that the time for bed has arrived, and negotiation is not acceptable. *It is bedtime.* If she gets out of bed, pick her up and take her back to bed. Turn on the flashlight and point it at a book and give it to her. Do not relent. The first few nights you may have to put the child back in the bed five or even 10 times, but do not relent. Keep smiling and stay calm, but do not give in. (You are the great wall of China, there is no end to you.) It may take a couple of nights, but stand firm. A couple of nights spent reinforcing the new routine will help you avoid years of future bedtime hassles.

Getting the Child Out of Your Bed and into Her Own

Now let's talk about another common situation. Many parents find themselves taking their baby to bed with them when they're infants as a means of both comforting a crying baby and still getting some sleep themselves. It can seem like a reasonable deal, and many parents do it. (I must point out that many authorities feel that having an infant in a bed with sleeping adults is a dangerous practice.)

However, when the child reaches toddlerhood, parents may find that they have a kid that won't sleep in his own bed. The child may even go to bed just fine—then, at 2:00 A.M., here comes the little one, crawling in bed with Mom and Dad! What to do now?

Take him back to his bed, tuck him in, give him a hug, turn on his flashlight, say, "Good night," and calmly leave. If he's talking, have him repeat with you that he will stay in bed.

The key here is to practice being calm. I know—it's the middle of the night and you're beat. I understand that you're frustrated, but so is your child! If you cannot be patient and calm at this stressful time, how can you expect your child to relax? A quiet song or back rub might be all that it takes at this moment. Rule #5 will come into play very effectively here. Do a few loving things and be amazed at how your love is the quieting influence that allows your child to drift peacefully and confidently off to sleep in his own bed.

Set out to make bedtime the most pleasant time of day and you will succeed! Your attitude might be the thing that needs changing, but *planning* for an enjoyable time always winds up *producing* an enjoyable time in the long run.

Chapter 4

Sibling Rivalry

"I'm pulling my hair out! Will my kids ever stop fighting?"

Kids are not born with negotiating, sharing, and compromising skills; those must be taught *before* they're in a fight. I'll talk more about sharing in a later chapter, but we can't talk about easing sibling rivalries without talking a bit about it here.

It's normal for kids to compare themselves with siblings. Kids will almost always look around for models upon which to judge their own behavior, and their worlds are fairly limited. They will obviously compare the treatment and privileges they see a brother or sister receiving with what they receive—and, because their ages differ, there are going to be differences! It is all that they have for comparison. They do not share the perspective of your years. They simply see another person being treated in a certain way.

It's your job to help them keep in perspective their place and their siblings' place in your world. Relax and become their guide. This is an exciting time in your child's development. Relax and enjoy it. Your relaxed attitude will come through loud and clear.

Situation 1: Getting Along in the Car

There was one day when our two sons were growing up that was a landmark day in our lives as parents. Our oldest, Drew, was about nine, and the youngest, Adam, was about three. We were taking a trip in the car to visit their grandparents, a pretty long drive of about four hours. We had only been on the road for a half hour when the inevitable fight began in the back seat.

We had heard it many times before. Adam started crying and yelling, "Drew hit me!"

Drew said, "He had it coming! He just spit on his finger and stuck it in my ear!"

Adam had mastered all the best techniques for annoying his big brother. He could dip his straw in a milkshake and flip a glop on his brother's face from 10 feet. He could "accidentally" flip a book closed and make it look like a real accident. He would get into his brother's games and mix them up or lose pieces just to annoy Drew. And he always had his "hole card" that could drive his brother crazy: he was the master of the "annoying low-volume, high-pitched squeak." He would make this noise under his breath, drive his brother crazy, but deny he was making any noise at all. And, as he had just shown, he was also the master of the "Wet Willy."

I think you get the picture, and you most likely have seen better techniques used regularly by your kids in your own home or your car.

So on that landmark day, I did what I had been doing for what seemed like forever (it can seem like forever even when your kids are just three, can't it?): I stopped the car and we separated them. We put Drew in the front seat and Barbara got in the back seat with Adam. Then we drove off in silence with two mad kids. (I was at least proud of myself for not shouting the traditional, "Quit crying or I will give you something to cry about!")

As we drove off in silence, it suddenly hit me: *What are we teaching our kids? Do I really want to teach them that if you don't get along with someone you love, you separate?* Ouch! When I looked around, it seemed to me that we already had enough of that in the world, and that certainly wasn't what we wanted to teach our kids!

Then I asked myself a really good question. "What *do* you want your kids to learn?" Well, I wanted them to learn to get along. And if I wanted them to learn to get along, that was an entirely different lesson requiring different action. It required teaching!

So Barbara and I set out on a very different mission. We actually took trips just for the purpose of teaching our kids how to get along! Your action might be similar, but tailored to suit your kids' ages and personalities.

For a week prior to taking a trip we would divide the teaching load. Barbara would talk to Adam, saying, "Do you always want your brother to slug you? If that's what you want, just keep annoying him—keep licking your finger and sticking it in his ear! Keep pulling the bookmark out of his book!

"But if what you want is for your brother to play with you and include you in what he's doing, try asking him nicely. Say to him, 'Hey, Drew, will you read some of your book to me?' When we're driving in the car, say, 'Hey, Drew, let's play the 'Ford/Chevy game.' You count the Fords and I'll count the Chevys and the winner gets to order the toppings on the pizza for lunch.'

"Say to him, 'Hey, Drew, let's play a game of Fish.'"

At the same time, Drew and I would be having a similar discussion. "Do you always want your brother to get your attention by sticking his slobbery finger in your ear? If that's what you want, just keep ignoring him, and he'll get your attention in the most annoying way possible. He'll annoy you until you're both in your 80s!

"But on the other hand, if what you want is for your brother to get your attention in a more pleasant way, you have to give your attention to him when he *seeks* it in a pleasant way. If he says, 'Hey, Drew, let's play the Ford/Chevy game,' play with him. It can be fun!

"When he says, 'Hey, Drew, would you read to me?' do it! You love to read. You can share the magic of your book with your little brother.

"When he asks, 'Hey, Drew, let's play Fish,' play with him! Have fun with him! A game of Fish will pass the time in the car, you will have a brother who really likes you—and you won't get a wet finger in your ear! You'll have a brother who likes to be with you."

We had months and years of wondering if all this teaching time was paying off, but believe me, it was worth it! Gradually our two sons became best friends. Jump ahead just a few years. We were gathered with family and friends at Mom's house for an engagement party for Drew and his wife-to-be, Maura. At one point Drew asked everyone to gather out on Mom's deck, then he got up on a chair and announced, 'I'd like to ask my best friend to be the best man in our wedding."

Barbara and I looked around at his friends, wondering who it would be. Then we were shocked to see Drew turn to his brother and ask, "Adam, will you do it?"

It was one of the proudest days of our lives. Our sons view each other as best friends! What an exciting revelation. Looking back, it would have been easier and more natural to just separate our kids when they argued or fought with each other. It took more thought and a lot more effort to teach them how to get along and celebrate their differences, but with a little bit more time, we shaped a friendship by teaching our kids *how* to be friends.

Our sons had a natural link because they are brothers, but it was certainly worth it for us to take the time to teach them how to be friends. Separating them and punishing them would never have taught them *how* to be friends.

It's natural for siblings to compete with each other and engage in some arguments and disagreements; it is not necessary that these disagreements become ongoing and permanent. *We can teach kids to get along!*

Teaching our children to get along with their siblings is one of the most rewarding jobs we parents can ever do. Now for some practical help in doing this!

Parents' Action

The first step in guiding siblings to work at being friends lies in *identifying exactly what specific behavior you want them to do* (Rule #1). Describe the desired action in *behavioral terms* that you can understand and then in terms that your children can understand. Of course, doing this for very young kids usually will involve more action than words—but then, the concepts will be simpler for very young kids.

Do not try to do this "on the run." By that, I mean don't try to devise your plan while your children are present and you are teaching. Frame your idea and your method of teaching well in advance. Write down exactly what you are going to do; writing helps you to be very specific. If you are teaching a child who is not yet speaking, it's even more important to think through your actions.

Because we have been verbal for most of our lives, we tend to think in verbal terms. I find myself continually doing this with our grandchildren. I try to explain an action to one of them with words that they don't understand. Just the other day I caught myself saying, "Listen to me!" to our one-year-old granddaughter. Well, she can listen to me, and she understands lots of words even though she isn't yet speaking, but that is a ridiculous thing to say to a one-year-old child! However, I am not around little ones constantly, and occasionally I slip up and try to give verbal instruction to a child who isn't verbal. I have to plan ahead to give nonverbal instructions.

With toddler siblings, you'll almost certainly attempt to teach about sharing toys. How will your lesson sound and look to your toddler? I suggest that you sit on the floor with your oldest toddler and practice the idea of "trading." Teach your toddler with words and actions that if she wants the doll you're playing with, she needs to find an equally attractive toy and say, "Trade?" As you play with her, she trades with you and you trade with her. Talk to her about using the idea with her younger sibling. Later, introduce the idea with the younger sibling present. Make no mistake: you'll need to be down on the floor participating, too. Both children will learn more from your actions than from your words. In the long run, you won't have to spend as much time refereeing. Sharing and trading will pop up spontaneously as a regular part of play.

Next, demonstrate words of respect like *please*, *thank you*, and *excuse me*. Encourage your kids to use these words while talking to each other—but more important, use these words yourself in the presence of your kids. Like I've said, kids speak the language they are exposed to. Rarely if ever do they learn language by actually being taught the words to say. Rather they simply observe the words being used and then repeat them. Make the language of respect the common language in your home.

The other day, I was visiting a childcare facility and was amazed at what I saw. The lady who runs the place is a wonderful, caring and highly effective educator; one of the most aware people that I've ever watched working with young children. She greeted me and told me that the teaching lesson for the week is saying "please" and "thank you."

"We are making this our goal for the entire week!" she told me. "By the end of the week, we will have every kid here saying 'please' and 'thank you' regularly!" I believed her and I knew that if she set out to do it, the odds were good that she would accomplish it!

Then a little boy climbed up on a table in front of us and she blurted out, "Jimmy, get down from there!"

Immediately she clapped her hand over her mouth and exclaimed, "Did you hear what I just said? And our lesson for the week is 'please' and 'thank you'!"

This lady is a trained professional who works full-time teaching lots of small children, and during a week when her goal was to teach kids to say "please" and "thank you," she had just barked a request for a child to do something in a gruff tone—and without a "please"!

As a parent, you must *always* be mindful of how *you* act and speak in the presence of children.

I know that kids often pick up the language of disrespect from other sources. That language is everywhere. I think that many cartoons aimed at a child audience model and speak the language of disrespect. Just remember that nobody is worthless, everyone can serve as a bad example to someone. Use those as times to stop and discuss other ways to say things.

Monitor video games with "trash talk." Either remove the game or better yet, teach your kids to talk back to the game and correct the negative words as they play. Make a condition of playing the game be that they must offer better words to use in place of the trash talk!

If your kids have friends who use some of the commonly accepted language of disrespect, it may be time to start a neighborhood parenting class to discuss neighborhood standards for respect and language. It's a rather simple concept that it's easier to teach your children something if their playmates are being taught the same thing.

It does take a village to raise a child. Build one! If you would like to get some information on how to do this, please visit our website at www.parentingwithdignity.com. This site is full of directions for setting up a community to raise children.

Peer pressure isn't something that only happens to teenagers. Make no mistake, kids who are just beginning to talk and walk can exert peer pressure on others their own age. Build positive peer pressure as early as possible. Recruit older brothers and sisters to teach their younger siblings proper ways of speaking. Allowing the older child some teaching responsibilities can work wonders to ward off sibling rivalry! It establishes in each child's mind the idea that they are not in competition, that each one has a role in relation to each other, which is very healthy. The older child sees acting properly and respectfully as part of his role, and the younger child sees that he doesn't have to compete with the older child and can accept the role of learning from the older sibling.

Aggressive Play and Fighting

Dear Mac,

We have two sons ages three and four. They are always fighting and wrestling. Everything seems to be one big competition. They play very aggressive "games" that they seem to have made up. They run and tackle each other. It scares me to think of what it will be like in two years. What will it be like when they are five and six? Where did this come from? We have never modeled aggressive behavior. They just seem to be drawn to competing with each other.

Is there any way to teach them to play in a less competitive and aggressive manner?

Thanks in advance if you can help.

Sincerely,
Caught in a trap

You may never have modeled competitive or aggressive behavior, but that doesn't mean your children are lacking for models of aggression. It's everywhere in modern American society—on TV, in advertising, in the workplace. Aggressive behavior is everywhere, and it's not necessarily all bad. The world your children will grow up in is pretty aggressive, and totally passive children will get walked on pretty badly.

The key to solving this dilemma lies in the answer to this parent's last question. "Is there any way to teach them to play in a less competitive and aggressive manner?" The answer is a resounding, "Yes!"

The key word, though, is *teach*. So how would you go about this? The key lies in Rule #1. You have to identify what you want the kids to replace the aggressive play with. You have identified what you do *not* want—now you must decide what you *do* want!

I know, I'm beginning to sound like a broken record, but the best solution to your problem lies in deciding exactly what you *do* want. I can't decide that for you, but I can offer a few suggestions based upon what I think that you might want.

Parents' Action

Let's imagine that you want your kids to play some quiet games—you know, games that do not involve tackling or hitting. Get out a game like Chutes and Ladders or some similar game rated for kids in your children's age bracket. Sit down with them and explain the rules. Most likely the rules will have to be taught by demonstration, given the ages of your kids. (I will say that I'm surprised that the creators of most kids' games write the instructions as if they are intending for adults to play! It seems to me they should write the directions to guide parents in teaching the rules to kids in the game's age group! But almost none of them do it that way, so it's up to you to devise ways to teach the rules to your kids.)

Before you sit down with your kids, familiarize yourself with the rules of the game. Devise ways of demonstrating the rules to your kids that they will understand. For example, if the game calls for rolling some dice, demonstrate this skill to your kids. If the game calls for spinning a spinner, let them try this activity numerous times before you try to play the game.

Play the games with each child separately before playing with them together, so they can get the idea without having the distraction of their usual aggressive play. Once you're ready to all play the game, establish the "game etiquette." Spend as much time teaching your kids how to *conduct* themselves as you do teaching them how to play. This is probably their first experience at playing a quiet and orderly game, so they don't know; it will all be new for them. As they learn how to play the game, they're also learning the rules for orderly play. (I have seen families who even build their own rules of conduct into games, with penalties in the game for loud or rude language, much like penalties in sports for unsportsmanlike conduct.)

73

They learned their aggressive play and now they need to learn orderly and quiet play. You will have to play with them and model the desired behavior. Show them how to sit cross-legged or sit in their chairs at a small table or kneel in a big chair at the dinner table. Show them what to do with their hands. Place them on the table and rest them quietly while waiting for their turn.

With aggressive kids, it would be good to play the game with little or no mention of winning. One of the biggest goals in teaching quiet play lies in teaching them about losing gracefully. Teach them to congratulate the winner and gracefully accept congratulations if they're the winner. You will not be undermining their desire to win, which is probably a good thing, but which needs to be tempered with the dignity associated with playing within the rules and accepting defeat gracefully. (Vince Lombardi's saying, "Winning isn't everything, it's the only thing!" can wait for another day.)

While you are spending some days or weeks practicing this instruction, select stories to read at bedtime or at naptime that deal with the fair and healthy playing of games. You might even edit a few of their books to insert a story line of healthy play in the stories. Find a few kid movies that portray healthy play and watch them together, using the pause function to talk about orderly play within the rules.

To put it as simply as I can, if you want your kids to play quietly and peacefully, you must teach them how to do it by playing quietly with them! You must give them experience with quiet and calm play!

He Got More! Hers Is the Biggest!

Dear Mr. Bledsoe,

It seems that our house is in a constant argument between our two kids about who got the most or who got the biggest. They have pieces of cake; it seems to be an immediate battle over who got the biggest piece. If one has a red Popsicle, the other one will not settle for a green one. It is so competitive and so pointless.

Can you help us?

Sincerely,

The parents of "I want more!"

First of all, I must say that I love the way these parents signed their letter. I have a lot of adult friends who could be their children! It seems to me that describes so much of America. Aren't we the "I Want More" society? I really had a good laugh over that.

I'm back in control now, so here's some simple advice to lay to rest the "I Want More" disease, at least until your kids become adults on the constant quest to have more than their neighbors!

We can learn a lot if we listen to grandparents. Our grandfather was a very bright man, and long on common sense. Any time there was cake to be divided among us grandkids, he would let one cut the cake and another decide who got which piece. Those were the rules! That system lay to rest many an argument about who got the most. The one cutting was totally careful to cut equal portions, knowing that one of the other kids would decide which piece would be his or hers. You might say Granddad was pretty good at keeping the piece. His technique sure kept us from fighting over who got the most or the biggest! He could teach parents a great deal.

I'm sure that if Grandad were alive today, it would be interesting to hear his comments about what I am going to say next. Another lesson needs to be taught when it comes to the issue of who got the most or who got the biggest. I feel positive that if I could speak to the man, he would agree that the only issue there is settling the argument peacefully.

The bigger lesson is that who has the most is really an irrelevant issue. In their lives, things will work out best for them if they can establish their needs based upon what they need and not upon what others have. Grandad told me many times that happiness was found in wanting what I've got, not in getting what I want! He never gave me the advice as an extension of the "who gets what piece of cake" lesson, but I believe they are very connected ideas and could be presented to children in just such a manner.

When children are given a piece of cake, help them to look only at the piece they have. "Look, you have a piece of the red flower in your frosting." Guide them away from comparing with others and help them see and delight in what they have right there in front of them. A two-year-old might not yet grasp the concept of happiness, but you can certainly help the child to focus on what is on her plate. Gradually, over the years you will raise a child capable of delight in personal accomplishment and personal possession independent of what others have.

Who knows, your child might reach adulthood and never enter the "Who Has the Most" generation!

Note: A Look into the Future

One last thought about sibling rivalry might bear mentioning, even though it probably requires a much higher level of reasoning than a toddler might manage. Looking into the future, I will suggest that it might be a good plan to help siblings celebrate their differences. With all of the rhetoric about fairness and equality that is being circulated, a concept that has crept into parenting is the idea that the ideal parent should treat every child the same. I believe that to be folly. Even identical twins are not the same!

Every child is unique and deserves to be treated as such. One way to ward off sibling rivalry is to develop different relationships with each of your children right from the start. Have activities that the whole family participates in, but also make it a point to have individual hobbies and activities that you do exclusively with each child. Let the others know about each other's unique interests and activities.

With one child, an early activity might be collecting dolls and doll clothes. For another, the activity might be collecting model racecars. Let them look for things for each other's collections.

Now those two examples are pretty obviously for children of differing gender, but it's easy to see that having differing interests doesn't hurt either one.

Now if the siblings are of the same gender, it's no less valid to encourage them to have different interests. If a two-year-old boy likes to play with cars and a four-year-old likes to play with Legos, it is just as wise to help each to develop individually. Let the older one celebrate his little brother's interest by letting him pick out a car and give it to him. (Sounds vaguely like Grandad letting one kid divide the cake and the other kid select the first piece, huh?) Then let the younger boy pick out some Legos for his brother. It doesn't have to be Christmas to give gifts. Let your kids give gifts all year round as a way of celebrating their unique and wonderful differences.

Sibling rivalry is natural. It takes some careful teaching on the part of parents to combat the tendency of kids to compete with siblings. When you do, it might be one of the most enjoyable accomplishments of your entire life, so don't give up! Keep trying and you will succeed!

Chapter 5

Eating Problems

"My five year old is a picky eater; can I ever expect him to eat normally?

Some balking at meal time is natural as growth spurts ebb
and flow, colds come and go, naps are missed, life gets too exciting, and so on. It's natural for children to be occasionally balky
at eating, but—and listen carefully here—most eating behavior
is learned! That's right: *Eating behavior is learned!*

Hunger is instinctual, but what a person eats and how they
eat is learned. Two thirds of the earth's population eats with sticks
or their hands! Over half the humans on earth consider insects a
staple of their diet ... not out of hunger exclusively; bugs are considered a delicacy!

So what is the point? The point is that *your* children will eat in
the manner you *teach* them to eat. I have said it many other places
in this book and I will say it again here: *Teaching does not necessarily
involve intent to teach!* A craving for sweets is learned. Granted,
once children have some experience with candy bars, they will
almost always develop a craving for them. Sweets are pleasant to
the human palate. However, a child who never tastes sweets will
not develop a craving for them. If you buy and serve sugar-coated
cereal to your children, you've taught them to want only sugar-
coated cereal. So many parents tell me, "All my kids will eat is

sugar-coated cereal." Baloney! They will only eat sugar-coated cereal if that's what they're served. If it isn't available, they'll eat other breakfast food. No children have ever starved with food on their plates.

Kids Can Learn to Desire a Healthy Diet

Boy, did we receive a lesson in the validity of all this by watching our daughter-in-law, Maura, as she and Drew encountered some severe allergy problems with their three sons. After a few years of constant runny noses, battles with eczema, and ear infections, Maura and Drew took the three boys to a doctor specializing in children's allergies. This doctor identified numerous foods and pets the boys were allergic to, including toddler staples: milk, cheese, soy, wheat, eggs, beet sugar, citrus, peanuts—the list goes on. So out went sandwiches, cheese, fruit, milk, toast, and most cereals. You get the picture: a dramatic life change for the whole family!

However, I observed that the boys all began to eat more! They have huge appetites at meals because they don't have the usual child snacks loaded with sugar and carbohydrates. Their snacks are now carrots, rice cakes, raisins, apples, pears, and two of the three boys could have oranges. Breakfast now consists of oatmeal with raisins, wheatless bread, and some days, sausage and bacon. They drink lots of water. They drink some white grape juice halved with water.

The amazing thing is that they now ask for those foods! When they visit, they will come to me and say, "Pappa, can I have some raisins?" or "Hey, Pappa, can I have some juice or water?" "Pappa, can I have a banana?"

At meals they tell *us* there are certain things they can't eat! They can also articulate that some foods make them sick, but when they grow up they may be able to eat them again. But they eat plenty and they're satisfied with meat, fresh vegetables, rice, and some fruits.

Drew and Maura's kids are no different from other people's children. They watch TV and are bombarded with advertisements for fast food. They still like to go to McDonalds and they love Happy Meals.

When the Happy Meals come, they're fine with either water or juice with their meal. They don't complain if they have no cheese on their burger, and they're just fine when their burger has the bun taken off of it. They love the plain burger.

As a parent of a young child, just remember that your children will eat exactly what you teach them to eat. We watched our grandkids being taught to eat a very healthy diet. Now, after about a year and a half of teaching, they crave the diet they have been taught to eat!

Now, do not think for a minute that I'm a health food fanatic trying to shame you into some fad diet or that I am telling you what to feed your children. *I am not!* Heck, I'm a carnivore who grew up eating beef daily, and so did my sons!

What you feed to your children is up to you. I'm just suggesting that you think about what your actions are teaching your children. Ask yourself what diet you want your children eating. Then serve that diet to them. They will learn to eat what is served to them. Hunger will still play a part, but the cravings for sweets and the dislike for fresh fruits and vegetables will take care of themselves if you serve only food on the list of the foods you decide upon. An occasional candy bar or food not on the list will not upset things. Rule #1: Your children will learn to eat the diet you have taught them! Rule #3: Tastes in food will change because the desired diet is served over and over. Remember that you teach by example—if you eat breaded fast food and a soda with no fruit or salad, guess what? Your children will do as you do, not as you say.

I was simply amazed to watch our grandkids' tastes change.

My gosh, look at the power in our hands if we change the eating habits of the kids in the next generation! Have you noticed what's happening in the fast food business recently? Low-carb diets have become popular, and look at the effect on fast food! Mind you, not everyone in America is on a low-carb diet, but now you go into a Wendy's, Burger King, McDonalds, Taco Bell, or other fast food establishment and all of them have low-carb offerings. Salads are a part of every menu. The other day I saw an advertisement for a lettuce-wrapped burger! We're not victims of the fast food industry: They serve us what we ask for and what we will buy. If enough people ask for Happy Meals with fresh fruit and fresh vegetables, McDonalds will serve them.

How Much Should Children Eat?

Now the next question is quantity. How much should we feed our kids? Let me go out on a limb here and say that I think we have raised generations of overweight Americans (adults, teens, and little ones) by telling children to *eat everything on their plates!* I know it was done with me. Most of you reading this book are probably younger than me, so for you it was probably a little different. I cannot count the number of times we Bledsoe kids were told to eat everything on our plate because if we didn't, we were going to have to address packages and send our food to the starving kids in China! You younger folks were probably asked to send your food to Bangladesh or some other third-world country.

In our family, there were four kids; I have an older brother and two younger sisters. Mom and Dad served our plates in the kitchen and we were told to clean them. As a little boy, I had a vitamin B deficiency and it negatively affected my appetite for a few years, but by age 7 or 8, I was a normal hungry boy and growing like a weed. My sister Janet, on the other hand, was and is a tiny person. Even today she's barely five feet tall. By the time I was in the eighth grade I was six feet tall; when Janet was in the eighth grade, she was about four feet tall. We were served the same plate of food and told to eat it all.

It used to really make me feel bad to see my sister in a constant battle with our Dad as he demanded that she eat everything on her plate. It wasn't a problem for me to eat everything on my plate—my body needed it! My brother Mike and I were eager to help her out when Dad wasn't looking, but most often she just struggled mightily to eat way more than her body needed.

The limit of what a child eats should never be the quantity on the plate! *The limit of what a child eats should be what their body needs.*

How do we know what our child's body needs? Watch and listen! Even a baby will let you know how much he needs: He will stop eating! Contrary to what you might think, your picky eater will not starve and become malnourished. Like I said, I was a big kid and probably due to a genetically high metabolism, I had a huge appetite. I could eat huge amounts of food; but I had an idea in my head that I didn't even know was there—and it was ruling my world. "Eat everything on your plate," my father's voice kept telling me. Wherever I went, I would eat everything on my plate. (Remember way back at the start of the book when I said that the ideas in your head will rule your world ... well, I had an idea that was ruling my world: "Eat everything on your plate!")

That worked just fine when I was young and leading an extremely active life. My body could burn up food. Then, a few years ago, as I grew older, my body no longer needed that volume of food, but I still had that same idea ruling my world. I began to pick up some unwanted extra weight, but I kept on stuffing food in my mouth to comply with that powerful idea echoing in my head. To stop adding extra weight I had to change the idea in my head. The same will be true for you and your children.

"Well, what do I do?" you ask. Read the next couple of letters and my responses, and hopefully you will get some ideas!

Our Kid Will Only Eat Sweetened Cereal

Dear Mr. Bledsoe,

Our daughter is three years old and she throws a fit at just about any food we set in front of her other than her favorite foods. What are we to do? At breakfast she will only eat her favorite, Coco Puffs. If I give her some toast or fruit, she just throws it on the floor or picks up pieces of the fruit and throws them at me. For lunch all she will eat is peanut butter sandwiches on white bread with the crusts cut off. If I leave the crusts on the bread, she will eat the middle of the sandwich and throw the crusts on the floor, or worse, she will throw them at me.

She will only drink pop. If I give her water, she throws the water on the floor. Sometimes when I give her juice she will play in it for a while, then she just pours it out on her tray or on the floor.

Dinner is the worst! She only will eat hot dogs and Tater Tots. Nothing else. We can't get her to eat anything remotely healthy. What are we to do?

We have had my parents over to seek their help and they have little more to offer than what we have already tried. We put good food in front of her and she simply refuses to eat it or she throws it and screams.

We are too embarrassed to have any of our friends see this behavior, so we simply will not accept invitations for dinner or invite others to our home during any mealtime. Help!!

Sincerely,
Buffaloed in Buffalo

This little three-year-old has trained her parents very well. She has taught them to do exactly as she pleases, and they do what she demands! I wish you could see my face. I am smiling as I am writing. I am not laughing at these parents; I am laughing because it's hilarious to see how well a three-year-old can teach adults to obey!

Now, let me tell you what I see going on in this family. First of all, how did the daughter discover she only likes Coco Puffs for breakfast? Where did she first get them? Did some alien sneak in and slip them in front of her while her mom prepared a healthy breakfast? While Mom wasn't looking, did someone steal the fruit and oatmeal and slip in a bowl of the sugar-coated chocolate cereal?

If this is a problem in your home, I'm pretty sure you parents are the ones who introduced your kids to sugar-coated cereal, so look no farther than yourselves for a solution. You taught them to prefer those foods; you buy them for your house. You are the ones who need to change, and your kids will change to match your actions and expectations.

Get the undesired food out of your house and don't buy any more. If you buy it for yourselves and you eat it in front of your child—or even if she just knows you have it in the house—then how do you explain why she can't eat it, too? That's a question you need to answer rationally.

Children do what works! If they do something, and you give them what they want in response ... then they've just learned how to get what they want from their world!

If your child has learned that by throwing food she doesn't want onto the floor—or just refusing to eat it—she will eventually get what she wants, you must now teach her a different action. It may be difficult for a few days or maybe even a few weeks, but it will be worth it in a few years when she eats healthily and acts respectfully to the people who provide her food.

Parents' Action

First, sit down together and decide what foods you want your child to eat. Make up a menu for the week. Plan exactly what you're going to serve for each meal each day. Purchase only those foods. Get rid of the undesirable foods in the house. The day before the new plan begins, have a rehearsal. Show your daughter what she will have for breakfast in the morning and explain to her that there will be no other foods offered. Explain very clearly and carefully to her that the next morning when you sit down for breakfast, you will all eat the same thing.

Tell her that anyone who throws food on the floor will get no more food. (Don't expect a three-year-old to listen and act upon simple directions like this. Giving the instructions is just the first step in teaching your daughter to eat a healthy diet with appropriate behavior.) Here's Rule #1 at work: explain that if she throws her food on the floor, she will be taken down from her high chair or down from the table.

The next morning do exactly as you said. Keep this idea running through your head: "My child deserves to eat healthy food," or some other positive statement so you don't revert to "she's driving me crazy" or "she has to eat something!"

Make no mistake: your daughter will probably throw a fit and throw her food on the floor. When she does, do exactly what you told her you were going to do. Simply lift her from her chair and set her on the floor. Quietly remove her food from the table. Do not explain to her what you are doing or why you are doing it. She is throwing a fit and she cannot even hear your words. Let your actions speak! Keep any anger out of your actions, even if she is crying and screaming. Quietly, quickly, and cheerfully remove her plate and sit back down and eat your breakfast. Ignore the fit.

Remember that for at least two of her three years she has screamed and thrown food—and been rewarded with eating exactly as she pleases. She's going to keep up the negative behavior until she's sure it won't work anymore. Whatever happens, do not get in an argument with her or try to reason with her when she is throwing her fit. She cannot listen or learn while she is in that kind of turmoil. Don't even talk to her. Simply ignore her.

If you can't stand to have her in the room while she is expressing her anger, give her a warning and then put her in her room if she doesn't heed it. However, *don't be fooled into thinking that putting her in her room is teaching her anything*. It's not. You have to *teach* her the desired eating habits. All you're accomplishing by putting her in her room is giving yourself a moment of peace.

Before the next meal, explain to her again exactly what's going to happen. You will serve the whole family and she can eat what's on her plate. If she doesn't eat what's on her plate, or if she throws any of it, she will be finished with that meal. Remain calm for this meal as well.

> *Say what you mean, mean what you say, and do what you said you would do.* Repeat this again and again to yourself until it's a mantra. Today is a new day! Be firm, be cheerful, but do what you said that you are going to do. Your actions will speak to your child louder than any words ever could.

A while back, two of our grandsons spent 10 days with us. It was good for me to actually practice what I preach and understand again how much resolve it takes to do what you say you're going to do! These boys had well-established eating habits when our son and daughter-in-law dropped them off at our house. It was hard not to fall into the old habit of giving them treats. Golly—grandparents *deserve* to give kids treats! In one day, I learned how quickly I could destroy what Drew and Maura had instilled in those kids. It's difficult when you love children and want to please them with treats. I caught myself lots of times wanting to give in "just this once!" It's almost like an alcoholic talking himself into just one drink!

Even though our grandchildren had developed healthy eating habits, they still could see the candy at the store and on television. They could still ask for it. However, it was my choice whether to give in. I know from experience, it will be difficult to stick to your guns, but, believe me, it will be worth it! You will teach your daughter to eat healthily. Doing this will be so good for her—and so empowering for you. You will learn that you are not at the mercy of the marketers and advertisers of unhealthy foods. You are in control! You may have a week or even two of unpleasant screaming fits as your daughter's negative habit is replaced by one of your choosing. Believe me, it will be worth it.

Have confidence; your daughter will not starve during her retraining. She may get a little hungry, but she will survive. Up until now, she has very effectively used your unspoken and well-meaning fear that she will be undernourished to get the food she wants. You can trust that she won't let herself starve. When those pangs of real hunger set in—she'll eat!

When she does eat some of the healthy food you have prepared for her, give her lots of praise. However, don't reserve your affection and love for only those times. As a matter of fact, when you are teaching something new and difficult and having to stand firm in the face of a child's anger and frustration, it is imperative that you express your love for your child even more frequently than you might normally express it. Otherwise, your child can interpret your firmness as a message that you do not love her.

She may throw that at you during her fits shouting, "Mommy, I hate you," or "Daddy, you don't love me." Just know that she is trying to "trip your trigger"—the same trigger she has had such easy access to for over two years. As soon as she is calm again, try to make some special time for her. Sit down and read a book; get out the Play Dough and make something; take a walk together; at the very least, share a hug and a loving moment.

Whatever you do, don't talk about what just happened. There is almost nothing to be gained in speaking with a toddler about past actions. Make sure all talk is about the next time.

How Do We Get Our Picky Eaters to Eat Enough?

Dear Mr. Bledsoe,

Thank you for your book. Without it I would be lost. I just have one question for you regarding the topic of mealtime. We have three kids all under the age of 4 and we are in constant turmoil about how to get them to eat enough. Do you have any tips?

Sincerely,
PPE (Parents of Picky Eaters)

I love their acronym, don't you? Before I offer any help with this common problem, let me say that if you're like this couple and you have three kids under age four—*go sit down!* With three kids under four you need a rest! I hope you live close enough to the kids' grandparents to allow them to help out once in a while. If you're a grandparent reading this and thinking that it is not your job to give your kids a break, that you are not a babysitting service, please relax and take at least one of the grandkids once in a while. Now let's talk about the quantity of food kids eat. How much food do we commonly put in front of kids at mealtime? Look at the volume in terms of percentage of body weight. If a child of three weighs 30 pounds and we give him a plate with four ounces of food on it (a small portion in many households), it would be the same as serving me two pounds of food! And I struggle to eat a quarter-pound burger or a whole dinner salad.

Here is an effective way to establish how much to give a child, which will also give your children an additional gift by teaching them a reasonable lifetime approach to deciding how much they should eat. Rather than loading the plate with what you think is a reasonable portion and then demanding that your child eat it all, simply put a bite of each food on the plate and let the child adjust the amount by asking for more.

They will then begin to listen to their bodies to establish how much to eat! Serve them one bite of the meat, one bite of the starch, one bite of the vegetable, and one bite of the fruit. (I am assuming that you are planning a well-rounded diet.) Then if they ask for more, only give them one more bite of each food group after the previous bites have been eaten. This will stop the child from eating all of their favorite food and then turning up their nose at the foods they don't like as much.

They only get more food in groups of bites from each food group. With this system, they cannot just eat lots of one food and leave the rest on the plate. When parents give large portions of each food on the plate together, what typically happens is that a child will eat all of their favorite food and become full.

For a week our four grandchildren stayed with us. Drew and Maura have been using this technique in addition to offering only foods that are not on their allergy prohibition list. On our second night with the kids, I was amazed to watch all four of them eating big amounts of broccoli at dinner. It has been my experience that broccoli is one of the most universally disliked foods among children, but these kids were eating it because they knew from experience that before they get another helping of any food, they must eat the small servings of each food on their plates. The kids come to the table with natural hunger. Their plates have very manageable amounts of food, and they eat the servings offered to them and ask for more, knowing that they will get more of everything. They eat their least favorite foods while they are hungry in order to get more of the foods they prefer. In the process they have learned to like many foods that they would normally have turned up their noses at.

Another point to be made here is that children go through phases where they don't eat as much. Their bodies grow in spurts, and their hunger mirrors those spurts by waning at times. On our grandchildren's most recent visit, one of them was simply not as hungry or capable of eating as much as he had only months before. Yet by feeding him a bite of each food group, we were ensuring that he was getting the needed nutrients from all of the food groups and letting him establish the volume by asking for more. He rarely asked for more on this visit, but he always ate a well-rounded diet!

Another idea that works is to give the same number of bites as the age; i.e., two bites of each food for a two-year-old. For a very young child, you are making the decision about eating a well-rounded diet, but the volume of food is left up to the child. If the child wants more, they get to eat more of each food.

At first this may be difficult to enforce as your child develops preferences for some foods and a dislike for others, but, believe me, there is a much greater chance of your children developing a taste for a wide variety of food if they *eat* a wide variety of food!

Kids will learn to eat what is served to them. Certainly, if all they get is sugar-sweetened food and peanut-butter sandwiches with the crust cut off, they'll develop a preference for those foods! If you give them a well-rounded diet, they'll learn to eat a well-rounded diet.

I Won't Eat the Crusts

Now let me offer a solution to the issue of the child saying "I won't eat the crust on my peanut butter sandwich! (or similar statements)"

Like the sugar-sweetened cereal, this is a learned behavior. The child will only learn different if you teach them different. Handle this just like the rest of the items placed in front of the child. Serve just one small slice of the peanut butter sandwich (with the crust) and give no more food until all of it is eaten. Do not engage in an argument about it. Like before, let your actions do the teaching. If the child whines, let her! But do not give more food until all of the first serving is eaten. Children will quickly learn to eat the food that is presented to them.

Note that almost all humans have specific likes and dislikes when it comes to food. It is okay and normal for a child to have foods that do not please their personal palate. We have instituted the "One Bite Rule" with our grandchildren when they visit. When something is served to you, you must try one bite. We talk to them about how your taste buds change and that something you didn't like a week ago can become a favorite food. They're secure in the fact that, if they honestly do not like a food, all they have to eat is one bite, which allows them to try new foods. We have been amazed at how many times we find our grandchildren deciding that they like something that they previously disliked.

One of them was positive he did not like crusts on bread. Now, he asks to eat the heel on a loaf of bread! How did he make the discovery that he likes the crust? He ate a bite one day!

Eating Disorders

I want to at least mention a problem that rarely shows itself in the early years but may take root in the toddler stage. There are real dangers for children in bulimia nervosa, anorexia nervosa, and binge eating. These syndromes are rare in toddlers, but if you suspect that an underweight child is showing signs of not eating in order to stay slim, it might be a red flag.

Also, if a child who is not ill often vomits right after a meal, it might call for a visit to the doctor. However, bulimia nervosa is very, very rare in children under age 10.

If you suspect your child may have an eating disorder, the best advice is to visit a pediatrician. If you begin to fear your child has a problem, whether the fear is founded or not, it can begin to drive some of your decisions and become part of the problem for the child. Eating disorders may be associated with depression on the part of the child. Worrying about a depression-based problem usually multiplies the problem. Seek professional help and guidance.

Modeling Mealtime Behaviors

I would like to mention one dynamic that can show up at mealtime and have an effect on eating habits. Children seek attention from their parents and siblings. Mealtime offers kids a *great* chance to receive that positive attention from parents and siblings. Making mealtime a happy and enjoyable time for children can often head off some eating difficulties. If mealtime is allowed to evolve into being only a time where you continually nag a child to eat, that's still attention! It may seem like negative attention to you—but to an attention-starved child, attention is attention, period!

In many homes where there are two or more children, the youngest can often feel left out because the more verbal family members dominate the discussion. A dynamic can evolve where the youngest discovers that a way to attract the attention is to stall in eating.

If the child feels the need for attention, be it because of a large number of siblings or because most of the talk is directed to others or about adult topics, the child will try to get attention in any way that works.

The solution to this problem does not lie in continuing to nag the child to eat! If you feel that your child is stalling just to get attention, the solution is to give attention at other times and in other ways. Ignore the stalling and let your actions speak for you. Explain that any food not eaten during mealtime will simply be removed. (Now, be careful here. You may be creating more of a problem than you are eliminating. Eating fast is not a virtue nor is it healthy. It takes the human body about six minutes, at a minimum, to perceive consumption and register satiation of hunger.)

If your child is a slow eater, most likely the best solution is for *you to slow down* rather than for the child to speed up. Set aside time for leisurely mealtimes.

It drives me crazy to hear parents justify the demands for kids to eat quickly because they are in a mad rush to get going! "We don't have all day to wait for this little person to dawdle with her food!" they say. To this I respond, "Slow down! The kid may be the one with the right idea. Eat slowly and savor your food and the company of the family's regular time to gather and enjoy each other!"

Most children who are sitting at the table and not eating with a plate full of food in front of them are fulfilling some other need by the action. Most are not aware of what they are doing. They are just stalling because it fulfills the need to get attention or it says, "Talk to me." Contrary to what some parents might contend, I do not believe that hungry children sit in front of plates full of food and starve themselves in some conscious effort to be contrary. If a child is not eating, he is either not hungry or he is meeting some other need by the action.

I worked with one family who complained that mealtime was a battle because neither of their children would sit down at the table and eat. They played with their food, stalled about eating, and continually got down from their chairs or climbed on the chairs and the table. I was privileged to view a week of videotape of their dining room. During that week, I never saw the parents sit at the table with their children! The parents were always in such a rush that they ate breakfast standing up while getting ready for work, filling their coffee cups, and cleaning up the breakfast mess. No wonder their children wouldn't sit down and eat! Dinner was a repeat of breakfast. The parents held their plates in their hands and ate on the run as they prepared the food for the kids and did other tasks. The television was always on.

Those parents told me that dinnertime was one of the most difficult times for them. They told me that their children just stalled and fooled around. They said that they just couldn't get the kids to eat during dinner but that they always wanted snacks after dinner. When I asked those parents to tell me about their children's eating habits, they told me that their kids were picky eaters who didn't have much of an appetite.

The solution to getting the children to sit and eat in an orderly fashion and eat their meals in a reasonable timeframe in this family was for the parents to sit down and do the same! Once the parents budgeted time to sit down and eat in a calm manner, the problem was solved. When the parents sat to eat, so did the children. When the parents were relaxed enough to sit and eat, the kids stopped "dawdling and stalling." The parents actually said that when they sat down with their children for a peaceful dinner, their children's appetites improved. I do not believe that the children's appetites changed one bit. What changed was the atmosphere that the parents created for their children at dinner.

The bonus here is that it actually took less time to prepare, eat, and clean up from a meal when the parents sat down and enjoyed the time than it did to rush, eat on the run, and nag at their children over and over: "Sit down! Eat! Hurry up!"

Remember: your children learn more from your backside than from your frontside. They learn more from watching what you do than they learn from what you say. Stop and ask yourself: What do I want to happen at mealtime?

Once you answer that question, and then teach it to your children, your problems will most likely be solved!

Chapter 6

Spanking, Time-Out, and Other Punishments

I was spanked as a kid and I turned out okay, yet so many people seem to outlaw punishment of any kind as a parenting technique. What should I do?

Don't panic. I'm not much of a believer in using punishment as part of raising kids either, but the real discussion shouldn't center on whether punishment is wrong or right but on *how well it works!* I don't think it works very well—if it works at all.

When I was a kid, I was sent to my room thousands of times for teasing my sisters. I was told to go and think about how to treat my sisters, and I sure did. I thought about how, as soon as I got out of my room, I was going to get them out behind the barn and hold their heads under water in the horse trough for tattling on me! I also thought about how my parents were not fair and how they always took my sisters' side in every argument, and I laid plans about how I was going to run away from home. I even concocted an idea that my parents hated me, and thus I hated them.

Sending me to my room didn't teach me how to get along with my sisters. The desired or intended result was a far cry from the real outcome. My parents' intention in sending me to my room was to teach me how to treat my sisters more nicely, *but what they got was far different from what they intended*. I do not believe they would have chosen any of the ideas running through my head to rule my world!

Proof That Punishment Does Not Work

Buck Minor, the cowboy on our ranch when I was growing up, always said, "If you teach an animal a lesson by meanness or cruelty, don't be surprised if the animal remembers the meanness and cruelty and forgets the lesson!" I remember him saying this repeatedly when I was young, and I was never quite sure what he was saying. Now that I am older, I can really see what he was telling me. His statement was about animals, but when I began teaching, the thought caused me to investigate for the first time the effectiveness of punishment as a tool for changing human behavior. Here's what I found.

First, let's define punishment. For the sake of our discussion, punishment is any artificially created consequence for a given behavior, which would include spanking, time-out, grounding, sending to the bedroom, removal of privileges, withholding of allowance, and so on.

Now, before we look at some common situations where parents use or consider punishment, let me give you a few reasons I do not believe that punishment works.

Punishment Guarantees a "Push-Back" Response

A "push-back" response is simply the natural human resistance to change. Any time we attempt to change a child's behavior, the child will resist. Adding punishment only ensures more resistance. If a young child is screaming when she wants something, punishment will most likely exacerbate this behavior. If a child is hitting another child, spanking that child will usually just make the child more secretive about hitting—and the fact that you hit the child only confirms in the child's mind that hitting is okay, and the pushback response simply gives the child reason to continue.

Punishment Shifts the Focus of Both You and Your Child From the Behavior in Question

When a parent resorts to punishment, both the parent and the child shift their focus to the punishment, its fairness, and its enforcement. The child stops thinking about the decision process and behavior that brought about the negative consequences in the first place.

The child is not engaged in developing a new thought process that will result in better decisions and behavior the next time. A spanked child will think about how their fanny hurts and how they want to run away from home. Seldom will he think about how to behave appropriately next time to avoid punishment. *And next time is the key!* If the child knew how to behave appropriately, he would have been doing it in the first place!

The younger the child, the greater the chances of behavior becoming a dysfunctional spiral. When we punish toddlers, they react very viscerally with their limited repertoire of emotions and reactions. They will cry, scream, lash out with fists, throw things, and they will begin to make comments like "I hate you, Mommy; I hate you, Daddy!" The child is expressing his extreme distaste for the situation and pushing back. He doesn't like the pain of being spanked, and he wants it to stop! He doesn't want to be in his room, and he wants to be let out! Being spanked or sent to his room doesn't teach him what to *do*, so rather than consider and change his behavior, the child pushes back against the punishment.

Punishment also stops the parent from teaching the desired behavior. Once you begin using punishment, you are caught in the trap of administering the punishment and maintaining control of the situation.

Punishment Focuses Anger on the Punisher

When adults resort to punishment, it gives children someone else to be mad at or someone else to blame. The anger interrupts responsible thought. They do not have to face their own behavior or the natural consequences of that behavior as long as they can be angry at the punisher. A child sent to his or her room will seldom or never think about how to behave properly next time, but rather will think about how unfair and mean his or her parents are. If the child had been able to independently think of the desired behavior, she probably would have used it in the first place.

A mom who sends her daughter to her room probably isn't seeking to plant "I hate my Mommy!" in the child's head, but that's exactly what she's doing. By sending the child to her room, the parent is very predictably putting that negative and unproductive idea in the child's head.

Behaviors Induced by Punishment Extinguish Rapidly

To be sure, punishment can sometimes prevent negative behavior. The child refrains from the negative behavior as long as the threat of the punishment is present. But because the reason for avoiding the behavior is the fear of punishment, the negative behavior can return when the threat of punishment—i.e., *the parent*—is absent. And shouldn't your goal be to teach your child good behavior whether you're there to enforce it or not?

You must include your children in developing the reasons for and benefits of the desired behavior. A child who was spanked for running beside the pool has not been taught how to reason, think, and make decisions. Next time, she will look around to see if anyone is watching and, if not, will take off running. The issue becomes a game of not getting caught. "If I don't get caught, I don't get punished." The child never confronts the danger of running beside the pool or considers better, safer behavior.

> Punishment may work to stop a particular action. If you send a fighting kid to his room, he'll stop fighting for the immediate present, and sometimes that's necessary to prevent injury—or a nervous breakdown!
>
> *The error comes when we think that our punishment has taught the child what to do next time.* It has taught the child what *not* to do, but it hasn't taught him what *to do!* Our job as parents is to teach kids what to do the next time—and how to decide to do it!

Punishment Traps the Punisher in Enforcing the Punishment

"You made the rules, now you must enforce them." Toddlers are really good at this game. They have unencumbered minds capable of complete focus on one thing. They will keep after you to see if you are going to be consistent. Toddlers are in a time of actively learning the limits on their behavior. They will test your resolve repeatedly!

You've probably heard the old adage, "Never argue with a three-year-old, because you will always lose!" I think there's a great deal of truth in this statement. Punishment engages the parent in an ongoing argument that they cannot win! Kids are too focused and parents have too much other stuff to do (don't you?) to maintain the argument. Eventually, the child wins, because parents just wear out!

When you introduce punishment, the child then may turn it into a game of seeing how much they can get away with without you catching them. A child sent to a time-out chair will continuously ask to get up to constantly test the parent's will to follow through. The parent is equally confined by having to ensure compliance!

Punishment Does Not Teach Accountability

Parents are responsible for seeing that their children's behavior changes. If parents use punishment, they have accepted *direct* responsibility for their child's *behavior*, saying loudly and clearly to the child, "You are not in control, I am." With this responsibility established, a child who has experienced only punishment has no ability to make her own behavioral decisions when the punisher is not present to take responsibility. My experience as a secondary teacher showed me that children raised under the constant threat of parental punishment and control were most at risk of making terrible decisions for themselves later.

Children have to learn to be accountable in the cold world outside your influence! And, believe me, the outside world is a tough teacher! Like I said, my years of teaching have taught me that children who must learn their own lessons by themselves, away from their parents, often make mistakes they have trouble surviving. The child who is punished for violence may only learn to avoid violence in the presence of Mom and Dad. The punishment has not taught the child any of the *reasoning* behind avoiding violence, and a boy who experiments with violence might never overcome that bad decision.

Toddlers might have a difficult time understanding "Do not hit," but a child can understand role-playing with Mom about other ways to express angry feelings. A child who is spanked for being mean to a sibling simply learns that the biggest person gets to hit! A three-year-old can learn that lesson with no words being spoken. The child punished for hitting accepts no accountability for hitting. The child has no thought of deciding to act kindly because it is a good way to act ... in that child's eyes, even adults don't act that way.

Punishment Blinds a Child to Real Consequences

The goal ought to be to let the natural negative consequences of the child's behavior do the enforcing. If your toddler runs beside a wet pool, falls, and gets scraped up, he has experienced the natural consequence. When he is comforted and bandaged, he is ready to be taught.

The real consequence of spilling on a carpet is that the child has to stop playing and clean up the mess, and the drink is lost and not replaced. A child who breaks a dish must pick up the pieces. A child who throws a ball carelessly in the house and breaks a picture frame must apologize for the error. It might even be a good exercise to take the child to the store to help buy the replacement frame for the picture to see that a bad decision can result in a long-term outcome.

Parents need to point out the negative consequences of negative behavior. We do not need to create artificial ones. Parents can help children best by helping them foresee potential problems, the natural consequences of their possible decisions, and then teach them positive actions to take.

The consequence of being mean to a sibling is that the child has made someone else feel bad. The child is viewed as mean and insensitive. Point out that consequence clearly to your toddler. Kids can feel empathy. Kids can feel remorse.

The key here is clearly for the parent to guide the child in appropriate action. When you resort to punishment, a child will simply deduce, by your action, that you are meaner than they are. (If the parent acts in anger, the kid might be right!)

> There are, of course, situations where it is unreasonable to let children incur the natural consequences of their own poor performance. If the kid's behavior is dangerous, intrusive, or an excessive disturbance of the peace, parents must be the adults!

Real Punishment, Real Rewards

The reward for good performance is ... good performance. Seldom is it necessary for us to provide the reward. The same is true for poor performance: the punishment is poor performance. As I mentioned in Chapter 2, the other day we were watching Dr. Phil, and a mother and father were seeking advice because their daughter had begun to lie. The daughter was fabricating stories to avoid punishment.

At first the fabrications were fairly innocent. But now she is 13 and has begun to lie about critical issues, such as where she is going when she leaves the house, about having a boyfriend, and what time she will come home. The parents were worried that this lying was not only unacceptable but dangerous.

Dr. Phil's advice was to establish who was boss by increasing the punishment: taking away privileges, confining the daughter to her room, and taking away more and more of her things until the daughter got the picture.

The father asked what I considered to be a very perceptive question: "So we just keep ramping up the punishment until it gets to the point where we are feeding our daughter with a straw through the keyhole in a room where she has no bed or clothes?"

Dr. Phil laughed him off and did not respond, but if you have even a mildly strong-willed child, you know that the father was describing a situation that you can easily picture yourself caught in. Once you choose the path of punishment, you are caught in an escalating cycle, upping the ante with every defiant behavior—and the child is the one in control. As long as the child is willing to take what you mete out (and this child was willing; she had been punished for 10 years), the child can almost always win that game. A strong-willed child will force you to up the punishment until you reach your limit and they win!

My advice is: don't go there! Direct all of your efforts toward *teaching the desired behavior!* Not once on that show did I hear anyone utter one word about honesty or the huge advantages of telling the truth. All the adults talked about was lying and the negative consequences of lying—mostly artificial consequences created by the parents. When they talked to the girl, all she could talk about was how unfair her parents were!

Isn't the goal to teach the child to tell the truth? I wish I could have been there to offer a different point of view. It is not the duty of adults to create new punishments but rather to point out the negative consequences of a child's negative actions. Most important, it is the obligation of all parents to teach positive alternatives.

Certainly, this young lady in the show is no longer a toddler, but the reason that I include her story is because the behavior began when she was three and has continued to escalate since then. The problem of lying began when she was a toddler, and the punishment that the parents meted out not only did not decrease the lying, it seemed to contribute to the problem, because the lying increased as the girl lied more to avoid the punishment.

If you have chosen this chapter as one of the first ones to read, you might feel like I have advocated that you throw away one of your only tools for working with your kids. Please don't lose hope! Read the other chapters and learn some techniques to use *in place of* punishment. You might find that you simply do not need punishment anymore!

Now let's look at some real situations to add a sense of reality to this issue of punishment.

We Are at Our Wits' End!

Dear Mac,

Every time our six-year-old son hits or shouts at his three-year-old brother, we send him to his room. When he gets to his room he shouts "I hate you!" at us and screams and throws toys. We have scolded him loudly and forcefully, spanked him, tried using time-out, and nothing seems to work. What can we do? We are at our wits' end.

Need help in Boston

To begin with, these parents have obviously proven to themselves that *punishment does not work!*

Let's go back to Rule #3. It says that you should repeat things to your kids. But Rule #3 also states that if you have tried to teach something three times and it is not working, you must remember these important words: "That didn't work!" Then you must find a new way to say it!

Where has this boy learned to shout at his little brother? Where has he learned to hit his little brother? His parents shout at him and hit him! (I know we've been taught to call it spanking, but I think that just legitimizes it. I prefer to call it hitting, because it's so much more descriptive of what's actually happening.) Remember that teaching something does not require the intention to teach. You're teaching your child every moment you're together! Children learn way more from your actions than they learn from your words!

Now is the time for these parents to try another way to say the same thing! I would suggest that they try to teach their son some other ways to relate to his younger brother—and try some other ways of teaching.

One problem here is that they wait until there is already a problem before they try to teach. It is almost impossible for a child to think or learn while he is mad at a sibling and mad at you because he has been spanked and sent to his room. Do not misinterpret what I am saying here. I'm not saying that you should be permissive or stop trying to teach your child to interact reasonably. But you must pick your moments, and try to teach the same thing in another way at a calmer moment! If you must send your child to his room to stop some violent or otherwise unacceptable behavior, fine, but don't allow yourself to think that sending him to his room has taught him anything. It stopped the behavior, that is all. The teaching is up to you at some calm moment later on, but *before* the next episode of negative behavior.

Parents' Action

Set up a time when you can be alone with your older child when both of you can be calm. Describe some acceptable ways he can express anger with his words. It might sound something like this: "I know that your little brother makes you angry when he gets into your stuff. A good thing to do is to give him something else to play with. Even better, what if you play with him? Rather than hitting him, try this. If he's in your room playing with your stuff, grab a ball and say, 'Come on, let's go in the other room and play catch.'"

This idea that he interact with a younger sibling in a more productive and reasonable manner is not one that six-year-olds would think up by themselves, but it just might work. It's definitely worth a try. Practice it with him. Role-play with him.

Next, suggest that the older child put breakable toys and possessions out of the reach of his little brother. Suggest that you go to the store together and buy a lock for a closet or a special box where he can keep his most valuable possessions. Then his brother cannot get into them unless the big brother lets him. Then let the older child teach his brother how to ask nicely to play with his toys. That might even be a special thing for the three-year-old.

Divide and conquer! If there are two parents in the home, one of you teach the six-year-old while the other teaches the three-year-old to respect his brother's things! Use this as an opportunity to teach the younger child to ask before grabbing toys and things that do not belong to him. This teaching will have to combine simple requests coupled with actions you have taught and role-played with him, such as saying, "please" or "Can I have a turn?"

The other can teach the six-year-old to comply with the request or to suggest alternatives. "Okay, we can play with my ball for a while. Then let's put it away and we can ...." Teach your six-year-old to say, "That was fun. I liked playing ball with you." You are teaching that the consequence of positive decisions is feeling positive.

You may be surprised to find that the time you spend on the floor teaching your sons will be enjoyable for you, but it's especially important for them. Teach them that in your family it's important for everyone to be nice and share. Continually verbalize and demonstrate by your actions what the desired behavior is. Get creative, but think clearly about what it is that you want your kids to do!

To Spank or Not To Spank

To close this chapter, if you're a parent who believes in physical punishment, I would like very much for you to think about the act of spanking for just a minute. I know that it's part of our culture. I was spanked as a child. I do not think that I was damaged in any way by it. Neither do I believe I was helped by it. It just happened to me. I learned the lessons in what preceded the punishment and what followed it.

I would like for you to consider a few questions as you contemplate spanking a child under age six:

On what basis have you decided that you are justified in spanking this little person?

- Are you spanking the child because you are bigger?
- Are you spanking the child because you are older?

- Are you spanking the child because you are smarter?
- Are you spanking the child because you are more experienced?
- Are you spanking the child because you know more?
- Are you spanking the child because you are angry about their behavior?
- Are you spanking the child because you want him to be more civil to others?

Please hang with me here and just listen for a second: to me, a "yes" answer to any or all of those questions would constitute a reason *not* to spank your kids!

Do you really want to teach your child that the biggest person gets to hit? That is what you will teach your child if that's your reason for hitting your child. Remember that your actions teach way more than your words to a very young child.

If you are justifying spanking your child because you are older, then get ready for your oldest child to feel entitled to hit his younger sister. You've taught your kid by your actions that you get to hit because you are older!

If you are spanking your child because you're smarter or more experienced, just watch your kids feel that the more education they have, the more they are justified in hitting and hurting those with less education.

If you're hitting your child because you're angry, don't be surprised when your child hits others out of anger. You're going to have a tough time teaching your child to control his anger if your actions show that you can't (or won't) control your own.

The Dignified Response

Please go back to the title of this book. *Parenting with Dignity* means that you are going to preserve not only the dignity of your kids, but also your own dignity!

I learned this concept from a dignified lady named Shirley Poe way back when I was in the army in 1970. Back then I was a lieutenant assigned the job of running the personnel office at Fort Eustice, Virginia, and that amazing lady worked for me as the office manager. She ran the office and set the tone for all of our business. Shirley's calm personality kept me sane despite the insanity of the army, and she also taught me a ton. (She remains a friend today and is still teaching me.)

One morning she was at her desk, greeting soldiers in her usual cheerful way, treating everyone with the same respect and dignity she used every day. Rank never made any difference to Shirley. She had arrived at her usual time, 10 minutes early. About an hour into the morning, one of the privates who worked with her came to me and said, "Lt. Bledsoe, did you see what happened to Shirley last night?"

"No," I replied.

He dropped the newspaper on my desk and left. On the front page was a picture of Shirley's home. There was a 10-foot cross burning in her front yard. It was a time of great racial strife in our country, and the Ku Klux Klan was very active in the area because of the government-enforced school integration there on the James River Peninsula. The cross burning had to do with a marriage planned in Shirley's family or something like that, which apparently didn't meet with the KKK's approval. Shirley is African American, and I believe they were angry that one of her relatives was marrying someone with lighter skin, or something equally ridiculous.

Simply put, Shirley had suffered a terrible and frightening indignity the night before. However, when I looked out my window and into the office, there she was, calm and cheerful as ever, even though it was common knowledge that the sergeant seated two desks from Shirley was a high-ranking officer in the local KKK. I was dumbfounded by her manner after such a dehumanizing experience, so I called her into my office. I pointed at the paper on my desk and said, "I just learned about what happened at your house last night, and, Shirley, you have to help me, because I don't understand something. How can you be on time to work, cheerful, respectful, and kind to everyone after something so terrible has happened to you? How can you treat people with respect and dignity when they treat you in such a disrespectful and undignified manner?"

She reached across my desk in that amazing and instructive manner of hers, patted my hand, and with her ever-present smile on her face she said, "Oh, Lt. Bledsoe, that's easy. In our family we are respectful and dignified not necessarily because the people around us are acting respectable or dignified: *We act that way because we are!*"

My life was changed forever! Shirley had just given me a standard to strive for. In all situations, I get to choose how I deal with other people. Their actions do not dictate my response: I do.

When we began to develop this curriculum, I felt that it was only fitting to title it *Parenting with Dignity*, because in our way of looking at it, parenting requires the same self-control that Shirley demonstrated daily. Your child may be acting rather undignified, but that does not mean *you* should lose your dignity!

Parenting with Dignity focuses on the dignified approach parents must always take in working with their children. Hitting children is simply undignified.

Chapter 7

Getting Dressed

"Morning is the hardest time of the day. Getting dressed is like pulling hair! She is four—will she ever dress herself?"

If you wait until morning when everyone, especially you, is in a hurry, getting dressed *can* be really difficult. Use Rule #1 to teach your children about getting dressed. Teach them what you want and, most important, teach them how to do it!

Lay the clothes out the night before while both you and your daughter are calm. Take your clothes into your daughter's bedroom and lay them out with hers. Having both sets of clothing ready will impart great calm to the next morning. While you choose and lay out everything from shoes to coat and backpack, explain to her what is going to happen in the morning. Get the new, calm routine in her head. Describe what you will say and the steps you both will go through.

When morning comes, allow yourself plenty of time so this new routine can be practiced with dignity. Wake her up with cheer in your heart at this new routine, and be excited about getting ready with her. If you have more than one child, get dressed all together. Go step by step. Put on an item of clothing and then have the child imitate you. Resist the urge to hurry them or do it for them. Ask yourself, "What is my goal?" If your goal is to get your children to dress themselves, let them do it.

If things move slowly the first time you try this, start earlier the next morning. Leave enough time to do the task. Remember, these are little kids and they are not yet capable of doing things in the rushed manner you have mastered after years of practice! Slow down and enjoy the peace and pace of being a kid again. This might be the best part of your day! Eventually, you might even be able to have some coffee with the minutes you save!

I experienced the amazing results of this technique a little while ago when our four grandchildren stayed with us for a week. They've been taught to dress themselves, and they lay out the next day's clothes each night. Each morning is a joy. The three older ones, ages two to six, dress themselves completely and they need no hurrying or coaxing. Our one-year-old granddaughter is almost there, only needing occasional help with a button or fastener. It's a fun part of the day, and they often beat me dressed. They really like that!

Your kids are an excuse to be young again and discover the unfettered joy of living. Enjoy this as you lead them on this great path. Getting dressed is one of those things you can enjoy with your kids for only a short while; enjoy it while you can and don't be too goal-oriented.

The S-l-o-w D-r-e-s-s-e-r

Dear Mac,

Our three-year-old daughter is slow as paint drying when she gets dressed every morning. She fiddles around until it drives us crazy. We don't have the time to wait for her to get ready every morning. How can we speed her up? We have tried rewarding her for getting ready quickly to no avail.

We have tried punishing her and it has no effect. We just can't seem to get her going in the morning.

What are we to do? We both work and even though our daughter is only three, she is making us both late to work. Not only that, we're afraid she's going to grow up driving everyone crazy because she never gets ready to go anywhere without us nagging.

We need help!
Slow Mo's Parents

All parents should rest assured that this *is* one of those things that, even if you do absolutely nothing, will take care of itself with time. Look around and ask yourself how many adults you see walking around naked! None? Well then, have some perspective here.

Are there some adults who take a long time to get dressed? Well, sure. Does it mean that they're miserable or bad people? Absolutely not!

Don't get me wrong. I'm not saying that you have to accept your kid taking an hour and a half to get dressed. But I *am* saying that between what this three-year-old is doing and what her parents have taught themselves to do, there's probably a reasonable middle ground.

Parents' Action

Consider that it may be *your attention*, positive or negative, that a child is seeking, *and getting*, with a slow pace! Look at this from your child's point of view. She knows that when she gets up and gets dressed she will soon lose you for hours.

Try getting up earlier and enjoying this time together. *Enjoy* this pace! Then, while you are relaxing and smelling the roses of the peaceful morning with your wonderful daughter, you might start modeling some more efficient ways of getting dressed.

Show your child how to do buttons efficiently, so he doesn't have to do them over because he got them started wrong. Teach her how to lay out clothes with the fronts facing up and pick them up so they're facing the proper direction, so she doesn't have to put them on and then turn them around. Sounds too simple, but those are things we do without thinking. A child is just learning, so guide her. Gradually she will get the picture.

Don't be surprised if getting dressed with your daughter in the morning causes the fiddling around to disappear. Giving her undivided attention in the morning may be what she wanted in the first place! Allow dressing time to be full of joy, sharing, and uninterrupted attention. You just made morning into a wonderful, *efficient* time of sharing.

Remember that dads can get dressed with daughters and moms can get dressed with daughters! Moms can get dressed with sons and dads can get dressed with sons. Don't make more of this than there is. Like Nike says, "Just do it!" When kids get older and feel the need for privacy, believe me, they will let you know. Cross that bridge when you get to it!

Look at Rule #5. It says that your most powerful tool for teaching kids to make good decisions for themselves as they grow older is making sure that they know you love them. Remember, kids spell love T-I-M-E! Even in your busy morning, you found time to spend with your child. As you continue with this comfortable time of sharing, you will find that your level of communication increases exponentially as you start each day together.

I guarantee you'll find it's worth getting up a little earlier—even if it means you have to go to bed a little earlier the night before. It's interesting isn't it? In order to teach your child to make good decisions, you must learn to make a few of them yourself!

Dressed Fit to Kill (Us)!

Dear Mac,

Our daughter is wanting to dress herself. We feel that's a good thing, but the problem is, she mixes her clothes up so that they don't match. She wants to wear sweat socks with her nice dress-up shoes. She is only three and she watches very little television, so we do not feel that she is trying to imitate some sort of style she is seeing on some program. She just seems to want to dress in some pretty unconventional ways.

We definitely do not wish to overreact, but when we go out and she is wearing a plaid skirt, sweat socks, white dress shoes and a Mickey Mouse T-shirt with a bright purple sweater, we just cringe. We are afraid other kids will start making fun of her. Some days her mixture of clothes actually embarrasses us.

Do you have any ideas for us?
Mixed up parents

Wouldn't it be nice if all people could be that confident and relaxed with their personal dress? Okay, I know that's totally impractical, but it doesn't hurt to dream.

Now that I am done dreaming, let's talk about this realistically. Humans are social beings. It is the same the world over. In every society, dress codes are enforced either by strict laws, religious guidelines, or loosely defined social mores, but all people are concerned with dress! Even people who profess not to care how they dress—dressing in sloppy old clothes from Goodwill—are concerned with how they dress. Imagine walking up to a 26-year-old young man at a grunge music concert wearing some baggy old work pants; old, worn-out tennis shoes; a t-shirt with holes and faded advertisement for some long-defunct sports team; and an old letterman sweater. If you asked him about his garb, he would probably contend that his dress is a rejection of being forced to dress in acceptable ways.

Now imagine that we walked up to him with a brand-new $800 suit, a tailored shirt, expensive belt, designer shoes, and a tie. If you forced him to dress in that suit, he would be just as uncomfortable in that "get-up" as you might be in his garb! How he dresses is important to him as well! All humans care about how they dress. Your children are just the same. They care how they look and dress. Your job is to teach them to dress in such a manner that they can be proud of how they look without making them overly concerned with trying to keep up with fads and fashions.

Parents' Action

This is going to be very personal for every family. I cannot give you hard advice with steps to follow here because your desires for your children's appearance will most likely differ from mine. But here are a couple of suggestions.

Teach your child about colors. Try to teach them what colors go well with other colors. Give your children guidelines about what messages their clothes send to others. A clothing standard that doesn't limit your child's opportunities or cause derision or undue ridicule would seem reasonable to begin with. Baggy clothes, wild colors, baseball caps—different people have different ideas about what's appropriate. Teach them that it is considered impolite to wear a hat in churches, places of worship, or at funerals. (Oops—I think you can see my problem in trying to define standards for you, because if you're Jewish, a yarmulke is not only appropriate but required [for males] in a temple or synagogue!)

I hope you get my message here. You must sit down and decide the dress standards you wish to teach your child, then figure out how to teach them to your child.

In the early years when their child is doing as they say, these parents might control her choices by limiting what she is allowed to choose from. They might only offer those clothes that they consider appropriate for the weather and whatever she will be doing. Don't take out the t-shirt and the sweatsocks when you're getting dressed for church. When you're going to the gym, get out the t-shirt and sweatsocks and don't touch the plaid skirt and the sweater.

Then teach her how to make selections that you deem to be appropriate. Show her how and especially *why* you made the decisions for her back before she started dressing herself. Get dressed together and talk about how and why you selected the clothes you're wearing. Over time she'll get the picture, and maybe even imitate some of your choices. Be careful not to kill your daughter's desire to express herself, but balance that with your desire to have her dress in a manner that does not close doors for her.

Fights over dress can tear a family apart. My advice, as your kids start to make decisions about how they dress, is to do a little research.

Get your old family albums or old pictures of yourself when you were growing up and take a good look. *How could you go out in public looking like that?* With that perspective, take another look at how your kids are dressing.

When they're toddlers, you can control how they dress by not putting anything you disapprove of in their drawers. However, that will soon come to an end. If you give your kids some standards to use in selecting clothes while they're toddlers, you may prevent some major clashes over clothes in the years to come.

Do remember this: The best way to make your kids look out of place when they start school is to dress them up like you! Kids don't want to dress exactly like adults, and that's healthy. It is a sign that they are beginning to express their individuality. Encourage them within boundaries that you can accept.

What About Wrinkles and Such?

Dear Mr. Bledsoe,

We are having a battle with our three-year-old daughter. It seems like every time we get ready to leave the house, she will have some wrinkle in her sock or some pair of pants "that just don't feel right," so we find ourselves being delayed and late for events while we sit and wait for her to adjust something.

We don't want to be pushy, but we feel she is getting to the age where she ought to be able to get dressed and get going with the rest of the family rather than making all of us wait for her to get everything perfect.

Sincerely,
Slowed down to a crawl

This couple is experiencing a common problem; their child is causing delays in their schedule and I know it can be annoying. I believe there may be a few things coming into play here.

Parents' Action

First, when they're getting ready to leave home, this little girl might feel uncertain or threatened. She may feel that, the minute they leave home, she loses her special place in her parents' world. At home, she is the center of attention; when they leave, she may feel insecure and left out. It might be a good idea to give her a little special attention when they get in the car by singing one of her favorite songs with her.

The little girl could just be going through a phase that she will outgrow. Patience is the key. When a child is dragging along and being slower than might seem necessary, try to simply allow a little more time. Help her to be more organized by laying things out ahead of time.

Slowness of this nature is often nothing but a problem of the child being easily distracted. Cutting down on distractions and making a routine out of your departures will often work well.

My dad did this with us. One of his pet peeves was our slowness in getting ready to go skiing. I can now see how effective his methods were because I still use one of them. He would make us repeat the necessities for a day of skiing like a mantra: "Skis, boots, poles, hat, gloves, goggles!" I still do it today, and it still helps me get ready to go skiing.

Try those types of things with your kids. Make little sayings about the sequence of events that must take place before leaving and watch the kids speed up because they don't have to think about every step as it occurs.

If wrinkled socks are a problem, let the child put them on in the car. Use the time in the car for "adjustments." Establish that as a normal part of the routine, so the child knows she'll have time in the car to make things perfect.

Getting kids dressed and on the way when time is short will remain a problem for almost every family. The key is to establish routines that make things easier by repetition.

One closing note bears making here. If you expend just a little time teaching your kids early in their development to be self-sufficient and do things on their own, then every day that goes by will become simpler for you. The more that kids can do for themselves, the less you have to do for them!

Our grandchildren can all dress themselves, and they can get into the car and buckle up their own seatbelts. It really does not take much longer to go someplace with them than it would with a group of four adults. They were taught early to do things for themselves.

The bigger and more far-reaching result of teaching kids to do things for themselves is that, when they get older and start making big decisions, they will be experienced in handling things for themselves!

Chapter 8

Manners

"Will we ever be able to eat in a restaurant again?"

To answer that, let me ask another question: Have you ever been to a fast-food restaurant? Of course you have, right? Well, think about what that has taught your kids about restaurants:

- You eat food from a bag, *with your hands!*
- Every one has a jungle gym!
- You get a toy with your food!

If you're going to a "sit down and eat with a knife and fork" restaurant, which is different from the restaurants your kids have visited previously, then you need to teach your kids the new behavior for the new place *before you go.*

Let me set the record straight, though: I'm not on a campaign to change fast-food restaurants. Shoot, I like them myself when I'm in a hurry or in search of what they offer: quick, predictable, tasty food. I don't condone the bashing these places get for raising an obese society. Parents are responsible for that! As a matter of fact, I enjoy taking my grandchildren to a fast-food place and watching them work up a sweat on the playground before or after their meal. I don't advocate this as a regular part of a child's diet, but they're not evil, either.

I just took my grandkids to a fast-food restaurant a few weeks ago and as soon as we got there they took off their shoes to play in the very elaborate two-story climbing maze! Not only was their behavior appropriate—it was stipulated in the rules of conduct on the wall!

My point is, if you have a desired behavior you want your children to exhibit in a particular environment, then it is up to you to take the time to *teach* that behavior to your children!

> *Kids can learn to behave appropriately ... but they must be taught to do it!* Good manners are not genetic; neither are rude behaviors. Of course, some "rude" behaviors actually come pretty naturally—eating with hands, grabbing food without asking, belching out loud, and so on. If we wish to have our children follow specific behaviors, we must teach them.

As I travel the country now, I make it a habit to approach families in restaurants, airports, parks, movie theaters, stores, and other public places and compliment them on their children's appropriate behavior. It's my quiet little mission: to let parents and kids alike know that someone notices children who demonstrate polite, appropriate behavior.

Now that I'm on the lookout for families who do a great job teaching their children high standards of behavior, I find it everywhere! So I *know* it's possible to teach this type of behavior! I've seen it!

Call for Back-Up

Grandparents can often be a parent's best ally in teaching manners! Many times kids will listen to grandparents about things like manners in a way that they may not listen to parents. As our kids were growing up, we saw to it that they spent lots of time with their grandparents—both Barbara's folks and mine—because we actually asked our parents to do some teaching for us.

Our two boys would often come home from a visit with GramBets and Grandpa Stu and start correcting us on *our* table manners! We would hear "please pass the potatoes" much more often after a visit with Gramma Maxine and Grandpa Dick. I also know that I'm much more aware—and thus much more effective—in teaching manners to our grandkids than I ever was with our kids! Now that I am older, I have more time to pay attention, and I have grown to appreciate manners more.

Both of our sons have repeatedly commented that, as they've gotten older, they've really appreciated the instruction on manners that they received from their grandparents. Each has been thrown into situations where they needed to know the finer points of manners and customs, and they were both very glad that their elder relatives had taken the time to teach them.

Many grandparents seem to be more willing than parents to invest the time and effort in teaching manners. They've learned the value of simple rules of conduct and have the patience to teach your children if you give them the green light to do so. If you're going to enlist grandparents to assist you, be above-board and let them know what you want them to do and how you want them to do it. (Sounds like raising kids, doesn't it? Rule #1: Tell your parents what you want them to do!)

Kids and Nice Restaurants *Can* Mix!

Dear Mr. Bledsoe,

When my wife and I were dating, we loved going to nice restaurants. We didn't mind the price; it was worth what we were paying to eat extravagantly prepared foods in a beautiful setting.

Then we had our kids, and for the past five years, nice restaurants have been out of the question. Now that our oldest is five and our youngest is three and a half, we would like to start going again, but we simply can't. We've tried on several occasions and had to leave because our kids behaved like monsters. We had become one of those families we used to hate! Everyone was staring at us wondering why we couldn't control our kids!

What can we do? We don't want to just leave them at home. We long to enjoy peaceful dinners in nice restaurants with our family, but it doesn't seem possible, the way our kids act.

Can you help us?

Sincerely,
Parents in the Parking Lot

This situation is not even close to being hopeless. Even children under age five can be taught to behave appropriately in public places. You can easily teach your kids basic manners.

After talking with this family I found that they had only given their kids the "fast-food training" that I mentioned earlier. Their kids had been taught by experience that a restaurant was a place to eat with their hands and play with toys.

Manners are behaviors that are specific to a time and place. If you want your children to adjust their behavior for a certain location, then you have to teach them how to differentiate. Manners on playground equipment are very different from manners in a formal restaurant, and those manners are different from the manners at a funeral. Help your kids select behavior that is appropriate to the situation *long before* they're in the situation.

The key concept here is the word *before!* Before you consider going to a nice restaurant, practice the appropriate behavior for the restaurant you will be going to. Spread a white sheet over your table to look like the tablecloth in a fancy restaurant. Set the silverware and fold the napkins to look like a restaurant's. Then one of you parents gets to play "maître d'." (If you're a single parent, enlist the help of a grandparent, mother, grandfather, aunt, uncle, or friend!) Have your children come to the front door and wait to be seated in the "restaurant."

If you want this to be really fun, dress up. Believe me, your kids will want to do this over and over, because you are actively involved in the activity. You might put your child in charge of speaking to the maître d', saying, "We have a party of four for dinner, and we would like a table in the main dining room, preferably by a window."

Have the maître d' seat you. Show your children that they are to wait by their chairs until everyone older than them is seated. Once seated, show them how to unfold their napkin and put it in their lap and sit up straight. Next, show them how to use all the silverware.

If you have access to a copy machine, run off a menu with a few options. Older kids may even recognize some words! Read the menu for younger children, just like you will when you take them to a real restaurant. Practice talking about the choices in a quiet voice and only read the choices that are available for your children. Teach them to look the waiter in the eye and say, "I would like to have the chicken nuggets, French fries, Jell-O, and orange juice. Thank you." Have a small plate of bread sticks or crackers they can practice snacking on while they wait for their orders.

I hope you're getting the picture. Practice what to do and say, from the entrance to the exit. Be sure to ask your children how they felt about themselves while they were acting so grown-up. The internal reward they'll experience is the important one: *Good decisions make you feel good!* Recognizing the feeling attached to making appropriate decisions is what will guide your children as they get older and make more critical decisions.

The problem of eating in a restaurant isn't earth-shattering, but it's common, and the answer is almost always the same. If you wish to take your kids someplace that has a special set of behavioral standards, as the adult in their world, you must teach them to meet those standards. You can never assume they will just know how to act.

Funerals and Other Solemn Occasions

Dear Mac,

We have a son age three and a daughter age four. We have had a tragedy in our family: my brother died in a brutal car accident this week. He was their favorite uncle. He was so full of life and fun ... the kids just loved him. They are broken-hearted, but I'm scared to death to take them to the funeral.

Our kids are very active, and they've never been to a funeral. I'm afraid they will cause a big disruption and it will look like they don't respect or miss Uncle Jim. I want them to be at the funeral, but I also don't want them to make a scene.

Do you have any advice?

Yours truly,
Grieving and Scared Sister

I definitely believe that this couple should take their children to the funeral of someone that they dearly loved. They, too, have suffered a monumental loss. Funerals are our way of dealing with the loss of loved ones, and they serve a purpose in the grieving process. They also present a great opportunity for you to teach your children about grieving.

Depending on who has passed, children may naturally be sad at a funeral. I later learned that this family did take their children to their Uncle Jim's funeral and that they were well behaved and showed genuine sadness at the loss of such an important person in their lives. That sadness, however, does not guide them in how to act. I've attended many funerals over the years and seen many *adults* who do not know how to behave. Just a year ago, we were attending a family funeral and we heard many people express outrage because one of the friends of the deceased showed up inappropriately dressed in what looked like work clothes. Many commented that this person was also disrespectful to the deceased because he talked loudly throughout the service.

The key, once again, is that you must *teach*. Children will certainly not know how to act at a funeral if they've never attended one. If you do not teach them how to act, there is a real possibility that they will misbehave. Strange situations often bring out strange behaviors in children. (Heck, strange situations often bring out strange behaviors in adults!)

So here is a plan for you. To begin with, if possible, take your children to visit the funeral home or church, perhaps on the morning of the funeral. Explain that when they return they will be attending the real funeral. This is an excellent way to introduce them to the atmosphere of the funeral. However, if this is impossible, as it may well be, there is still much you can tell your children that will help them understand what to expect and how to behave.

Explain that most of the people at the funeral will be very sad. Explain to them that when someone dies, it makes people sad because they will miss seeing that person. Explain that when people are sad, they talk quietly and may cry. Practice whispering with them. Explain that everyone will be expecting them to be very quiet, and that sitting still will be the way for them to behave. Actually practice some words for them to say. "I am really sorry that Uncle Jim died," or, "I miss my Uncle Jim very much."

Tell your children that it is okay to cry if they feel like they need to. This is always a very new experience for children, but they will learn a great deal by attending. They will have many older people to watch and model their behavior after.

If your children are prepared for what they are going to experience, they will be much more likely to handle the experience appropriately. Do not be deluded into thinking that one practice will ensure perfect behavior, but you will greatly increase the odds of good behavior if you prepare them with some practice and some expectations of what is coming.

Talking about funerals may seem a little far afield for a discussion of manners, but it really is not. Manners are a set of rules for proper behavior in the proper place. As your kids grow up, teach them very clearly that what is appropriate in one setting is not okay in another setting. No matter what occasion you're preparing your child for, what you're *really* doing is making your children socially aware, so they can behave appropriately in *any* given setting.

A funeral is a very specific setting with a set of pretty well established behaviors universally accepted. Teach your children what is expected of them before they attend, and you will dramatically increase the chances that they will meet those expectations.

Please and Thank You

Dear Mac,

We have twins who are almost three. We have been trying to teach them to say "please" and "thank you" for the better part of two years and they seldom follow our instructions. We have to remind them almost every time. Did we start too young? Is it hopeless? Or can you give us some help?

Sincerely,
Nagging Parents

My granddad used to say, "A 'please' will open ten times as many doors as 'thank you,' and either will open more doors than any key!" This couple definitely did not start too early. They've just found a few ways to teach "please" and "thank you" that didn't work. They need to find some other way. They don't say how they tried to teach those words to their children, but I will bet that they just told the kids what they wanted.

I would ask this couple if they always use 'please' and 'thank you' when talking to each other or their kids. I'll bet their answer would be, "No, not all of the time."

If you want your kids to use words like "please" and "thank you," they have to learn them just like they learned the rest of their language. Your children will repeat and use the words that are used regularly around them. If your children don't often say words like "please" and "thank you," it is most likely because they don't hear them regularly.

Teach them when to use the desired words. Describe the situations at home when you will expect them to use the words. Have them describe to you, in their own words, some situations when they will say "please." Then, do not even acknowledge that they are talking unless they say "please" or "thank you" at the appropriate times.

If they ask for a snack by just saying, "Can I have a cracker?" act like the child has not even said a word. Your actions will teach far more than your words. Do not get into a series of reminders like, "What's the magic word?" or "I can't hear you if you do not say 'please.'" Doing that doesn't teach them to say "please" at the appropriate time. It teaches them to say it when you tell them to. There is a big difference. Teach them how to select the appropriate time to choose to use the right words. Once you have taught them how and when to say those words, they will say them all of the time—even when you're not there to remind them!

I'm aware that manners can easily take a back seat in the high-speed life many of us live today. Manners may be low on the list of things parents are willing to spend time teaching, but many people outside the family will be watching and judging your children on their manners! You can say that manners are old-fashioned, but that doesn't change the importance other people attach to them.

Failing to teach manners to your children can close many doors to them. They can be reprimanded and criticized at school and in play situations for lack of manners and be totally puzzled because of their lack of awareness. Later in life, they can lose out on social opportunities and even job opportunities because they were never taught the necessary social skills and manners.

Chapter 9

Appropriate Language

"Our son sounds like a truck driver; he picks up every word; can we ever expect him to speak appropriately?"

Kids learn vocabulary at a phenomenal rate. It's not extraordinary for a child of two to double her vocabulary each week! Be careful what you say in their presence. (Please note that I mean no insult to truck drivers. Some of my friends drive trucks, and they are wonderful people who use very appropriate language! Those were the words of a mother writing to me about her son.)

Kids speak the language they are exposed to! Like I have often said, kids raised in Japan speak Japanese. Kids raised in France speak French. Kids raised in my home will speak English and they will use the vocabulary they hear regularly. Move the Japanese child to the French home and she will speak French within six months. Raise the French child in the Japanese home for a while and he will speak Japanese. This is not difficult to understand. Kids speak the language they are exposed to.

As a matter of fact, it has been well established that young children are capable of learning language at such a phenomenal rate that they often need only hear a word once in the proper context in order to add that word and its meaning into their vocabulary! They will learn the subject/verb agreement they hear.

To ensure that your children use appropriate vocabulary, you must expose them to that vocabulary. It's pretty simple, really. If they regularly hear you cursing, they will curse—and with surprisingly well developed diction and feeling! If a child never hears you curse until you are angry, they will likewise refrain from cursing until they are mad—but then, look out! If you allow yourself that leeway in your own behavior, don't be surprised to hear such language pop up in your children's vocabulary.

> It is simply unreasonable to hold your children to a higher standard than the one you hold for yourself!

So often I hear parents tell me, "I was so surprised when our son just let go with the 'F-word' when he got mad at a toy! We have no idea where it came from!"

Well, they might not have a clue where it came from, but I do; odds are pretty good that their son was in the room when Dad hit his thumb with a hammer and let go with the "F-word." The child may not have even looked up or been consciously paying attention, but the lesson was learned! Later when the boy was angry, just like Dad had been, he let loose just like Dad did!

I think that teaching appropriate language gets down to a simple matter of what you, as the parent, model for your children. If you swear in front of your children and you do not wish for them to swear, then you must explain why you are different and have a different standard for yourself! (I must note that I think this will be a very hard sell!)

What About Language in the Media?

"So what about television, radio, music, the internet and movies?" you ask. Well, take a page from my Granddaddy Mac's book. He used to say, "Nobody is worthless; anybody can serve as a bad example to someone!" The danger comes when the other medium is the only voice in the room.

If you're worried about what your kids are hearing at a young age, then get a television with an off button and a channel changer. Place limits on what they watch and when they watch. Again, time becomes an issue because you need to watch and listen with your children rather than turning on the TV and leaving them alone with it. I am amazed at the number of "put-down" phrases and the disrespect for authority figures in some cartoons and children's videos. I believe that it would be dangerous to leave children alone with that programming. On the other hand, if the parents are in the room, those cartoons provide an opportunity to discuss those statements and why you don't use words and phrases like that in your family.

I firmly believe that what you teach your children is up to you. I try to teach parents the *method of teaching* and leave *what to teach* up to them. My next comments are simply my own opinion. I find much of the language on some children's programming to be more offensive than any of the 14 to 17 curse-words banned from the airwaves! To me, hearing a children's cartoon character say, "You wanna piece of me, you slimebucket!" is far more damaging to a child than hearing the same character say, "Damn!"

I don't want to get into a sermon about what should or should not be allowed on children's broadcasting. I do not believe in censorship. What I am saying is that, before you allow a child to select any cartoons to watch, you should watch the programming carefully yourself. Consider the number of violent actions and violent statements made in a half-hour program. Then ask yourself, "Is this program presenting ideas that I want in the head of my child?"

Don't just look for a few bad words. Look at your morals and your values and ask if the programming fits what you want to teach your children. If your kids are exposed to any particular program, they will pick up some of the language and actions. If the program is not what you want your kids to think and the characters use language that you don't want your children to use, *then turn it off!*

As your children grow, begin to increasingly involve them in selecting the programs they watch. Get them thinking at a very young age by asking them, "Is this show about good ideas? Does this show demonstrate the manners and beliefs of our family?"

As you know if you have read what I have been presenting in this book, I am not much of a believer in controlling children's behavior by controlling their environment. You can't protect your children from the world; you must teach them to live in it! However, language development is such an instantaneous thing with very young children; I think it's reasonable to limit what they see and hear in these very early years.

Teach Them the *Right* Words

Controlling the words your kids learn at an early age will have a lasting effect on their future language and expression. But you can't control their whole world. Kids will hear more and more words, phrases, and ideas. You cannot protect them forever, and you cannot protect them completely.

As soon as possible, teach your children how to select what words, phrases, and ideas they will use in expressing themselves—but don't expect them to ever "unlearn" a word, phrase, or idea. Do not be deluded into thinking that just because they do not use the words you have forbidden, they haven't learned them. If they have heard you use the words, believe me, they have learned them. Children will learn just about any word, phrase, or idea they hear!

Most of the time what happens is that children simply learn to avoid using the words around you, but they will use them elsewhere. In order to teach a child to not use certain words, phrases, and ideas it is necessary to teach them *why* it is wrong to use those words. *You must teach them how to make good word choices.*

It is very hard to *unlearn* the bad habits of making poor choices in words, phrases, and ideas.

This process can start at a very young age. Kids who have learned how to make appropriate language choices at an early age are far less likely to pick up inappropriate language habits when they inevitably hear bad language later in life. You must begin the ongoing task of teaching your child *how* to select the words, phrases, and ideas with which they express themselves. Teach them *why* certain words should be avoided, not just *which* words to avoid.

It works best if you tell kids *what to say* rather than *what not to say*. When they use an offensive word, especially in moments of anger and frustration, let the emotional moment pass. When they are calm, model for them the same situation with your choice of appropriate words. (Humor helps!) Teach them how to express those thoughts and ideas in an appropriate manner.

Your child may see a movie where a character says, "F--- you!" At this point, you enter into the conversation and say, "Ohhh, that's not the best way for him to express his feelings. He could have said, 'Boy, am I mad at you! What you did was really not fair!' See how much more specific that statement is?"

Use Rule #1 and end the criticism with a positive statement of the expected behavior. Give your child another example to follow, and then role-play with your child.

Rule #3 is also very important in teaching appropriate language to children. The more they hear a word or phrase, the greater the chances they'll choose that word or phrase. Keep repeating appropriate language in the presence of your children, and you will increase the chances of them speaking in an appropriate manner.

Another important part of teaching children to use appropriate and approved language is to get them to verbalize their desire to use language appropriately. Get them to say, "I do not use bad words!" This will be very personal for your family. Be sure to establish guidelines your children can understand, and then live by those guidelines yourself!

Children Speak the Language They Are Exposed To

(The following letter was handwritten. I have tried to print it here as it was written, with little punctuation, no capital letters, and all of the original misspellings.)

dear mac,

my husband uses relly foul language. i cant convince him that his behavyer is having a bad afect on our children. our oldest is in grade 2 and he came home from school with a note pined to his shirt (i found this an odd way for a school to comunicate with parents) stating that "this boy's language is terible. if his language does not improve some very strict punishment is in order!

my husband's response was to say, well, i'll just give him a whipping for cussing at school! I do not think he is reasonable.

to make maters worser yet we have two more children ages 3 and almost 1. The three year old is allready learning from his second-grade brother and as the younger one begins to speak i just know she will learn from her older brothers.

I am at my wits end and I don't know what to do can you help? we are a good family but everyone in the comunity must think we are terible just because of the way our kids talk!

thanks,
mother of trash talk

My response may have been pretty hard for this woman to read, because I pulled no punches. In a letter that is critical of her *husband's language* and the language that her child is using at school, she had countless misspellings and a total lack of punctuation and capitalization!

Your children will grow up learning the language they hear and read. Both parents must take care to use the language they want their children to use. You can't expect your children to do something that you're not willing to do yourself. If you have one standard for your own behavior, it is nearly impossible to hold your children to a higher standard. Even if you have trouble writing, you must expend the effort to write correctly! Get a small pocket dictionary. Use it often. Let your children see you doing this. Tell them, "Please, please, pay attention to learning to write and speak properly. People will judge you by the way you talk and the way you write!"

Parents' Action

But this frustrated mother is asking for help with something else, and you may be having a similar problem. Here's a family game that might help everyone recognize and address the problem.

1. Give each family member $2.00 worth of nickels every Monday.

2. Make up a list of forbidden words. The key is for the kids to be involved in making the list! (Here you are using Rule #4: getting them to say it for themselves.)

3. Read the list out loud and then post the list someplace in the house where everyone can see it. (One family we know put the list on their refrigerator in bold red letters. They would also point out the list to visitors, to let them know that those words were not allowed in their home!)

4. Place a jar with a slot in the lid on the dining room table. Any time a family member is caught using a forbidden word, he or she must throw a nickel in the jar.

5. Any money that is not put in the jar at the end of the week will be theirs to keep. (I recommend that you get each kid a savings account for storing his or her money, but piggy banks are fine—and fun—for starters.)

6. The family member with the most money left at the end of any week gets to hold onto the money from the jar.

7. At the end of the month, the family member with the most money in his or her piggy bank gets to decide how to spend the money in the jar! (Soon, because so few banned words will be used in your home, you will need to save the money for weeks to even gather enough to buy just one soft drink!

An "almost one-year-old" child most likely will not be able to play this game, but by the time she is old enough to play, it probably won't be necessary to play the game or have a jar. She will have learned appropriate language by being continually exposed to it!

After a few weeks of this game, you will be surprised by how markedly your children's language has improved. The key factor will be their awareness of what is appropriate and what is not. What's more, this game usually makes parents equally aware of *their* language, how often they had been swearing in front of their children—and how aware of it their children are!

I know that it worked for a coaching staff I was on once. We decided to play the game to set a good example for our students. Man, we were all shocked at how many nickels we were throwing in the jar! It made us aware of our own language, and when our language cleaned up, so did our team's!

Your children will speak with the vocabulary that is spoken to them. Pay attention!

Swearing in Anger

Dear Mr. Bledsoe,

Our children have learned to use cuss words in anger. It is not a super big problem because they are rarely angry, but both our daughter and our son let out with some pretty rank vocabulary when they get mad.

Any suggestions?

Yours,
Offended mom

If parents allow themselves to swear when they are mad, it's no surprise that their kids do, too. Your children's language and behavior will follow that of the adults around them. If you yourself are *always* mindful of your language—and remember, kids will pick up an occasional slip as easily as a constant barrage of angry cursing—then find out where they are learning the offensive language. Kids do not dream up this vocabulary themselves!

I must admit that between the time our sons left home and our grandchildren arrived, I became a little lax in my use of "colorful" language. Our son and daughter-in-law had to mention to me that I had used a couple of angry epithets when our grandkids were listening and they were picking it up. A little reminder from my son was all I needed to see the influence I was having. You may need to do this also when you find the source!

If your children hear appropriate language almost all the time at home, but every once in a while they hear a spicy word in a time of anger or frustration, they will learn to use those undesirable words only when angry or frustrated—just like you do.

Parents' Action

Here's a suggestion. Make up some new words for your family to use when you feel the need to express "strong feelings." At a time where you might be tempted to swear, say, "Blast that blatterat!" or "Shh-ugar!"—you get the picture. My grandfather did that for the four of us kids. A comedian at the time had made up some funny words to use in place of cursing. Granddad picked them up and used them around us, and we picked them up quickly.

"Dirty packaloomer!"

"Dirty brackafrash!"

"Oh clamahamens!"

Those nonsense phrases are indelibly locked in my vocabulary!

Facial Expressions and Tone of Voice

Dear Mac,

Our daughter of three uses the most ugly tone of voice when she speaks to us. She continually whines and speaks with an angry tone that is so disrespectful. She shouts her demands at us and her facial expressions are really nasty.

We try to correct her by telling her to use her "nice voice" and her "pretty face" but it doesn't seem to make any difference.

Can you help?

Sincerely,
Parents of "the Devil"

Well, for starters, these are not the "parents of the devil"! They have a daughter who has learned a language. Along with her vocabulary, she has learned the unspoken language of facial expressions and tone of voice. I don't believe she's being disrespectful. She's just using what she has heard and what works.

My training and experience as both a speech teacher and as a speaker has taught me that *how* you say something is often more important than *what* you say. This little girl has learned *how* to say things and it is working. Her manner of saying things is causing her parents to listen to her in a way that they might not otherwise have.

My first suggestion to these parents is that they pay careful attention to how they speak to their daughter and how they speak to each other in her presence. I would be willing to bet that this young girl is imitating a tone of voice that has been used by the adults she is watching.

I would also contend that once the little girl used her whining tone or her undesirable facial expressions, she probably found that they worked better than a conversational tone to get her parents' attention.

Parents' Action

If you are in a similar situation with any of your children, there are two corrective actions to take.

First, be extremely careful to monitor your own manner of speaking. Stand in front of a mirror and look at your own facial expression. Listen to your own tone of voice. It's very easy to speak in a nasty tone of voice and allow your facial expression to show anger without knowing it. Many people who actually take a look at what they are modeling for their children find that they speak much more nicely to the lady serving coffee at the quick-mart than they do to their own beloved children!

In a videotape of a family that I was helping, I saw parents shout, "You speak nicely to your sister!" at their son in exactly the tone of voice that they were forbidding their son to use! These parents were shocked to watch themselves. They did not realize that they were speaking to their son in that manner until they saw it on tape. Their son's behavior with his sister was a masterful imitation of his parents.

Children will use the tone of voice that gets attention. Pay attention to the tone you want to hear, and that will be the one your children choose!

The second corrective action to take in teaching proper tone of voice is to pay attention to what tone of voice you respond to. Many times you will find that the child is simply using the tone of voice that works best for getting your attention.

I helped another couple by watching them carefully. When their son asked for assistance or made a comment in a conversational tone of voice, he was often ignored. Then the boy would resort to a louder and much more whiny voice. The parents would then admonish him for his whining and say, "Stop whining. Now, tell me in your nice voice." The boy would then make his request in a nice voice and the parents would do what he requested.

This small boy had figured out how to get what he wanted from his parents. Whine first to get their attention, and then say it nicely!

My advice was to ignore any whined request. "Ignore it and walk away," I told them. Never respond to the whined request. Only acknowledge comments and requests offered in the desired tone of voice. I told them that the key to changing their son's tone of voice was to respond to conversational tones. "If you ignore a conversational comment, you are telling your son to try another tone because that one didn't work."

Your kids learn the language that they are exposed to. Be careful of what you say in their presence. Never hold your children to a higher standard than you hold yourself to.

Chapter 10

Dealing with Interference from Relatives

"Will our parents ever realize that we have a plan for raising our kids and that we are very capable parents?"

Your parents can't know your plan if you haven't shared it with them. Your parents may need a little parenting at this stage. Give them a role in your plan, but don't forget to listen to *them*, too. After all, they've done what you're doing, and it may not be necessary to reinvent the wheel! Many of the older folks in your life do know something. You don't have to do everything they say, but you may have something to learn from their experience.

I sincerely believe that the key to dealing with family members who try to interfere in raising your children is to effectively communicate exactly what your plan is. In order to do this, you must establish clearly in your *own* mind exactly what your plan is! (Does this sound familiar? Sounds vaguely like Rule #1, doesn't it?) The more complete your plan is and the more clearly you can relate it to different situations, the less likely you are to have problems with others trying to give advice or get in the middle of your interactions with your kids.

That's right, I believe the first step in dealing with family and relatives who wish to be involved in raising your children should be communicating to them precisely what you want from them. Communicate what your goals are. Help them understand your methods for reaching those goals. Express those ideas in language they can understand. Remember they had different models for their ideas. They grew and learned in a different era. They had different fears and different dreams. When you openly share your objectives, you'll often find that you share the same goals.

This is an ongoing process, and it isn't always easy. When you communicate with your parents about your children, the roles are suddenly reversed. You were the kids, but now you're assuming the role of parents. This may be awkward and may take time, but with patience and open communication, it can evolve into a very natural relationship.

The key is to think through your plan, be firm and committed to it, and then communicate that plan to them in a kind but firm manner. Use Rule #3 with your parents just like you do with your kids! You will, almost certainly, have to repeat your plan more than once. If you repeat it three times and they still aren't getting it, then *change the words*, just like you do with your children. Say it in a different way, but keep saying what you need to say! Stick to your plan and express it until they get it.

Remember one thing as you discuss your plan with older people: they have experience that may differ from what you have learned. This doesn't mean that you must *prove* they are wrong! What you must do is communicate your plan and communicate that you are very firm in your desire to follow that plan. Acknowledge that your ideas may be different from theirs, *and then move on in implementing your plan.*

Whatever you do, do not let yourself be baited into arguments! This is *much* harder than it sounds (as you may already know), and it will take real dedication and patience on your part. Calmly maintain your strong commitment and stick by your guns. Once you have taken your stand, it will gradually become easier each time. Keep in mind that almost everyone attempting to give you advice is doing it out of love and concern for you and your children! Keep the anger out.

Let me repeat that the key to effectively dealing with people who try to interfere or give you advice lies in having a well thought-out plan for raising your children! The more complete your plan is, the less likely you will have ongoing problems with others attempting to get in the middle of your actions. At the same time, you will receive meaningful tips that fit with your plan.

Smoking and Other Bad Habits

I will get into some specific ideas on how to take your stand in a little bit, but there is one other general area in which relatives and friends can affect how you raise your children: personal conduct.

It's one thing to have relatives and friends trying to give you advice. It's a whole other issue when someone who's close to your family models behavior that violates or contradicts your plan for raising and teaching your children.

Let's take smoking, for example. You probably want to teach your children to live their lives free from the cigarette habit. If you have a relative who smokes, it's reasonable to ask him or her to do it outside or away from your children. The same goes for vulgar language, improper manners, and just about any other negative or questionable behavior.

An effective phrase in these types of situations begins with "In our home ..."

"In our home we don't allow smoking in the house, car, or around our children."

"In our home we do not curse. We have made the commitment to our children to speak only in appropriate language."

"In our home we do not use violence as a means of solving problems; we always find some way to negotiate."

"In our home we only watch or listen to certain movies, television shows, and music."

Suppose someone comes back with, "Man, you can't protect your kids from the world. What will it hurt if I smoke?"

You have a great answer! "I know that we cannot completely protect our kids. Ultimately they will have to make their own decision about that issue, but what I said is, *'In our home we do not smoke!'* All I ask is that you please respect the rules of our home."

Notice that that request is not at all confrontational. You are not passing judgment on them or asking them to change their thinking or their actions anywhere but in your home.

Pushy Parents

Hi Mac,

We love your book and your video series. However, we have a problem with my husband's Mom. We are a new modern family and we hope to raise sweet, considerate, and sensitive children. But Mother-In-Law is not helping us at all, Mac.

She is basically a screamer. There is really no other way to describe her. She screams for the sugar; she screams for plates to be passed across the table; and she screams at me for allowing my child to play with Play-Doh. I can ignore her screaming at me, but I do hope my sons will not follow in her footsteps and learn to scream for everything. I want a mild-mannered child, not someone who doesn't know how to control his volume. (We live with these in-laws, by the way.)

Besides, I don't want to instill fear in our children. We can see our eldest child becoming a fearful and scared little mouse in response to his grandma's constant shouting. Our second and youngest child is still brave and fearless. I seriously think that both kids' confidence and fearlessness will start diminishing if this screaming and threatening goes on any longer.

Please help soon,
Non-Screaming Parents

This mother has very observantly recognized that children *become* exactly what they live. A child who lives with constant screaming will probably grow up screaming! There is also a definite risk that he will lack the self-confidence to make strong decisions for himself. *Recognizing the problem takes us halfway to the solution!*

The second part of dealing with the problem lies in establishing in our children's heads exactly the desired behavior we want them to use. This desired action must be described in behavioral language that the child understands.

This letter does contain one very difficult but powerful dynamic that is definitely in play in this situation. It is very difficult to establish desired behavior for your children if you are not living in your own home! Because it is the home of the mother-in-law, this mother does not have the right to establish what is the accepted model for behavior.

The first thing I would suggest to this mother is that she take action as soon as is possible to move out of the relative's home and into her own home. I am aware of the difficulty of this for many families, but at some time it is just natural for a family to establish an independent home for their children. As long as you are living in someone else's home, it is much more difficult for you to ask for cooperation. If you're in this situation, then you must negotiate an agreement. If you were in your own home I would simply advise you to say, "In our home we speak in a civil, respectful, and conversational tone of voice." That is a bit more difficult when it is not "your" home.

Until then, your statement might go more like this: "We are attempting to raise our children to speak in a civil, respectful, and conversational tone of voice, so we would sincerely appreciate it if we could all model this in the presence of our children."

Even if this situation doesn't apply to you, you would be well served to use a similar statement when you visit someone else's home, as you almost certainly will. You are asking for help in teaching specific behaviors to your children, and allowing them to serve as models of the desired behavior.

Additional statements will help. Saying, "Our children admire you and look up to you so much. They always talk about you and how much they admire you. We continually see that they are shaping their behavior to match yours. Whether you know it or not, you are a teacher every moment that you are around them. Please help us to teach them well!"

Try getting difficult, bossy, or downright abusive older relatives on your side by saying, "In today's world, most kids don't respect their elders. We are teaching our sons to respect their elders and we want your help. We teach them to show respect by obeying quiet instructions from people who are older than them, so please express any commands to them in a calm tone. If they don't listen carefully and obey you, please let me know and I will make sure they do in the future! We all have a responsibility for the actions of children and we need to teach them how to respond to reasonable requests. In order to do that we must give them practice. You present a wonderful opportunity for our sons to practice respect, and I need your help!"

Pushy Parents, Part 2

Dear Mac,

I love your book and I sincerely believe that I should teach my kids to be independent thinkers and that the way I should accomplish this is to do as you say, and "put them on the seat of the bike and put the handlebars in their hands and then give them a shove!" I am really trying to do this, but my problem is that both sets of grandparents are so critical of me for doing this.

My parents are very loving, but also very domineering. They think that putting my kids in charge of things around the house is just letting them "get away with murder" as they put it. They feel that I should be more controlling and put my foot down more often.

My "ex-in-laws" are also wonderful people, and just because my former husband and I couldn't get along doesn't give me the right to keep them out of their grandsons' lives. My boys love them and so do I. The problem is that they believe in lots of restrictions and punishment. They grew up in that era of "spare the rod and spoil the child!" When I put one of the boys in charge of a task and he doesn't do it just like I would, they believe I should "come down on him."

Let me give you a couple of examples so you can see my dilemma.

Last week my folks were coming to dinner and I put my oldest son, Billy, in charge of setting the table. I told him that he was to have it set by 6:00 and there were to be six places at the table. Billy waited until the last minute, then he just put a stack of silverware in the middle of the table along with six glasses and a pile of napkins. My mother came unglued. She said he was so disrespectful to her and to my dad. She came right out in front of Billy and told me I should send him to his room for being rude. She really got in my face and Dad backed her up.

I felt the problem with Billy setting the table was that I had not specified clearly enough what was expected, so I gave him a little instruction on exactly how to set the table, and I also explained to him that setting it like he had was often interpreted as being too casual for a sit-down dinner with friends. He was respectful of my wishes and was very diligent when I had him set the table properly as I had just explained it.

But my mom just wouldn't let it go. She took me into the next room and proceeded to lecture me about how I was letting Billy get away with this now and in the future it would come back to bite me. "He needs to know that you are boss!" my mother scolded me.

Then, a few days ago, my ex's parents met us to go to a neighboring town for dinner at a favorite restaurant. We all got in our van and headed out. I put Sam, my ten-year-old, in charge of the route to the restaurant. (I remembered that you had mentioned that as a way to let children learn how to make decisions.) Sammy had gotten online and found a "scenic route" using back roads and city streets to get to our destination. Grandpa came unglued when I listened to Sam rather than to him.

Grandpa said, "I have lived here all of my life and I know a much shorter way to get there. It is disrespectful for you to let this youngster's whims run the show. He should respect me and my knowledge."

147

In both these cases arguments ensued, and I felt like my desire to teach my children to be independent thinkers was being seriously challenged by both of the sets of grandparents. they all come from the old school and are not in tune with what I am trying to do! Mac, what should I do?

I do not wish to be disrespectful of my parents or my ex's parents but I think I am right in handling my sons as I am doing. Please can you give me some direction?

Sincerely,
Frustrated in Fresno

I feel this mother's pain. If my mail is indicative of what is happening to young parents all over America, people in this dilemma have lots of company. I also am aware that having company does not give you any solace, so here are a few ideas for you to use to help you to deal with this situation constructively.

First and foremost, it is important to recognize that many parents have extended families that care deeply about the younger generation. *Be thankful that you have grandparents or relatives who care about your children's instruction.* Their comments, although they may not always be in support of your techniques, are clear indications that all of them care deeply about the moral upbringing of your children.

That being said, they need to also understand what you are attempting to do with your children. They need to know that you have a plan, and they need to know what that plan is. They will never know if you do not teach them!

Parents' Action

Pick a time when your children are at school or away from home, and invite the grandparents (or whatever friend or relative you're butting heads with) to sit down with you and hear your plan. Assure them that you are not being lenient when you put the kids in charge. Assure them that the contrary is true. Let them see that by putting your kids in control of parts of their lives you are teaching them to be responsible for their own actions.

Make your explanation brief, concise, and well thought out. Ask for their support. Then give them tasks to do with your children! Tell one that you would appreciate very much having them give your children instructions in table manners, using whatever technique they choose. Invite them to have your children over for dinner, or take your kids out to dinner. Tell them that you need their help in teaching your kids proper manners.

Give another the task of teaching your children to respect the older generation and their contribution to the freedom now being enjoyed by the kids of today. Ask them to take the kids to museums and to read about important sacrifices of the older generation.

If you explain what you're doing, you're much more likely to be successful in gaining their support. Even if they do not agree with you, it will really help them to be more supportive if they know what you are attempting to do. Also, it will define their roles for them. Giving them a role in teaching your children will empower them, and they may not feel as strongly the need to interfere.

If relatives still insist on being "in your face," it may be necessary to let them know the rules in your house. You may need to be "in their face" a bit by telling them that when they are in your house, they may not contradict you in front of your children. Explain that if they insist on doing so, they simply will not be invited back. Here are some words you might use, "In our house I am in charge of raising my children. I have given lots of thought and consideration to what I am doing, and I expect you to respect that when you are in our home. When we are in your home, you are in charge, and we will live by the rules that you impose and I expect the same respectful compliance from you when you are in our home."

Leave it at that the first couple of times. Then, if they still insist on contradicting you, you might need to add, "If you cannot abide by the rules in our home I will be forced to ask you to not come here. I am imposing similar self-discipline on my children and I respect you enough to hold you to the same standards in our home. Please live by the rules of our house or stay away." It might be uncomfortable at first, but not for long! The fact that your elders are expressing concern is proof that they care deeply about your children. They will rapidly come around and become your biggest supporters in your honest attempts to do a great job of raising your kids. As they begin to see your plan and their active role in it, they will become a big help.

Aging Grandparents

Dear Mac,

We have a problem in our family that is tearing my heart out. We have two kids ages three and four. I was born late in my parents' lives. Mom was 41 when I came along. That meant that my parents were in their 70s before our kids were born.

Mom died suddenly and unexpectedly last year and the problem is Dad. He is a wonderful man. He was a very loving and wonderful dad, but he is now 74 and getting around is difficult for him. The problem is that he would love to be a much more connected and involved grandpa, but he just doesn't know how.

My kids like him but they don't know how to be when they are with him. He simply cannot get down on the floor and play like they do. He moves slowly and he doesn't hear too well anymore because of hearing loss from his work at the mill.

How can we include Grandpa in our children's lives?

Sincerely,
Love My Dad in Chicago

Including elderly people in children's lives is critical. One of the most wasted resources in America today is the vast knowledge of our elderly citizens. It is not hard to include an elderly grandfather in the lives of very young children, but it does take a conscious commitment on the part of the parents.

I've talked continuously in this book about the wisdom of my grandparents. I actually have to be careful not to make that the whole focus of the book, because it could be! My grandparents were all wise and wonderful people. I am so thankful that my parents made time for us to be with them as we were growing up. Even so, I nearly missed some valuable lessons.

My father's father was quite a man. To meet him one would never have guessed what he had done in his life. He was quiet and soft-spoken and played his accordion at most family gatherings. He rarely spoke of politics or world affairs. I knew that he had been in the Navy and had retired as an admiral, but as a child I didn't even know what that meant.

Granddad was not a man to talk of his accomplishments. He gave lots of wisdom in little sayings he passed along in letters and such. He taught me to always be on the lookout for a good joke and to seize any opportunity for a good healthy laugh. He taught me how to remember a joke. He said, "Kid, just remember two really good ones. Tell them to everyone until someone tells you a better one and then replace one with the new one and keep telling them. By the time you're done telling a joke ten times, it will be permanently stored!"

I loved that man, and just like the grandfather in this lady's letter, he was about 70 by the time I was 5. He could not play catch or run with us but I still relished being with him. He taught me how to sharpen a knife to a razor's edge, and he started me on a lifetime habit of carrying a pocketknife. I carry one to this day, and every time I pull out my pocketknife I think of him and one of his many lessons.

When I was teaching an American history class in about my third year of teaching, I came to World War II and was searching for a way to bring the era alive for my classes. It came to me that Granddad had served in that war. I asked him if he would mind if I asked him a few questions about his experiences and videotaped them for my class. Due to a stroke, he was not able to come to my class in person. He agreed to be taped only if I gave him the questions well ahead of time.

Wow, I have never been so surprised in my life. This quiet little man was one of the most decorated war heroes in the Pacific theater of

World War II. I did not know it because he never talked about that part of his life. Man, was I glad I had asked. It would have been a shame for all of that man's knowledge and experience to have never been shared with me and other generations of our family—not to mention my history class!

Parents' Action

The lesson that I learned from this experience is the importance of asking grandparents to share their wisdom with your children. I must tell you another reason why I feel so strongly about expanding the role of grandparents. During all our years of teaching, one thing was a constant among almost all of the kids we worked with in middle school and high school: when we asked them who were the people they felt most certain loved them, they all answered, "Grandma and Grandpa," without hesitation!

If all of our students were telling us that grandparents are the most common source of unconditional love, why wouldn't you make lots of opportunities for your children to get as much of that as possible?

Be the stimulus for this kind of sharing between generations in your family. Set up situations for your children to simply sit and ask their grandparents questions. Following family dinners, remain at the table and ask your parents specific questions about their experiences growing up. If they were alive during the Korean War, ask them to give their thoughts. Ask your parents to tell where they were when President Kennedy was shot. Ask them their thoughts about the Vietnam War.

Yes, I know, when your kids are three and four they cannot understand much of what Grandpa says about the past, but you are establishing an idea in your children's heads that elderly family members are respected people with worthwhile ideas. Your actions say, "Listen to these people—they have important things to say!"

I would strongly advise all parents to give grandparents specific tasks with your children. If they live in another city, when you visit ask

Grandpa to take the kids to the museum. Search the newspaper calendar for fun events that the grandparents can take your children to when they are in town. This lady's father could easily take her children to a circus, a car show, a movie, or a fair. Set everything up so that it is easy for the grandparents to do. If they are too old to feel comfortable doing this alone, go with them.

This lady could set up a checker board at her house so her dad could teach her children how to play that simple game. Then she could teach her children to ask Grandpa questions while playing. "Grandpa, how did you and Grandma meet?" Then she should pray that Grandpa cries when he tells about meeting the love of his life.

She could prime the kids with good questions for Grandpa. "Grandpa, how big is God?" "Grandpa, now that Grandma is with God, will she be glad to see you again some day?" "Grandpa, why are you proud to be an American?" "Grandpa, can we go and throw rocks in the creek when we finish playing checkers?" "Grandpa, where did you live when you were my age?" When Grandpa answers these questions, it will be like storytime for your kids. They will love the stories just like they love to be read to. In the process your children will be learning some valuable lessons and family history.

I will offer another observation to consider. When you give your kids questions to ask your parents, you should try to listen, too. You most certainly will learn something. Many parents tell me that this activity has been one of the most important steps for patching up old wounds between them and their parents. For many parents, this is the first time they've ever actually stopped and listened to their own parents. Try it—you may like it!

Views You Can Use

There is a wealth of knowledge in the experiences of the older generation. Use it! The only way that you can get that valuable information is to listen. When older people talk about their experiences raising children, listen to them. You don't have to do what they say, but every time you listen you learn valuable information that might help you form your plan for raising your children.

In raising your children it is not necessary to "reinvent the wheel." Many of the experiences of those who have gone through it all before can be very instructive. Even though that young lady was having trouble with her parents in some areas, this does not mean that she cannot learn from them. In the one area of giving her children responsibilities and letting them learn from those experiences, she may differ with her parents, but she may find that by keeping an open mind she can learn some great tips on dealing with many other situations.

For example, I had a great conversation with a young mother whose parents had been headed down that path of interference when she took a stand similar to what I advised in the earlier situation. She explained her plan for raising her children and her parents balked for a week or two, but rapidly got in tune with her plan for teaching her children to make decisions. The young mother kept her lines of communication open with her parents, and learned a technique that her parents had used in raising her that she was totally unaware of. She has been using the technique with her own kids ever since they turned twelve and started attending boy/girl parties at friends' homes.

The technique is called making the "Chips Call." Every time one of her kids is invited to a party, she makes her "Chips Call" to the parents at the home of the party. (She does just what her parents taught her that they did when she was growing up.) She calls the parents and says, "We had a gathering at our house a couple of days ago and we have about six bags of chips left over. I'm calling to see if you would like me to bring them over for the party this weekend?"

She says she gets one of two answers. The other parents either sound shocked and ask, "What party?" or they say, "That would be great!" In either case she has information to help guide her own kids.

If the other parents don't know about the party, they're probably going to be out and the party will be unsupervised. She can talk with her kids about the dangers of attending a party where parents are not present. She has headed off a difficult situation without being nosy and prying the information out of her own kids. She saves face for her kids by not calling other parents and questioning them about a suspicious party.

If the parents are going to be home and supervising the party, the mom has a perfect excuse to drop by to drop off the chips. In the process, she gets to meet the parents and talk with them without seeming to pry.

Even though this mother has a clear plan for raising her own children, she has kept the lines of communication open to draw on the wisdom of her parents for augmenting her plan. She says she has the best of both worlds.

Now you most likely will not be calling the parents of your toddler's friends to check on parties, but the idea would be a good one to sock away for a time in the near future when you might. The point in including the example here is to point out that you can even learn new things from your own parents! These parents raised this mother and used a technique that she was not aware of until they told her. Most people who are willing to listen to their parents will learn some valuable lessons.

Even if your parents were abusive and dysfunctional parents, you might learn from them. I do work in prisons, and every time I go to a prison to teach parenting skills, I always learn something from at least one prisoner. Certainly all of the inmates that I meet have made some terrible mistakes, but many have some wisdom to offer if I just keep my eyes and ears open.

Extended families and relatives can be a huge asset to you in raising your family. Put them to good use!

Chapter 11
Learning Disabilities

"Is it ADD or just bad behavior?"

I have another name for ADD ... I call it intelligence! Whatever you do, do not try to make your active toddler behave like every other child. If your child is active, give her more to do. Give him ways to make constructive use of that energy. You will probably have to plan ahead because you will not be able to think as fast as your child does.

Please, please, please, do not jump to conclusions here and stop reading. I am not dismissing learning disabilities as nonexistent. They are real and come in varying degrees. What I am saying is that with a child under the age of six, it is really foolish to jump to such far-reaching conclusions and make sweeping diagnoses based on those kinds of differences.

Still, with so much talk about Attention Deficit Disorder these days, anyone with a normally active toddler is probably wondering if his or her child is really "normal." It's easy for a worn-out parent with too much on her plate to think there must be something "wrong" with this toddler who will not wind down. "Who put the Energizer battery in this kid?"

Let's use Attention Deficit Disorder /Attention Deficit Hyperactive Disorder (ADD/ADHD) as the most common example and discuss it in a bit of detail—though you will see that I detest slapping labels on children.

Learning Disabilities and Toddlers

Why am I including a chapter on learning disabilities in a book about kids who aren't yet in school? Two reasons: first, because so many parents of toddlers come to me wondering about very young kids and hyperactivity; second, because the success rate for teaching coping and adapting skills for learning disabilities goes up exponentially if the process is started early.

Because there is so much talk about Attention Deficit Disorder, many people are frightened about it. The biggest mistake I see parents making when it comes to ADD/ADHD and other learning disabilities is thinking that the diagnosis of a learning disability and labeling of a child with the name of the "disease" somehow helps someone! It seems to me to be a universal dilemma to find someone who has been diagnosed with ADD who has been given tools for coping with the diagnosis!

I meet kids and adults all the time who tell me, "I (or my child) have been diagnosed with ADD/ADHD."

I always ask, "What is your number one strategy for dealing effectively with your situation?" Most everyone answers with a blank stare. Someone has diagnosed a problem but done little or nothing to teach compensation or adaptation skills!

When I ask for a definition of ADD/ADHD from these parents who are scared of it, everyone seems to give me a different definition. Not many people have a clear picture of what they are dealing with. As a matter of fact, I spent three entire days on the Internet, trying to find a clear definition of ADD/ADHD. I found myself in the same fix I was in as a teacher. I saw an extremely vague label being used to make decisions about teaching children. I went to 33 websites dealing in various ways with the syndrome, and only one had a definition of ADD/ADHD I could use to identify whether a child had it.

It's not too surprising that this was also the one authority who had solid procedures for helping a child adapt to this unique way of perceiving the world. That one wonderful article helped me understand why so many people have trouble working with kids who are diagnosed with ADD/ADHD. I have since met Dr. Ned Hallowell, who wrote the article, and he and I share many beliefs about raising self-sufficient, self-reliant kids. Dr. Hallowell has not only studied ADD/ADHD, he *has* it, so to me, he's a real authority. He helped me to understand I was not wrong to think of ADD/ADHD as a unique level of talent and intelligence. In fact, the "disease" has been one of the major contributors to his success!

With his permission, I have included his article on what it is like to have Attention Deficit Disorder.

What's It Like To Have ADD?

by Edward M. Hallowell, M.D.
Copyright (C) 1992

What is it like to have ADD? What is the feel of the syndrome? I have a short talk that I often give to groups as an introduction to the subjective experience of ADD and what it is like to live with it:

Attention Deficit Disorder. First of all I resent the term. As far as I'm concerned most people have Attention Surplus Disorder. I mean, life being what it is, who can pay attention to anything for very long? Is it really a sign of mental health to be able to balance your checkbook, sit still in your chair, and never speak out of turn? As far as I can see, many people who don't have ADD are charter members of the Congenitally Boring.

But anyway, be that as it may, there is this syndrome called ADD or ADHD, depending on what book you read. So what's it like to have ADD? Some people say the so-called syndrome doesn't even exist, but believe me, it does. Many metaphors come to mind to describe it. It's like driving in the rain with bad windshield wipers. Everything is smudged and blurred and you're speeding along, and it's reeeeally frustrating not being able to see very well. Or it's like listening to a radio station with a lot of static and you have to strain to hear what's going on. Or it's like trying to build a house of cards in a dust storm. You have to build a structure to protect yourself from the wind before you can even start on the cards.

In other ways it's like being super-charged all the time. You get one idea and you have to act on it, and then, what do you know, but you've got another idea before you've finished up with the first one, and so you go for that one, but of course a third idea intercepts the second, and you just have to follow that one, and pretty soon people are calling you disorganized and impulsive and all sorts of impolite words that miss the point completely. Because you're trying really hard. It's just that you have all these invisible vectors pulling you this way and that which makes it really hard to stay on task.

Plus which, you're spilling over all the time. You're drumming your fingers, tapping your feet, humming a song, whistling, looking here, looking there, scratching, stretching, doodling, and people think you're not paying attention or that you're not interested, but all you're doing is spilling over so that you can pay attention. I can pay a lot better attention when I'm taking a walk or listening to music or even when I'm in a crowded, noisy room than when I'm still and surrounded by silence. God save me from the reading rooms. Have you ever been into the one in Widener Library? The only thing that saves it is that so many of the people who use it have ADD that there's a constant soothing bustle.

What is it like to have ADD? Buzzing. Being here and there and everywhere. Someone once said, "Time is the thing that keeps everything from happening all at once." Time parcels moments out into separate bits so that we can do one thing at a time. In ADD, this does not happen. In ADD, time collapses. Time becomes a black hole. To the person with ADD it feels as if everything is happening all at once. This creates a sense of inner turmoil or even panic. The individual loses perspective and the ability to prioritize. He or she is always on the go, trying to keep the world from caving in on top.

Museums. (Have you noticed how I skip around? That's part of the deal. I change channels a lot. And radio stations. Drives my wife nuts. "Can't we listen to just one song all the way through?") Anyway, museums. The way I go through a museum is the way some people go through Filene's basement. Some of this, some of that, oh, this one looks nice, but what about that rack over there? Gotta hurry, gotta run. It's not that I don't like art. I love art. But my way of loving it makes most people think I'm a real Philistine. On the other hand, sometimes I can sit and look at one painting for a long while. I'll get into the world of the painting and buzz around in there until I forget about everything else. In these moments I, like most people with ADD, can hyperfocus, which gives the lie to the notion that we can never pay attention. Sometimes we have turbo-charged focusing abilities. It just depends upon the situation.

Lines. I'm almost incapable of waiting in lines. I just can't wait, you see. That's the hell of it. Impulse leads to action. I'm very short on what you might call the intermediate reflective step between impulse and action. That's why I, like so many people with ADD, lack tact. Tact is entirely dependent on the ability to consider one's words before uttering them. We ADD types don't do this so well. I remember in the fifth grade I noticed my math teacher's hair in a new style and blurted out, "Mr. Cook, is that a toupee you're wearing?" I got kicked out of class. I've since learned how to say these inappropriate things in such a way or at such a time that they can in fact be helpful. But it has taken time. That's the thing about ADD. It takes a lot of adapting to get on in life. But it certainly can be done, and be done very well.

As you might imagine, intimacy can be a problem if you've got to be constantly changing the subject, pacing, scratching and blurting out tactless remarks. My wife has learned not to take my tuning out personally, and she says that when I'm there, I'm really there. At first, when we met, she thought I was some kind of nut, as I would bolt out of restaurants at the end of meals or disappear to another planet during a conversation. Now she has grown accustomed to my sudden coming and goings.

Many of us with ADD crave high-stimulus situations. In my case, I love the racetrack. And I love the high-intensity crucible of doing psycho-therapy. And I love having lots of people around. Obviously this tendency can get you into trouble, which is why ADD is high among criminals and self-destructive risk-takers. It is also high among so-called Type A personalities, as well as among manic-depressives, sociopaths and criminals, violent people, drug abusers, and alcoholics. But it is also high among creative and intuitive people in all fields, and among highly energetic, highly productive people.

Which is to say there is a positive side to all this. Usually the positive doesn't get mentioned when people speak about ADD because there is a natural tendency to focus on what goes wrong, or at least on what has to be somehow controlled. But often once the ADD has been diagnosed, and the child or the adult, with the help of teachers and parents or spouses, friends, and colleagues, has learned how to cope with it, an untapped realm of the brain swims into view. Suddenly the radio station is tuned in, the windshield is clear, the sand storm has died down. And the child or adult, who had been such a problem, such a nudge, such a general pain in the neck to himself and everybody else, that person starts doing things he'd never been able to do before. He surprises everyone around him, and he surprises himself. I use the male pronoun, but it could just as easily be she, as we are seeing more and more ADD among females as we are looking for it.

Often these people are highly imaginative and intuitive. They have a "feel" for things, a way of seeing right into the heart of matters while others have to reason their way along methodically. This is the person who can't explain how he thought of the solution, or where the idea for the story came from, or why suddenly he produced such a painting, or how he knew the short cut to the answer, but all he can say is he just knew it, he could feel it. This is the man or woman who makes million-dollar deals in a catnap and pulls them off the next day. This is the child who, having been reprimanded for blurting something out, is then praised for having blurted out something brilliant. These are the people who learn and know and do and go by touch and feel.

These people can feel a lot. In places where most of us are blind, they can, if not see the light, at least feel the light, and they can produce answers apparently out of the dark. It is important for others to be sensitive to this "sixth sense" many ADD people have, and to nurture it. If the environment insists on rational, linear thinking and "good" behavior from these people all the time, then they may never develop their intuitive style to the point where they can use it profitably. It can be exasperating to listen to people talk. They can sound so vague or rambling. But if you take them seriously and grope along with them, often you will find they are on the brink of startling conclusions or surprising solutions.

What I am saying is that their cognitive style is qualitatively different from most people's, and what may seem impaired, with patience and encouragement may become gifted.

The thing to remember is that if the diagnosis can be made, then most of the bad stuff associated with ADD can be avoided or contained. The diagnosis can be liberating, particularly for people who have been stuck with labels like, "lazy," "stubborn," "willful," "disruptive," "impossible," "tyrannical," "a spaceshot," "brain damaged," "stupid," or just plain "bad." Making the diagnosis of ADD can take the case from the court of moral judgment to the clinic of neuropsychiatric treatment.

What is the treatment all about? Anything that turns down the noise. Just making the diagnosis helps turn down the noise of guilt and self-recrimination. Building certain kinds of structure into one's life can help a lot. Working in small spurts rather than long hauls. Breaking tasks down into smaller tasks. Making lists. Getting help where you need it, whether it's having a secretary, or an accountant, or an automatic bank teller, or a good filing system, or a home computer, getting help where you need it. Maybe applying external limits on your impulses. Or getting enough exercise to work off some of the noise inside. Finding support. Getting someone in your corner to coach you, to keep you on truck. Medication can help a great deal, too, but it is far from the whole solution. The good news is that treatment can really help.

Let me leave you by telling you that we need your help and understanding. We may make mess-piles wherever we go, but with your help, those mess-piles can be turned into realms of reason and art. So, if you know someone like me who's acting up and daydreaming and forgetting this or that and just not getting with the program, consider ADD before he starts believing all the bad things people are saying about him and it's too late.

The main point of the talk is that there is a more complex subjective experience to ADD than a list of symptoms can possibly impart. ADD is a way of life, and until recently it has been hidden, even from the view of those who have it. The human experience of ADD is more than just a collection of symptoms. It is a way of living. Before the syndrome is diagnosed that way of living may be filled with pain and misunderstanding. After the diagnosis is made, one often finds new possibilities and the chance for real change.

The adult syndrome of ADD, so long unrecognized, is now at last bursting upon the scene. Thankfully, millions of adults who have had to think of themselves as defective or unable to get their acts together, will instead be able to make the most of their considerable abilities. It is a hopeful time indeed.

Address Correspondences to:
Edward M. Hallowell, M.D.
142 North Road
Sudbury, MA 01776
DrHallowell.com

Turning a "Disability" or Disorder into a Strength

All work with children diagnosed with ADD, ADD/ADHD, and other learning disabilities must focus on *strategies* to help them compensate and adapt rather than just slapping on the label.

I see so many parents, teachers, and others make fruitless attempts to force these children to act like every other kid. It is futile. This approach is about as logical as trying to make a short kid tall or make a tall kid short! "Go stand in the corner and grow!" Few people would be foolish enough to say that to a child, yet I often see adults telling a kid with difficulty focusing on one task, "Pay attention! Put that magazine down while I talk to you. What is wrong with you? Can't you focus?"

Nothing is wrong with the kid! He simply needs help harnessing his amazing ability—and his need—to focus on more than one thing.

I certainly do not intend for this chapter to cover all learning disabilities, nor do I pretend to cover the topic completely enough for you to stop researching and learning if you suspect that your child has a learning disability. Read, study, and listen! A label is not a solution; a label is only a start. By itself a label does not help anyone! In most cases, a label by itself usually does damage.

Can Medication Help?

Doctors prescribe and parents give medications to kids with difficulty focusing and think that using medicine to calm them down has helped the kid. Look back at Dr. Hallowell's description. Having ADD is much like having bad windshield wipers in rainy weather. All the medication can do is clear the windshield. Once the wipers have cleared the windshield, the driver must still be taught to drive.

That's our job. We must teach kids to do what's expected of them in spite of the fact that they perceive the world in a little different way. Keep in mind that your goal cannot be to make the kid like everyone else; it must be to teach them how to do what the world needs them to do!

I would not pretend to practice medicine nor would I try to overturn a doctor's recommendation or challenge the trained professional's recommendation of use of a drug such as Ritalin (Methylphenidate) or any of the other drugs that are now being prescribed. If you are considering the very serious step of putting your child on medication, please do your research. Read, read, read! Visit your doctor prepared with intelligent questions, and listen carefully to the answers. If your doctor is offering medication as a solution to your child's difficulties, make sure you also ask about the coping and adapting techniques that will accompany the medication. These techniques are a component of your child's treatment that are every bit as important as the medication in teaching kids to effectively use their unique way of perceiving the world. If the person does not offer any, I would strongly suggest looking further!

If you have any doubt that these drugs are powerful, just look into the use of Ritalin (Methylphenidate), Paxil (Paroxetine), Adderall (Mixed Amphetamine Salts), Dexedrine (Methamphetamine), and a number of the other drugs being prescribed for ADD/ADHD. I was shocked a number of years ago when I actually found out what these drugs are and what they do. If you do not believe that these are powerful, mind-altering substances, just look at how many of them are the drug of choice of addicts seeking a powerful high. In many schools across America, Ritalin and Adderall are drugs of choice for getting high at school. Many kids who have prescriptions for these drugs are selling them to friends for a very handsome profit.

Like I said, I am not attempting to practice medicine, but I sincerely hope that you do much reading and research before you follow a prescription for a mind-altering substance. Don't be panicked into a rash decision especially when your child is so young. Start learning the many techniques being used to teach kids to use their unique way of perceiving the world to live effectively. Always get a second opinion. If a doctor is recommending a drug, ask a trusted counselor, teacher, or psychiatrist for their professional opinion.

Help Them Make Meaningful Connections

If your child is showing signs of attention deficit, make sure that she is surrounded with people who make her feel connected. Go to our Rule #5 and make sure that you express your love to your child in a different way every day! Dr. Hallowell agrees. "I had Attention Deficit in first grade and I was also dyslexic. I couldn't read but my teacher always sat next to me during reading and she put her arm around me. I was the most enthusiastic nonreader ever!" Look at him today! He is a world-renowned child psychologist and author!

I wouldn't contend that Dr. Hallowell reached his esteemed level of accomplishment just because his first grade teacher put her arm around him. He got where he is because of a ton of hard work and training, but that might not have been possible if he hadn't felt unconditional love and a meaningful connection with his world as he worked his way through life! The end of his progress could easily have been an unaware first grade teacher who was not tuned into his real needs.

Now let's look at some specific situations that you might be encountering with your child.

A Shocking Diagnosis

Dear Mr. Bledsoe,

The counselor and teacher at our son's preschool has diagnosed our son as having ADD. This devastates us. We don't know what to do. We don't want our son to be in Special Education and we do not feel he is in need of medication. How can we deal effectively with his school?

Sincerely,
Frustrated Parents

The guilt and recrimination parents feel when this label is applied often becomes its own disability. If your child feels guilty and stupid, then those feelings, too, become the disability. Remember that both Dr. Hallowell and I regard ADHD as a sign of great intelligence, and we both applaud the special ability of an ADHD child to do several things at one time. Celebrate the fact that your child is unique and then get about the business of teaching him to use his way of perceiving the world to his advantage.

Even with a formal diagnosis of ADD, this is not a time to label and fret over the labels. First, their son is very young, so those parents are lucky to get such an alert early in a child's development, but you should remember, if your child receives such a diagnosis, that it isn't written in stone. Your child could rapidly learn to adapt and do what is asked of him very effectively! He may have a way of perceiving the world that is different from some other children's, but it isn't wrong or bad. It is also very similar to some of the world's most effective and important people!

As a matter of fact, in many ways your child will have an advantage over others. Do not let this label scare you. The only significant question is, what are the strategies you, his teachers, his counselors, and his schools will use to teach him? If the discussion ever digresses into how you can all team up to control the young man, that's when you should step in and refocus everyone on the real task of teaching your son the subject matter. The only reason to discuss the control element should center on the curriculum. We must quiet "the noise," "clear the windshield," so he can learn. Remember, clearing the windshield does not teach him to drive, nor will giving him medications teach him to read! Giving your son more than one task at a time may allow him to concentrate better, but still we must focus on what we are attempting to teach your son, not just on his need for more stimulation.

Parents' Action

Now let's get specific. Now that the counselor has offered you this diagnosis, it is time for you to start asking, "What are the strategies you advocate for dealing with our son's unique ability?" If the counselors/teachers are unable to offer specific strategies to help your son focus, then it is time for you to advocate steps for them to try. It always works best if you have used them and you can document their effectiveness.

Your child is not yet of school age, but start trying various techniques now! I will give you a few, but your new job is to become the expert on behalf of your child. Start reading, start meeting people, and start learning.

One of our dearest friends did exactly what I am recommending to you. She had a son the same age as one of ours who was diagnosed with ADD even before he started school. She became the authority on her own child. (Who better than you to be the authority on your own kid?) She read and read. She attended workshops. She called and visited educators and doctors. She learned the letter of the law about the education her son was entitled to. By the time her son was in second grade, she had educated most of the teachers in her son's school about effective teaching techniques for kids with ADD. It was amazing to watch. Her son graduated from college with a degree in education and is now a teacher and a coach!

You know your child better than anyone. What strategies that you've used at home have been effective? All some kids need is more stimulation. Others need schedules, lists, and calendars. When I was teaching school, if I had a student who seemed to have a difficult time focusing while I was talking or while we were in a listening exercise, I would try giving the student a group of papers to alphabetize. I also would put a stopwatch on my lecturing; if I talked for more than a quarter of any class period, I changed the lesson. (Just a note, I would not recommend that you try to change a teacher's lecture style.)

I always instructed the child that they were responsible for paying attention and keeping up with what the rest of the class was doing and for any assignments. For some, alphabetizing papers wasn't enough stimulation, so I would give them materials to organize and arrange on a bulletin board, or books that needed new stickers put inside the cover, or paper that needed to be shredded—something that involved physical activity. I never gave any of these tasks without a reminder that the secondary activity was in no way a substitute for the academics in the classroom.

If having a second simple task helped to "clear the windshield" or "still the wind" for the kid, then that became a routine. My approach was to let the activity "clear the windshield," but the goal was always to teach the kid to drive! My goal was always to teach the child the lesson of the day. Your goal should always focus on teaching your child to get along in the world.

The Big Struggle

In his book *Driven to Distraction*, Dr. Hallowell often speaks of "the big struggle" that erupts in families with children who have ADD—a battle that I believe often *unnecessarily* erupts between parents and children with learning disabilities. The parent wants what is best for the child, and the child wants to do what the parent wants, but due to the distraction from his unique perception of the world, he simply forgets or finds himself doing something else.

Learning what will work in these situations while your child is still at a young age will help you avoid the big struggles as they grow. Here are a couple of possibilities (a complete list would fill an entire book).

Give More Than One Task at a Time

If your child is easily distracted from tasks such as picking up toys and putting them away, give her an additional task to perform while picking up the toys. Have the child call out the names of each toy as he puts it away. Or give the child another object to manipulate while picking up the toys. Give the child a basket to carry while picking up the toys. Putting each toy in the basket is a way of giving the child a constant object to manipulate while doing the other task.

Have the child pick up the toys with a flashlight in a dark room. The flashlight gives the task a new focus. The flashlight may help the child to operate because it occupies the need for sensory stimulation.

Finding techniques like this will help the child make focusing on the task at hand become a habit over time.

Make Lists of Things to Do

For many kids with ADD, it helps to give the child a plan. (This is Rule #3: it's a different way of saying the same thing.) By making lists of tasks to perform, you teach the child to focus.

We just had two of our grandsons visit us for a week. I don't think either of them has ADD, but we still used this approach. They are both nonreaders and nonwriters under the age of four, but they're capable of making lists of things to do. They draw pictures and cut out pictures to put on lists. We sat down and planned out our day with them. They drew pictures of things and cut out pictures of things they wanted to remember to do that day. It worked!

Laying out a schedule often "quiets the noise" for kids who struggle with ADD. The schedule allows them to focus their amazing concentration on productive action. If it works for your child, start early to help them make it a lifetime habit—and note that it helps you budget your time, too!

Have Your Child Repeat Instructions Back to You

Here you're using Rule #3 in giving the child another repetition and Rule #4 in getting the child to say it for himself. For many kids with ADD, simply saying something out loud creates a memory key that works. Many authorities call this *original awareness*. Many with ADD are capable of hearing something while thinking consciously about another idea and don't really hear the new thing being said. Having the child repeat the instructions can often make this new idea or request rise to the level of prime awareness.

Partner with Your Schools

So often when I encounter parents whose children have been diagnosed with ADD or some other "alphabet disorder," I see a reaction just like the lady in the letter. Parents become upset and anxious because the perception is that someone has just told them that their cherished child is "retarded" or "stupid," which the parents intuitively know is not true. Many panic when they hear the words *special education!*

Then I watch them get into a battle with the school, demanding that their child not be put in special classes. This fretting and effort is wasted and the animosity between the parent and the school is off track and is definitely counterproductive. Worse yet, all of this conflict is confusing for your child, who needs the constant message that *they can learn*.

I strongly recommend building a team with the school to decide what works best for your child. Start trying strategies at home, until you find a set of actions that work well for your child. This book is not intended to be a manual for parents of kids with ADD/ADHD. You are going to be spending extra time with professionals anyway, so find the experts who make sense to you, and learn coping and adapting skills to teach your child. Work with the professionals at your school to build a plan that works so that your son can participate effectively in learning!

There is an amazing lady up here in Montana. Dr. Marlene Snyder is a nationally recognized authority on ADD/ADHD. She has long proposed having well-informed parents deal with learning disabilities by changing schools from the "bottom up." She believes that most school districts resist change not because they don't want what's best for children, but because they rightfully seek to resist changes that merely follow whims and fads, and seek to follow valid research and proven techniques.

Dr. Snyder's book is specifically about ADD/ADHD and teen drivers and isn't directly applicable to parents of kids not yet in school, but what she proposes is very applicable to parents of very young children. If you suspect that your child has indications of Attention Deficit Disorder, begin very early in finding techniques that work for your child. Then devise a method of documenting your successes with your child to give to your child's teachers and schools.

Both Dr. Snyder and I strongly advise you to use caution as you approach your child's school. If, during the three years prior to your child reaching school age, you determined that it helps him to focus and stay on task if there are routines to his day, that is valuable information for a teacher who is overloaded with new kids. That teacher might have 10 parents tell him/her that they suspect ADD in their kids! From the teacher's point of view, this may be overwhelming. The teacher is anticipating problems from this class, but—voila!—here you come with a few suggestions that work! You might establish yourself as an advocate for your child as well as for the teacher. At the same time, you are educating the teacher about techniques you've *proven* are effective for teaching kids who experience difficulties in focusing!

Dr. Snyder coaches parents on logical approaches for parents as they contact schools and school personnel in order to teach them what works with their own kids. Let me say it again, both Dr. Snyder and I strongly advise you to use caution as you approach your child's school. You can go from a "respected helper" to a "meddling invader" very rapidly, so proceed with caution.

A Parting Comment

I would like to close this chapter on learning disabilities with a general comment for all parents. As I taught for 29 years, I gradually gained a perspective about children and learned the lesson of remaining calm. I know they are your children and they are the most precious things in the world to you, but you must remain calm. Be reasoned in your approach to raising and educating your kids. Remember, the world is run by C students! The only class I was ever kicked out of in my 17 years of formal schooling was English—and I ended up teaching it for 29 years. Now I'm writing my second and third books!

Think about this for a second; if your child is somehow assigned to be in special education because of a difficulty he or she has in a particular manner of learning, it is not the end of the world! In schools I'm familiar with, the most dedicated teachers have been the special ed teachers! They are the warmest, most nurturing, and most willing to adapt their style of teaching to meet the needs of the kids they teach. Wouldn't you want your kids in the care of people like that?

I believe that every state in the entire United States mandates that every special education student must have an IEP. ("Oh no!" you are fretting, "not another of those alphabet diseases!")

Please stay calm and let me explain that acronym. IEP stands for individual educational plan. I don't know about you, but I would have liked for my sons to have had an individual educational plan tailored to their particular needs and learning styles. I often wonder why we don't have an individual educational plan for every kid! Why do we reserve the best that education has to offer only for kids with special education labels?

Relax and be calm. Practice working with your child until you know at least three effective techniques, and then calmly and efficiently share those techniques with the people who are going to act in a nurturing manner with your kids. You will teach your children to live in a complex world and to use their unique abilities to become effective, self-directed, and fully developed adults!

Chapter 12

Sex Education

"My gosh, our son is three. Is it too early to start talking about sexual issues?"

If they're old enough to ask, they're old enough to get the answer. At three kids don't need the whole course, but they can understand that it is a normal human behavior. The real course you ought to begin very early is Relationship Education!

I have an opinion about sex education that may surprise many parents: I don't happen to think that sex education is particularly difficult or complicated! The basic function of the human body is pretty simple. The complicated course to teach children is relationship education. That's a course that should begin when your child is born—and continue for a lifetime.

I don't believe you need to teach very young children too many details about sexuality, but any details you *do* teach should be dealt with in a very natural and matter-of-fact way. Sex is *not* the most pressing issue for very young children. What ought to be on the minds of parents of toddlers is "How does this topic fit in our broader educational plan for our children?"

The 24/7 Relationship

Just as certainly as children will speak, walk, and grow, they will arrive at puberty and experience the awakening of their sexual lives. It's a fact of human development. However, prior to this awakening, it is critical that children receive some very clear guidance in how to conduct a relationship with a sexual component to it! Teach your children that sex is only a part of a meaningful relationship.

Our culture has evolved to a point where our media, at least, seems to portray a sexual encounter as the same thing as a relationship. Wow, that is so misleading to children on the way to inevitably becoming sexual beings. The important thing to address—and demonstrate— for small children is to show them what a couple does the other 23 hours and 50 minutes of the day. As they get older, you can more fully discuss the role of sex in that "24/7" relationship.

Children observe and learn from *that* part of the relationship—*your* relationship, assuming you have a two-parent home—every day. What are they learning from what they see and hear? Do they see respect, joy, affection, compromise, gentleness, sharing, meaningful touch and interaction? Do your children regularly see their parents hugging and kissing as a part of their day-to-day interaction, or do they never see their parents as a physically connected couple?

If children see sex treated as dirty, casual, or wrong, that is what they will learn. If they see loving adults interacting respectfully, affec-tionately, and showing healthy touching and hugging, they will learn to act that way when their sexual being comes to life!

I sincerely believe that the most important part of the sexual edu-cation of very young children lies in allowing them to regularly see their parents modeling healthy and affectionate interaction. The time will come for them to understand the physical act of sex, and it can be very natural and easy if they have watched an ongoing relationship between loving and respectful parents who openly enjoy each other's company.

The "Facts of Life"

A child under the age of five certainly ought to know the proper names for the parts of the human body. That's pretty straightforward, and you should approach it the same way you taught them the names of the other body parts. You should probably also explain that these parts of the body are not generally discussed in every setting! Small children can understand that some things are private and only discussed with family, in private. They'll probably learn that naturally by the fact that they do not hear *you* regularly discussing those body parts. Kids learn language and its usage by being exposed to it. Just as children learn to use proper subject and verb agreement, verb tense, and other complicated nuances of language, so, too, will they learn that there are certain words and terms that they do not hear commonly spoken.

Don't make the mistake of thinking that teaching a child the names and functions of body parts constitutes sex education. That would be as foolish as teaching a child the parts of a car and what they do and thinking you have taught the child to drive! However, getting too involved or intense in these discussions can only mystify and lead to confusion for children on the whole topic of sex. The key is for you to be relaxed and natural as you talk about these topics. Use the terms in a sensible manner in the presence of your children. If they hear you appropriately using the terms and names of body parts, they will use them the same way. They will learn not just the words, but the context in which to use them.

Their questions will be a guide. If they ask, "Where did I come from?" you might respond, "Where do you think you came from?" Let them clarify whether they've heard something about penises and vaginas, or are just wondering if they're from Wisconsin like their friend at preschool. If their response leads in the direction of anatomy, again ask, "What would you like to know?" They may just want a simple "yes" or "no" to a question.

I always advise, if they're old enough to ask, they're old enough for an answer. If your answer is, "You're too young to ask," they will seek answers elsewhere. Think ahead about the questions to come, and discuss them with your spouse or other significant adults in your child's life. You'll be better prepared to answer simply, without the details your child *isn't* ready for!

I think the car metaphor is a good one. Kids ride in the car, gradually learning the parts and functions and the appropriate and acceptable behaviors. They don't need to learn to drive until they reach the age and have the maturity to handle the responsibility. The most important way they learn about driving as small children is from observing how *you* drive. Do they see you being attentive? Do they see you obeying the rules and laws of the road? Do they see you ensuring the safety of everyone in the car with you? They will imitate you as soon as they begin to learn to drive. In the early years they learn the attitudes of safe driving and the context for the later lessons of actually learning to drive a car.

The same is pretty much true of children learning to become sexual beings. In the early years they learn the context for a sexual relationship and the attitudes important to a relationship. As they get older they can learn the rest of the details.

Believe me when I say that the hardest part of the sexual education of a child is not teaching them how their bodies function sexually. The hard part is teaching them how to conduct the meaningful relationships of which sexuality is a part! Remember, there is a wise Samoan concept that you must teach your children *even* if you must at times use words! Words are most likely the least important part of teaching children about sexuality.

My experience as a high school teacher and Barbara's experience as a middle school teacher has only fortified my contention that relationship education is the important topic, not just sex education. We cannot count the number of young girls we have seen get pregnant during our careers. All of those young girls and the fathers of their children had figured out how their bodies work, but none of them had any idea how to build a relationship! Very few of those thousands of pregnancies ended with anything resembling a meaningful relationship. The majority of the relationships ended as soon as the pregnancy began! And from our point of view, these pregnancies were just the tip of the iceberg. Many more kids are harmed by casual, immature, or promiscuous sexual behavior than are brought to light because of pregnancy.

As a parent of a very young child, this ought to be a sobering thought for you to ponder as you take on the job of raising and educating your children. I advise you to put a great deal of emphasis on teaching your kids how to build meaningful relationships.

Questions, Questions, Questions!

Dear Mr. Bledsoe,

Our three-year-old daughter seems to be asking lots of questions about bodies and body parts. She has a boy cousin of a similar age and we spend a good deal of time with his family. The kids play together and have had baths together. She has noticed that she is built differently from her cousin and asks questions about the differences.

We just do not feel comfortable talking with her about such topics at such an early age! How old should a child be before we start into sex education?

Sincerely,
Wondering in Washington

Kids who are old enough to notice the difference are old enough to know the names of the body parts. Why not? They need to know the correct names! If you don't teach the correct names, they'll learn some from someone else, and you might not approve of the names they learn from playmates. Teach the correct names as soon as they ask.

Parents' Action

If you begin talking "matter of factly" with your child at an early age, you, too, will become comfortable with the topic. As you both become comfortable, it will be a very natural part of educating your children.

Gradually, children will learn to become private about their bodies. That will come naturally as they grow up learning that girls and boys use different restrooms, locker rooms, and so on. The important thing right now is to give them accurate information!

If you have an extended family or just close friends with whom you spend a lot of time, it's important that you get together with the other parents and discuss what you wish to teach your children, establishing some reasonable guidelines and timeframes for doing so.

The key is to have this open conversation with the adults who are raising your children's playmates, so that all of your children hear and see similar things as they grow up. Discuss at what age you think children should stop taking baths together. (Even if you don't establish an end to bathing together, your children will probably let you know when they're no longer comfortable with it.) The open discussion will simply keep everyone aware of the fact that your children are growing up and in need of instruction.

Involving the Extended Family

Strong extended families are a wonderful instructional aid for raising well-balanced young people who are comfortable about their own sexuality. The cool thing that your children learn as they spend time with the extended family is that there are people from all stages of life, and seeing positive, loving, fun interactions between adult men and women will serve as models for their own behavior as they mature. If it is possible, keep participating in your strong extended family!

The more couples of different ages that your children see maintaining loving, respectful relationships, the better! If your children can be around loving and happy grandparents, aunts, uncles, and others who have meaningful relationships, you greatly improve the chances of your children seeking such relationships!

This does not mean that, if there has been divorce in the family, you hide from it. My gosh, divorce is a reality in America, so if there has been divorce in the family, try to treat it as naturally as possible. Use those situations as real life examples for your children. Talk honestly about what happened to cause the relationship to break up. Don't take sides or expose your children to all the sordid details of an ugly and contentious divorce, but talk about how people sometimes grow apart if they are not careful to cultivate a happy relationship. Teach them that creating a lasting relationship is hard to do. Let them see that sometimes people have disagreements and arguments but that it is often possible to work them out.

The relationship education you will be giving will far outweigh any talk about body parts that you might have. Too many people discuss sex with children as if it is a separate and different thing from a meaningful relationship between two people. Children need to see that sex is just a part of a good relationship.

All too often we talk about and focus on problems. Problems force their way into our lives. Don't let that happen in your family. Sure, there may be divorce and discord, but there is also another side of the coin. If you have older friends and relatives who have been married for a long time, be sure that your children get to spend lots of time around those people, too. Talk about how they have achieved their long-lasting relationships. Kids do not need to just see and hear that half of the marriages in America end in divorce; they also need to see, firsthand, that half of all marriages end in long-lasting, happy, and meaningful partnerships! Be sure that they spend lots of time around people who have made it work.

Playground Sex Education

Dear Mr. Bledsoe,

Our son is attending preschool and he is only four but he has been coming home from school with some of the most alarming language. He is not just coming home with the seven forbidden words; he is coming home with phrases describing sexual acts! We were shocked. He used some language that my husband and I have never used. We have never let him hear anything like that on TV, and we know that none of our friends have ever spoken that way in front of him!

We are really distraught over this latest development. Should we withdraw him from the school? Should we demand that the preschool pay closer attention to the kids in their care? Should we try to identify the child who used the offensive language and demand that this child be removed from class?

We are so scared about the future if this is starting in preschool!

We need help,
Scared in San Jose

These parents are justified to be alarmed, and lucky to get such an early wake-up call! What they have just experienced is a great lesson in the reality of life. We cannot protect our children from the world, so *we must teach them to live in the world!* That is one of the main lessons of the entire Parenting with Dignity approach to raising children. Kids will run into things that you may not approve of, so your job is to teach them how to deal with them. But I am way ahead of myself; let me answer these very common questions as directly as I can.

Parents' Action

These parents ask if they should withdraw their child from that school and my answer is a resounding, "*No!*" If all the parents who have high moral standards for their children's behavior were to withdraw them from school, it would be disastrous—first for the families of the children who are bringing that language to school! They need help and guidance, and parents with high standards are a positive force in their lives and their children's.

Just think about this for a minute. If you remove a child from school every time he's exposed to something you disapprove of, you would have to move your child from school to school 10 times a year, if not more! My mother used to repeat a wonderful old saying: "Bloom where you are planted." (As a matter of fact, she still says it to me from time to time!) She was telling us to let the world see the good in us no matter where we found ourselves. Do the same for your family. Teach your children that the conduct of others does not determine their conduct.

Now let me discuss another of this parent's questions: "Should we demand that the preschool pay closer attention to the kids in their care?"

To begin with, I don't think you should ever start a conversation with anyone working with your kids with the word *demand*. You have the right to expect high standards from those people, but you'll have much more luck if you start by simply informing them about the language your son used when he came home. They may be totally unaware. Then listen and watch to see what their strategy is. It will tell you a ton about their program. Moving your child is your hole card, but letting the school personnel act is always the best place to start.

Then, if the teachers' strategy is ineffective, you can move on to more involvement. I suggest you invite the staff of your preschool to attend a parenting class that you start. (To read about starting a Parenting with Dignity class, go to Chapter 16.) Approach them by saying that there is a group of families getting together to discuss some standards of behavior to teach their children to use at school. Tell the preschool administrators and teachers that you would like to have their input. Invite them to attend. Any good preschool staff should welcome that kind of parental involvement. If they do not choose to attend, then you have learned some valuable information about the school!

Now for the final question, "Should we try to identify the child who used the offensive language and demand that child be removed from class?"

This is a great time to develop a whole new and productive attitude about raising your children. Here is an idea that you must wake up with every day: from now until your child leaves your home to live on his own, *he will spend more of his waking hours with other people's children than he will spend with you!*

That is shocking, but nonetheless true. So your most important strategies—in *all* areas—must be to teach your child how to make good decisions about his *own* behavior, *regardless* of others who may not have the same standards!

It now must become your priority to teach your child the standards you want him to follow in making good decisions! He will be in the presence of other kids from this day forward who will continue to exert powerful influence and pressure on him to behave differently, so he must have strong values and standards to follow as he makes good decisions. (Again, there's more on this in Chapter 16.) To do this, you must know with great certainty what values and standards you want to guide his life. They must be crystal clear enough for you to write them down, prioritize them, and *express them*.

Your next step must be to develop a network of parents with similar standards. This may sound difficult, but it's really a simple concept— and one that will actually simplify your task. After all, it will be easier for you to teach *your* child if she's running with children who are learning similar standards!

Because sex education seems to be a common question and concern, it would be a great topic to stimulate interest in a parenting class. I strongly suggest that you consider using our Parenting with Dignity curriculum. It lends itself well to a small group of parents like you might draw together from a preschool. Spreading the use of appropriate language will be just one of the benefits of holding this class! Right now, in the early years, your children will benefit from spending time with children with similar ideas ruling their worlds. Later on, as these children grow up and begin to date each other, they'll benefit because they will have been taught similar dating behavior.

Growing Up Together

Dear Mr. Bledsoe,

We have been through your entire nine-tape Parenting with Dignity Program and it has helped us more than we can express. However, we have come upon a problem and we have no idea what to do. So here goes ...

Our three-year-old son and his buddy have literally grown up together. We only live one house apart on the same block in our quiet little town. We have become best friends with the other boy's parents. The two boys are like brothers. Since they are only-children they play together constantly. It really works out great for both families since we can rely on each other if one of us needs to run an errand or keep an appointment. We even take turns having the boys sleep over so that the other couple can have "Date Night." We feel that between the two families we are providing much-needed support for each other.

We do everything together. Right now we are having a real hot spell so our two families went together and bought a wading pool for the boys to play in. This is where the problem arose. The pool is in our back yard, and it is a private yard, the boys are young so we usually let them swim without clothes. The other day, the other mother and I were on the back deck drinking a lemonade and watching our sons playing together in the pool when all of a sudden we were shocked with what we saw them doing!

They were sitting on their towels beside the pool and our son said to his buddy, "Look at my penis, it's standing up!" He was pointing to his budding little erection. His little friend said, "Mine does that, too!" He grabbed his penis and pulled on it a few times and he had an erection, too. The boys were not aware that we were watching.

We were absolutely shocked. We didn't know what to do, so we did nothing. That night, we got together with our husbands after the kids were in bed. When we told our husbands about what we saw, both of them laughed at first, but we were all confused and unsure about what to do.

Is this odd behavior or is it natural? Should we stop future behavior like this? Are we wrong to let our children play together without clothes? Should we tell them that it is wrong to discuss things like erections with others?

These boys are only three. Is this an indicator of what is to come?

Sincerely,
Two shocked families

Welcome to the real world of raising children! Of course, these children are normal! They saw something and commented upon it!

I would be more worried if something like that happened and they did *not* comment on it. That's how the male body naturally works. And, although they were confused, these parents did not overreact, and that is good.

They're also very lucky to be sharing this period of raising children with another couple that is also paying attention and trying to do what is best. With open lines of communication, they can honestly discuss events like this and arrive at the best plan of action for their kids. A group of parents experiencing similar situations is one of the greatest aids to effective parenting.

Next, I want to commend these parents for their support of each other. Sharing the load during errands and having an evening for the parents to be alone is a great way to deal with the hectic pace of raising children. I believe that sharing the care needs with trusted friends is superior to childcare. Having their sons spend time with a trusted friend in a familiar setting is so natural and it is so comforting to the child. I know socialization is a key issue, but that will come as their sons move into preschool and later into school. It is really nice for those boys to have friendship and companionship in this early stage in life.

Additionally, I would like to commend both families for not resorting to a "blame-game" where both families try to somehow blame the other for what has happened between the two boys. That could be and often is devastating for the two families, but even more so for the children. What happened was a very natural thing. Children are curious about their bodies and nobody is to "blame" for that! Be supportive and open as your children grow and learn.

Now let me answer their specific questions. First, "Is this odd behavior or is it natural?"

Again, this is not odd behavior. These are normal little boys noticing the world and specifically in this case they were noticing their own bodies. It would be odd if they did not notice. The key is to not overreact. At some quiet time, it would be a good idea to communicate to the boys that it is inappropriate to discuss their private body parts with others—however, don't overdo it, and certainly don't make them feel ashamed of their bodies or ashamed of being aware of them. Try to explain what happened as naturally as you might explain how an elbow works.

"Should we stop future behavior like this?"

The key is to help your children develop a healthy view of their bodies without exposing them to embarrassment should they behave similarly in some other setting. In other words, let them know that it is natural for their bodies to work that way, while at the same time letting them know that it is not acceptable to discuss that function openly in all situations. Let boys know that, although having an erection is natural and okay, it is also not something to be discussed at dinner or with Grandma's bridge group. It is important for children to accept themselves naturally, but limit things to their appropriate social setting.

Also, rest assured that these parents have done nothing wrong in letting three-year-old boys play in a wading pool without clothes. They will have the rest of their lives to worry about wearing clothes. Relax, take a deep breath, and move on to bigger things. The question is not whether you should (or can!) prevent them from being aware of their own bodies. The question is, "At what age should we be teaching our children appropriate dress and conduct?"

Parents' Action

As your children become aware of the changes in their bodies, it will probably be good to get them learning by doing. In other words, a great way to teach them to keep private things *private* is to let them practice at home. Let it be seen as another step in the process of being more grown-up, rather than tying it to the erection incident. Make it natural and your kids will perceive it as natural. For example, they can learn to close the door when they go to the bathroom and to get dressed in the privacy of their room.

Should you tell children that it's wrong to discuss things like erections with others? Well, it's certainly a good idea to teach children to keep certain subjects for private discussions with Mom and Dad. In a perfect world we could immediately answer every question and allow every comment from our children, but you can't raise children in a bubble! Socialization is one of your key jobs as parents—to teach your children the appropriate behaviors for the appropriate situations.

It would be far more damaging to avoid telling your child something is inappropriate than it would be to scold him for it. It could be devastating for your son to blurt out "My penis gets stiff sometimes!" in front of Grandma's bridge group. If their reaction is shock, it could be hard for a child to understand. If their reaction is laughter, it could teach him that this is great entertainment! Either way, he's learned something you'd rather he hadn't.

A Time and Place for Everything

As I have said before, your children will rapidly understand that they don't hear you talking about such things in all situations, even as they learn that you know the words and what they stand for. As they learn that verbs have tenses, so, too, will they learn that there are topics to save for private times. It can be very natural if you can treat it naturally.

Accurate information is the key. There are lots of good books and in-formation out there. Do a simple search and find books and resources that support what *you* think is appropriate as a parent. Three books that Barbara and I liked were *Where Do Babies Come From?* by S. Mayes, and *Where Did I Come From?* and *What Is Happening to Me?* by Peter Mayle. We read and reread these to our boys (and we found out later that their babysitters read and reread them, too).

Children have an insatiable curiosity about *everything*, including their bodies. Their questions will challenge you, intrigue you, and may even embarrass you—but one thing is certain. They will keep coming only if they get good answers! *The surest way to have your children be confused about their sexuality is to just say nothing.* Answer honestly and simply, and if you don't know the answer, tell them you will find out—then do it!

Chapter 13

Bullying

"Is it normal for kids this young to hit, kick, and bite? Is my child a bully because she grabs toys from other kids?"

Just about any behavior can be learned, but some seem to be more innate. A child grabbing a toy he or she wants from another child is pretty natural. Offering a toy in trade for the wanted toy is *not* so natural—and that's where parents' teaching skills come in. You have to *teach* the desired behavior.

Now I don't want to overreact in a book about raising toddlers, but bullying is real. A two-year-old pulling a playmate's hair doesn't constitute bullying, but some of what we overlook as innocent play may also be the beginnings of bullying. Bullying often begins very early, and it can often be averted by early awareness and proactive guidance from parents. Some bullying behaviors begin as soon as a child begins to talk. Authorities working with the problem in schools also tell us that most bullying in the middle school years is rooted in early childhood.

I believe that parents must be on the lookout for bullying behavior in their children because our society provides so many opportunities for kids to learn bullying. Kids have many models for this behavior, cartoons being just one example. Kids learn phrases such as "You wanna piece of me?", "Butthead!", and "Sissy!" to shout at friends. Kids learn that the way to deal with conflict and frustration is by calling names and using putdowns. Very young children may bully by choosing one child who always has to be "it" or always has to have the inferior car or doll. If the bullied child doesn't comply, the threat is that he doesn't get to play.

That being said, I believe even more strongly that the best way to ensure that our children are not bullies is to teach them a better way to act. They simply won't need to bully if they have learned more successful ways to get what they want from others. If we teach and encourage respectful, dignified, and effective skills at an early age, most kids will use what they have been taught. If we wait until the bullying has appeared, we're most likely going to have real difficulty in stopping the behavior.

The following is from the United States Department of Health and Human Services on their National Mental Health Center Website.

What Is Bullying?

Bullying involves repeated acts of physical, emotional, or social behavior that are intentional, controlling, and hurtful. Bullying is a learned behavior, evident as early as two years of age. Bullying can be either direct or indirect. Direct bullying usually is seen and felt readily. Indirect bullying (deliberate exclusion, name calling, etc.) is much more difficult to identify, often is more difficult to remedy, and should be clearly seen as different from direct bullying. Boys are more typically engaged in direct bullying and girls in indirect bullying, but that is not always the case. Just be alert and consider the following:

1. Bullying is defined by a power imbalance between the bully and the target.
2. A bully's power can be derived from physical size, strength, verbal skill, popularity, or gender.
3. A bully's target feels tormented, helpless, and defenseless.

4. Bullying can include hitting, name-calling, threatening, intimidating, kicking, spreading rumors, teasing, pushing, tripping, excluding someone from a group, or destroying someone's things.

Why Stop Bullying?

1. Bullying interferes with learning in school and may lead to increased absenteeism and dropout rates.
2. Students feel less safe and less satisfied in school when there are high levels of bullying in the school.
3. Bullying children may become bullying adults and are more likely to become child and spouse abusers.
4. The longer bullying lasts, the harder it is to change.
5. Bullies identified by age 8 are six times more likely to have a criminal conviction by age 24.
6. Bullying may be linked to other delinquent, criminal, and gang activities, such as shoplifting, drug abuse, and vandalism.
7. The targets of bullies grow socially insecure and anxious with decreased self-esteem and increased depression rates, even into adulthood."

Preventing bullying is far more effective than stopping the problem after it has reared its ugly head.

How Do We Prevent Bullying?

So, "How do I prevent bullying from becoming a problem for my children?" you ask. That is a great question!

The answer is not simple, but it is not really very complicated either. The first step is to decide what behavior you want! Describe how you want your children to relate to others. I have some definite ideas for my own kids and grandkids, but deciding how you want your kids to behave is a personal issue.

Here is one idea that I try to have dominate the behavior of my children: *Do unto others as you would have them do unto you!* Ah, yes, you say, the idea commonly known as the Golden Rule. Often it is called old-fashioned. I do not believe that it is old-fashioned; it is *old*, period. Old-fashioned implies that it has somehow worn out and is no longer applicable. I believe the Golden Rule is old because it has stood the test of time. Down through the ages this rule has applied to meaningful human interaction. The Golden Rule is often not practiced, but it is still applicable, and, if practiced, the simple concept of treating others the way we would like to be treated would certainly improve the world. If you teach your children this one idea, you would probably never have to teach them about bullying! If they are doing one, they can't do the other!

Let me demonstrate how I would go about teaching the Golden Rule. Even if this is not an idea you choose to teach your children, you will still be able to duplicate the process outlined here in teaching your chosen idea.

As I go about teaching an abstract idea like this to a young child, I always begin with the adage, *Actions speak louder than words*. The concept of "Do as I say, not as I do" has set parenting back more than any other single statement. Kids will almost *always* do what you do and *ignore what you say!* Therefore, the best way to teach a young child to treat others the way they would like to be treated is to treat them that way: treat your children the way you would like to be treated!

Be polite to kids. Ask them to do things in a conversational tone. Smile at them continuously and listen to them respectfully. Share with them continuously. Tell them often, "In our family, we say 'please' and 'thank you' because it's the right thing to do. In our family, we don't yell; we speak in a nice voice." Make "in our family …" a regular introduction to describing expected positive behaviors.

Read the following letter I received from a parent who believed her son was out of control in his treatment of his little sister. Before you read my comments, stop and think about where the child learned the bullying behavior he was exhibiting regularly with his little sister.

Bossing, Name-Calling, Pushing, and Shouting

Dear Mac,

Our problem regards our five-year-old son, who is a tyrant with his three-year-old sister. He continually yells at her. He shouts instructions at her in the meanest of tones. If she does not follow his commands, he hits her and calls her names. He shoves her. Sometimes he drags her or shoves her into her room and closes the door on her. She cannot reach the doorknob so she shrieks as he confines her in "prison." I am becoming worried for our daughter's safety.

Our son will start school next year, and my husband and I are very worried that this aggressive, bullying behavior will get him in trouble—or, worse, and maybe of more importance he will injure one of the kids at school.

We have tried everything. We have sent him to his room for time out. We have spanked him immediately every time he hits or yells at his sister. We very sternly tell him not to treat his sister like that. Sometimes I feel like a broken record because I am constantly telling him to stop! I get so frustrated that I yell at him even though I know I shouldn't. He can see that it makes me mad when he treats his sister like that, but he just keeps on. We are at wits' end.

I have been through your course and I know that your Rule #3 says that we should repeat our instructions to our children but we have told him to stop so many times that I feel like it is all I say to him.

Can you help us, please? We feel like we are raising a monster.

Sincerely,
Beth and John

What advice would you give these parents? They certainly seem justified to be alarmed and should be commended for recognizing a dangerous trend in their son's behavior. They *should* worry about the safety of their little girl—and not just her physical safety. They should worry about her emotional safety as well! She could develop permanent scars as a result of her older brother's bullying.

But let's take a look at how to change this alarming behavior. Let's look at the letter and what it actually said.

Our son hits his sister and we have tried to stop that by hitting him.

Our son shouts at his sister and we have tried to teach him to be different by shouting at him.

Our son locks his sister in her room and we have tried to change him by sending him to his room for a time out!

Where do you think this child learned his bullying behavior? His parents' actions are speaking so loudly that he cannot hear their words! Their actions have taught him how to act. If you want to teach your children to behave differently, you have to start acting differently yourself. This is true with almost everything we teach children, but it is the *only* way to teach kids how to treat others!

> I have said it before and I will say it again until it sinks in: *Kids learn more from our backside than they do from our frontside!* Children learn more from our actions than they do from our words!

You must do some soul searching and clear thinking here. If you act in a way that you will not let your child act, then you are obligated to explain to him *why* you are acting in a manner that is unacceptable for him. If you shout at your child (or at each other), then you must be able to explain, *in a manner that she can understand*, why it is okay for you to shout and not okay for her. If you tell your child he must not hit, then you must explain why it's all right for you to hit him. I know, people use the word *spank*, but I use the word *hit* because it is so much more descriptive of what you are doing. I tend to believe that calling it *spanking* attempts to legitimize it.

If a parent can explain either of these to a child, I would like to hear it, because I don't believe I could! (It might be interesting to note that I e-mailed back and forth with this couple a few times and they never did try to justify yelling or hitting.)

It might be easier for these parents to justify putting a child in his room for a time-out, while still explaining why you are denying him the right to use this strategy with his little sister. You are using time-out to stop dangerous behavior. You are using time-out to give him a chance to calm down. Parents have the responsibility to make the home a safe place, but he is not in charge of safety, so he is not to use that technique himself.

Parents' Action

Begin by phrasing ten common instructions for your child in words that are polite. Practice saying them in a conversational tone of voice. The key word is *practice*, for the same reason that your child must practice appropriate behavior: You have to overcome some unhealthy habits! You may be surprised by how difficult it will be for you to make this change. Be aware of this difficulty; your son is going to need a lot of positive repetition and endless patience from you to change his behavior.

I even suggest that parents practice giving instructions to each other after the kids go to bed. Practice it with a pleasant, conversational tone of voice and a smile.

Make an agreement that you will speak only in a polite manner. Vow to never yell at each other. Promise to always use "please" and "thank you" when asking anyone to do anything. Your children will begin to imitate this behavior! (Hasn't this boy imitated his parents' yelling long enough?)

Use statements like, "In our family we do not speak like that to each other; we always speak in a quiet voice!"

Constantly practice this new way of acting, especially at times when your children are not in the midst of turmoil or conflict. Do not expect overnight results, but your children will watch how you behave and will begin to behave that way, too.

Teach Respect by Being Respectful

Polite, considerate treatment of others is a learned behavior. It is learned by exposure to it, like a language. I wouldn't have believed this myself for the first eight years of teaching. I set myself up as the enforcer, and I shouted and yelled with the best of them! I had over three full pages of rules for my classroom, and I was in control. Well, many of my students looked at that and said, "He designed the game, so I will play and win!"

The day that I started acting in a respectful manner toward my students was the day my classroom became a respectful place. When I presented respectful behavior as a choice, my students began to behave respectfully towards each other and towards me. Respect is so much easier to get if it is first given.

I know that many parents who read this are experiencing a strong push-back response to what I am saying, because loud, often disrespectful, and even violent commands with children is so accepted. Remember what I said to this couple about their son being bossy and mean to his sister. The first thing that needs to change is the behavior of the parents. The first step in teaching children respectful, dignified behavior is treating the child in a respectful, dignified manner.

Please, please, please do not misinterpret what I am saying to you. I am saying that you should treat your children in the manner that you want them to treat others. I am not saying that you must be permissive or that you should not be forceful and demanding of high levels of behavior. What we are talking about here is the manner in which you go about teaching excellent behavior to your children.

My work in prisons only further confirms my belief that teaching civil and dignified behavior to people must first begin by treating them the way you want them to act. I have visited prisons where all rules are enforced with firm, swift, and sure punishment by custodians who treat the men with disdain. These are places of constant confrontation and violence.

Then I visit prisons where the overriding philosophy is to treat the inmates with the utmost respect and dignity. The atmosphere is so different that it's like a different planet.

At the Bristol County Correctional Facility in Dartmouth, Massachusetts, Sheriff Tom Hodson has established an atmosphere where inmates are treated with respect and dignity. His standards for behavior are as high or higher than any prison I have ever visited, yet the place is amazing. I won't try to paint an unrealistic picture. Just like other prisons, they have some inmates who are so hardened that they must be kept in solitary confinement, but the rest of the inmate population is really something. When I visit that institution, I am always amazed at the respect that is shown to me by the inmates.

They have been taught respect, not by confrontation or by power struggles, but by being treated with respect. To teach these men how to treat someone the way they would like to be treated, it was first necessary to treat them the way their custodians would like to be treated.

Well, your toddlers are not criminals, and they certainly do not have the background of violence or abuse of many of the men I meet in prison, so it should be easier to teach your children than it is to teach the prisoners.

Chapter 14

Sharing

"Is it reasonable to expect a child of two or three to share with other children?"

I have read many parenting manuals that propose that teaching a child under five to share is unreasonable. I beg to differ. Kids can be taught to share very early.

If a four-year-old is grabbing toys away from a two-year-old, ask yourself, "What behavior do I want the four-year-old to use in place of grabbing the toys?" If you cannot answer that question precisely, how can you expect your child to do so? What behavior do you want? Do you want your child to offer another toy in exchange for the one the younger child is using? Do you want the older child to simply respect the younger child's right to play with the toy because she had it first? Or would you like for the two to play with the toy together?

Once you decide precisely what you want, you must then devise a strategy for teaching that behavior.

I Want It!

Let's say you have decided to teach your four-year-old three different strategies for when he sees his younger sibling playing with a toy he wants. In one case, you want the older child to recognize that his younger sibling is already playing with the toy, so he should respect his right to continue to play with it. How will you teach him to recognize this situation?

Offer the older child three ways to identify that his younger sibling is really playing with the toy and should not be interrupted. Describe these methods of identification to your child using both words and role playing. First, explain that if his brother's eyes are looking at the toy, that means that he's really playing with it. Get down on the floor and pretend you're playing with a toy. Ask the older child to pretend that you are his little brother and ask him to look at you and tell you whether your eyes are focused completely on the toy. If they are, he must let you play with the toy. If, on the other hand, you're playing with the toy but looking distractedly around at other things, then it's okay for the older sibling to begin to barter for use of the toy.

Next, explain that if the younger child has just picked up the toy, then that is another good reason to let him have it for a while. Role play again, showing the older child that soon the little brother will lose interest in the toy and begin to play with something new, making it okay for him to have the toy himself. Just like before, get down on the floor and demonstrate that often waiting takes almost no time. Play with the toy for a short while, put it down, and start playing with another toy. (In fact, explain to him that, by waiting patiently and quietly, he may even get the toy sooner, but if he demands the toy, his little brother may cling to it even more tightly!)

A third way for your child to see if a trade can be negotiated is to see if the younger child can be tempted. Show big brother how to find another toy and play with it right in front of the younger sibling. If the younger one watches, then it is a good time to negotiate a trade of toys. Get down on the floor and play with a toy, pretending to be the younger child again while your older son plays nearby. At first, keep your eyes on your toy and ignore him. Point out that this is not a time to try to trade toys. Next, look over at the older child and watch him play with his toy. As soon as you do that, tell big brother that now he can negotiate a trade. Make sure that you establish in the older kid's head that if the younger child does not want to trade, that decision must be honored.

Repeat these scenarios a number of times over a period of days. Let the child demonstrate that he can identify each of these behaviors as you pretend to be the younger sibling. In the repetition you are practicing Rule #3! By repeating these behaviors, you are imprinting clear ideas and strategies for the older child to use with his younger brother. Then watch the kids play together. Pay attention and watch for opportunities for the older child to practice with his little brother. Kneel down beside the older child and whisper in his ear, "Your brother is playing with a toy; can you tell if this would be a good time to try to trade?" You might even do a little coaching. Whisper, "Are his eyes on the toy? Move over in front of him and see if he looks up at you."

Now comes the most critical part. If he has some success and works an effective trade with his little brother, jump on this experience and apply Rule #4: get him to say it for himself. Say to him, "See? How does that feel? You found a good time to trade and when you offered to trade, it worked!" This first time, you are only asking if he agrees. The next time, ask a question that cannot be answered with a "yes" or "no." Ask, "How does it feel to be able to see when your little brother will trade, then actually trade with him without a fuss?"

As you can tell, you cannot affect this kind of permanent and self-sustaining change without allowing a *lot* of time for repetition. But, trust me, it's worth it! The alternative is to spend the next 10 years (or more) being continually engaged in preventing squabbling, hitting, tears, and sometimes mayhem. Which expenditure of your time would you prefer?

The goal is to get your older child to act in the desired manner for his own reasons—not just for your approval! You want to teach your children to act in the desired manner because it works, not just because you are demanding the behavior. The desired behaviors then become self-supporting habits. I firmly believe it is a mistake to hover over your children offering constant "attaboys" and "nice jobs" to them. Doing so teaches kids to act appropriately for the approval of others, rather than because good decisions work and it feels good to act in that manner.

Acting only for the approval of others would be a good thing if you could ensure that your child will always be in the presence of people who recognize appropriate behavior. You can't. What if your child comes in contact with people who give approval for inappropriate behavior? I know we're talking about toddlers here, but think ahead to when your child starts school. You would like the sharing behaviors to continue into the school years so he can identify times when he can share or trade toys, school supplies, or ideas with other children.

You can expect in the early school years that your children will come in contact with kids who haven't been taught to share, and kids will gang up on each other with some bullying (see Chapter 13). Your children will encounter other kids who will encourage your child to join them in taking things from others. You won't be there to give the positive comments and guidance, so you must hope that your child will stand his ground and not participate in such behavior. If he has only learned to do things to get your approval and you are not there to offer it, he will be much more likely to seek the approval of his classmates.

Sharing for Its Own Sake

Dear Mr. Bledsoe,

I am a single mom with two children, both girls ages four and two. I am so busy supporting myself and the girls that some days I feel overloaded. My four-year-old is so demanding of her little sister, and the biggest thing is that she will not share anything with her sister.

Our day-care provider says that it is a constant battle at her house, too. She says that Cindy (my oldest) constantly grabs toys from LuAnne (my youngest). It's disheartening, too, because she doesn't grab toys from other children; she only grabs from LuAnne.

I heard about your Parenting with Dignity program from a friend. She told me I could write to you and that you would answer, so here is my question. Can I expect my four-year-old daughter to share with her sister or should I just wait until she is older to try to teach sharing?

Sincerely,
Nearly Burned Out

First, I must say that this woman is a hero! I could not imagine being a parent to two children under the age of five and also being the sole support for the family. If you are in that situation, you are justified in occasionally feeling worn out. I would advise you to stop and congratulate yourself for the amazing thing you are doing. Please give yourself a big pat on the back for me. I admire you more than words can express.

Allow me to give one piece of advice to other single parents: Please do not try to do your job all by yourself. Enlist help! If you live near some extended family, please ask for their help. Develop a cadre of friends who are willing to help you with parenting your children. By no means is it an admission of weakness or being incapable. It's just smart parenting. Read Chapter 16 about forming a class. You won't believe the strength you will gain from the others who go through the class with you. It will be an investment of time now that will save you years of tears, frustration, and fatigue later.

Now to this woman's specific questions. Can you expect a four-year-old to share with her sister or should you just wait until your child is older to try to teach sharing?

That is really two questions. The answer to whether you should wait until she is older is a resounding and definitive *no!* Start teaching your children to share right now and do not ever stop teaching that most important life skill. If you want your child to learn to share, then you must start teaching it right away. Every day you wait is another day of instilling a bad habit of not sharing.

Now for the real question: Can you expect a four-year-old to share with a sibling?

Absolutely, a four-year-old can learn the concept of sharing! First, follow Rule #1 and define what you want the behavior to look like. In order to teach a child to do what you want them to do, you must first decide exactly what the desired behavior is! Then you must be able to describe it in terms that your child can understand. You also must be able to give her a "sales pitch" that very clearly shows her how she will personally benefit from following your instructions.

This will be very personal; you will need to decide exactly what *you* want the sharing behavior to look like. I will give you an example of how I might approach this task.

To me, sharing involves two basic actions. First, sharing means giving up something one has to someone else (in this case, Cindy giving something to her sister, LuAnne). To describe this in terms Cindy can understand, I would set up several situations over several days. I would never try to teach this new and rewarding action too quickly; instead, introduce it in small increments over a period of time.

> Never try to teach a positive behavior at the same time as stopping a negative behavior. Trying to teach sharing when two kids are locked in conflict over something is almost impossible. The time to teach is long before a negative behavior has arisen. *Place the desired action in a child's head at a calm time apart from the action.* Try to set the picture of the desired action in your child's head, then orchestrate or watch for an opportunity for the child to put it into action.

Parents' Action

I would tell this mom to take Cindy aside one morning and begin to teach the desired behavior. Use Rule #2. Praise her and keep her action separated from her self. Begin by saying, "Cindy, you are so kind to your sister. She is so lucky to have a big sister who is so thoughtful." Most children have a strong ability to see themselves in a good light. Ask her to describe some good things she has done for her sister lately. If she struggles, be ready with a couple of specific examples to prompt her. You might say, "You are so cheerful with LuAnne at breakfast," or, "You are so nice to your sister at bedtime. You always give her a big hug before bed." The idea is to call to mind the positive things she already does, so she is saying to herself, "Yeah, I *am* pretty kind to my sister!" Rule #4!

Now, begin to describe the desired behavior. "Cindy, when you're playing with your sister, rather than taking something from her, it would work best if you *trade* with her if she has a toy you want. Today when you're playing with her, this is what I want you to do. If you see LuAnne playing with a toy you want, pick up another toy and start playing with it in front of her. Wait until she seems interested in the toy you're playing with, then ask, 'LuAnne, how would you like to trade?' Hold your toy up for her to have. Wait until she takes the toy you offer her, then say, 'Okay, now that you have that toy, can I play with this one?'"

Then practice with Cindy. Say, "I will pretend to be LuAnne. I will start playing with this doll. Now, you pick up another doll right here in front of me and start putting the clothes on it. Watch my face. When I look at you, ask me if I would like to try dressing this doll. As soon as I start, then you ask if you can play with the other doll."

Practice with different toys. Once you have practiced a couple of times, get the girls together and watch them playing. When LuAnne is playing with a toy, whisper to Cindy, "Try it now." As soon as she makes her offer, watch carefully. LuAnne might not go for it on the first try. Say quietly, "Try another toy." In doing this, you are coaching your daughter to be persistent and to not give up on the first try.

The minute a trade is negotiated, be ready to give the sales pitch! Say to Cindy, "Isn't that fun?" The key here is to get her to say to herself, "That worked, and it felt good to be able to trade with my sister without hurting her feelings or making her cry!"

You have just practiced an application of Rule #4. The sales pitch helps the child verbalize the positive feelings she derives from the desired action. Once Cindy feels the power of working a trade, and the positive payoff of feeling good, coupled with getting to play with the toy she wants, the behavior has a high likelihood of being repeated!

Continue to find opportunities for your child to share and feel the benefit of doing it. Every desired skill you teach requires time, time, and more time—and you will find your child *loves* the time you spend teaching her.

Be sure you reward yourself with your *own* internal sales pitch: Spending this time with my child feels good! She has learned a new skill from me and she and her sister are *sharing!*

Chapter 15

Sports

"Is three too young for organized sports? How about five?"

This is a question often directed at me, since we have two sons who were both heavily recruited high school athletes, had a great deal of success in their college careers, and finally our oldest son has had an illustrious professional career as an NFL quarterback. However, I do not believe that our experience gives me any special authority to speak on the subject other than to say that we certainly didn't hurry to get our kids involved in sports at an early age!

Keeping It Loose

When our sons were very young, they had no opportunities to be involved in organized sports. I'm not sure how I felt about that at the time, but looking back I now believe that it was a blessing in disguise! We lived in small rural communities that had only the most basic sports programs, with nothing organized for kids under age seven or eight.

The lack of organized sports was really an advantage for our children.

"How could it be considered an advantage to not have any chance to participate in organized sports?" you ask. Well, with no organized sports or pressure to be involved, our sons were completely free to explore events and activities as they came along. Drew, our elder son, was free to enter a Bike-a-thon to benefit our local United Way, where he rode his bike on a three-mile course and raised money for each lap. He had a blast attacking this cause-driven activity. There were almost no rules; he just had to follow the course and check in at the starter's table each time he finished another lap. He rode at his own pace, but got to test his ability against others, learn about his limits, and test his determination. One lap would have been a success; as it turned out, over 30 miles was not enough to max out his desire. He got into the riding so much that after all the other riders were finished and it began to get dark, the organizers had to come out and ask him to stop! He was on about his tenth lap of the course, having fun and learning about the joy of civic volunteerism!

The boys also got to participate on a summer-only swim team as soon as they could swim the length of the pool. Lots of participation opportunities, lots of ribbons, and not much stress.

From the time they were two-and-a-half, Barbara would drop off our sons at the high school where I was coaching football to just hang out while I was doing my job. Talk about unstructured! Some days they would play with the balls with other kids who dropped by. Other days they built forts with the blocking dummies. Much of the time they just played tag and "hide-and-seek" with friends. At times they would stand by me as I did my job, listening and watching and then crawling through the huddle. My players were great with the kids, and I could not have found better role models for our sons than Keith Badten, Steve Dorsey, Ricky Dunn, Mark and Blaine Bennett, and countless others on my teams. I believe the key was that I never tried to organize my boys' play or involve them in anything that they did not choose to be involved in. They got to seek their own interests and their own readiness.

When they did get old enough to participate in organized games, these were little more than supervised games of "work-up" baseball and pick-up basketball. Parents were almost totally uninvolved. Umpires and referees were usually volunteer parents or high school kids, there just to keep the game moving and instruct the kids on the rules. Uniforms were jeans and t-shirts, and teams were adjusted by the week according to which kids showed up. Kids would play for new teams just to even up the sides. I believe that this loose structure was good for my sons. The games had almost no pressure involved.

Now, don't get me wrong, I am not one who thinks that we should tear down scoreboards and just play for the love of the game. I believe that the love of the game includes winning, but at early ages, kids can play a game to win and keep score without winning becoming the primary focus.

While we were living in Benton City, Washington, our son Drew was privileged to play in a basketball league where all of the fundamentals were taught to the whole group by high school athletes before any division into teams took place. The kids would rotate around the gym from drill to drill and the high-school athletes' focus was on fun and lots of repetition. Little spontaneous games would spring up in these drills. Laughing was at a premium and skill development was the result of simple participation. Games were short and loosely organized. It wasn't a perfect program by any means, but the keys were the focus on fun and the loose organization.

Take Things at Their Own Pace!

I'm opposed to most organized sports for kids who are not yet in school. For too many kids those programs are too structured and tightly controlled by the parents and coaches. There will be time for skill development as kids get older. What kids need in the early years is a chance to participate and have fun. They're not developmentally ready to attempt proper manipulation of the balls and implements of most sports.

When adults get carried away and begin teaching sophisticated skills to kids who are three, four, or five, all that happens is that the child learns bad habits they will spend the rest of their lives trying to break. A three-year-old child is incapable of properly shooting a basketball or throwing a football. I hate to hear parents saying things like, "Little Billy is just a natural quarterback, look at him throw!" Baloney! It's actually impossible to spot an athlete at that early age. Take a look at our son, Drew. He was being told that he had no future as a quarterback as late as the seventh and eighth grade! Even the junior-high coaches could not yet detect any potential! But look at him now.

I believe the best way to expose small children to sports is by having the mitts, balls, bats, hoops, sticks, pucks, skates, rackets, and so on as just another toy in the toy box. Let them pick them up just as they would a toy fire truck or a doll and play with them at their own pace.

That being said, kids can join some sports at a very early age—sports with little competition done almost totally for simple enjoyment. For me, skiing and horseback riding come to mind, but bike riding, skating, and swimming also fall into this category. I'm sure many families find that sports like fishing and camping also make for good family fun. The key lies in letting kids enjoy activities at their own pace. Encourage them to enjoy an active lifestyle. Let them gain a desire to participate in activities at an early age and let the skill development and participation in organized sports come later.

Take skiing for example. Very young children can master skiing and enjoy the exhilaration of the speed, turns, and jumps. The problem arises when overzealous parents try to get the sport organized and force races and competition on these little ones. When this happens, the sport often loses its attraction for the children and progresses into work. If you are going to get your young children into a sport like skiing, let them establish when they're ready. Make it available and let them establish for themselves when they want to pursue it.

I know that classes are available for kids in sports like skiing. If you are thinking about involving your children in such classes, observe the classes before enrolling your children. Watch the instructors' teaching style. Are the lessons designed for the kids to have fun? How do the instructors teach the skills of the sport? Do they explain with words and good examples the children can understand? Do they break a new skill into components? And again, is all of this fun?

We have a very instructive bit of videotape of one of our boys playing in a t-ball game. I think the content of the tape can be very telling even if you're not seeing it. Our son is playing third base and a batter has just hit the ball for the other team. The batter is in a mad dash for first base while about six of the players on our team are in a wild chase for the ball. A runner on the other team is running for third—but she has to stop to ask our son to put the base down! As the action was taking place, he was checking under the base to see how it was held down! He set the base down, the girl stepped on it, then she ran home and scored. A run was marked up in chalk on a make-do scoreboard, and the game went on!

I think that episode says a ton about youth sports! First, there wasn't an adult screaming instructions at the kids. The kids were playing the game. Our son, while he was participating, was just curious about how bases are held down. When the girl came to the bag, they were able to work it out and, while a score was being kept, it certainly wasn't the total focus of the game. Nobody waged a protest about the "cheating" third baseman. Youth sports need to be that loosely organized!

Spotting Athletic Talent

Dear Mac,

You have a son who is an NFL quarterback, and we are wondering, how old was Drew when you first began to see his potential to be a great quarterback?

The reason I am writing is because our son is two and he just wants to throw everything and I think he is a real natural!

Sincerely,
Proud Dad in Boston

Well, Drew was about 10 games into his second year in the NFL when I thought he might make it as a quarterback in the NFL. Until then, I was always worrying that the dream would end and I would wake up to find that it wasn't real!

Honestly, Drew did not show exceptional ability to play sports until he was in about the tenth grade. Sure, he said he would like to play sports just like many kids, but he didn't show any special talent. He participated in the "sport of the season," from swimming to wrestling to soccer to baseball to football with great enthusiasm, but showed no exceptional skill other than tremendous endurance.

I do not believe that it is possible to spot ability at an early age. For every dad of a professional athlete who will try to tell you that their child was a natural, I can find you ten million dads who made the same claim only to be disappointed. Enjoy what your child is doing, but don't try to predict. Parents' expectations will more than likely just make sports less enjoyable for their kids.

To back up my statement that organized sports and skill development should be left until later, let me just offer one physiological reality. Until your son's hand is big enough to allow him to hold a football in the proper throwing position and then flip it violently so the tip of the ball goes from facing forward and backward, he cannot physically throw a football properly. If your son is not able to throw a football properly, it's impossible to predict how he will be able to throw it when he is able to do so with correct technique.

Now here is the really important thing for you to know: if you try to have your child throw, shoot, swing, or perform some other skill before he or she can do it properly, you will teach the kid bad habits that may never be overcome. If a child throws a football every day but throws it *improperly*, he will develop an improper muscle memory that will be almost impossible to overcome when he does gain the size and maturity to throw properly. The same is true for manipulating implements and balls in any other sport.

Make sure your kids have lots of opportunities to play with all kinds of balls and sports equipment. Play with them and help them naturally develop general skills like throwing and catching. The key is for your kids to develop a happy enjoyment of athletic activity. Just teach them to love to *play*, and don't worry about playing *games!* Just play!

Here is one guideline you might find helpful. Once you believe your child wants to do more than just play with the implements of sports—balls, mitts, bats, sticks, tees, pucks, and so on—make sure that he has implements he is capable of handling properly. Get small implements that allow him to duplicate approximations of proper actions for the sport.

In the meantime, just enjoy your kids and their zest for life!

Coaches at Any Age

Dear Coach Bledsoe,

Sir, I have many very fond memories of my four years playing for you on the Waterville High School football team years ago. Playing football was a landmark experience that shaped much of my character. Now we have our son, Cameron, age one, and I really want him to have a similar enriching experience when he gets old enough to participate.

Even though we get together three or four times a year to share family time, I have simply never thought about this issue until Cameron was born. Now I have a question for you.

I remember that your sons, Drew and Adam, were almost always at our practices. Now that I have a son of my own, it has caused me to think about you and your role in the lives of your sons. I was wondering if you ever stopped and gave them instruction about the game of football and football skills when they were visiting practice. I don't seem to remember you doing that, but that may be because I was not paying attention at the time.

Whatever you did must have worked because they both turned out to be such great athletes. I was wondering if it was the early instruction that they received while at practice that made the difference for them.

Sincerely,
Shawn Woods

I have been so proud watching Shawn being a great dad. He and his brother, Shane, were always our boys' favorite babysitters. Even as a young man, he always loved kids and had time to play with them. Shawn's letter is further evidence of my belief that he is one of the real "thinkers" who passed through my classrooms. That thoughtful approach to being a parent shows that he'll do a great job as a dad, because he's always seeking information that will make him better!

But the answer to his question is, "*No!*" I rarely if ever stopped to give my sons much instruction while they were at my team practices; they weren't old enough and really weren't interested.

I must say, however, that the biggest instruction my sons got at that period in their lives was from the young athletes on my teams! Our boys were very fortunate to have them to look up to and emulate. While visiting practices, our sons learned a work ethic, teamwork, sportsmanship, and character! As my players worked on their skills, some little eyes were watching and a couple of young brains were soaking up lots of good ideas about how to conduct themselves. They were learning how hard they would have to work in order to be athletes when they grew up. They were learning what it meant to be a member of a team.

They watched the high school athletes work in practice and never had illusions that they could be good at sports without tons of hard work, sweat, and determination. Even today our sons have a clear picture that to accomplish anything they have to work hard like they saw those kids doing every day. Those *athletes* were the teachers our kids had when they visited practice.

Here is a true story. On the day Drew was drafted #1 by the New England Patriots, Chris Berman was interviewing him for ESPN. Chris had done some homework and found out that my friend Shorty Bennett and I had run the All Northwest Football Camp for years. In his research, Chris found out that many NFL players came to our camp as guest instructors. He mentioned a few of the more prominent names—pros like Fred Biletnikoff, Jim Plunkett, Jim Zorn, Steve Largent, Kenny Easley, Clint Didier, Ronny Lott, Warren Moon, and others. Then he asked Drew, "With all of those NFL players in your dad's football camp, I'll bet some of those stars were your heroes."

Drew's answer kind of shocked Chris. (I must say that it kind of surprised me, too!) Drew said, "Well, what I learned from those famous players was that NFL players are just regular people. However, Chris, if I'm really honest, my heroes when I was growing up were Shawn Woods, Ricky Dunn, and Mark and Blaine Bennett! Those guys were the quarterbacks on my dad's football teams when I was growing up. I wanted to be like them!"

While your kids are in their formative early years, don't worry too much about teaching specific skills. Just make sure that they have heroes they can see up-close and look up to, just like my sons looked up to my young players. And you don't have to be a coach to ensure that your kids have young role models to follow. Visit practices, meet high school athletes in your community, and let your kids meet them. Do volunteer work at your local high school and take your kids along, just to make sure your kids see the conduct of committed young people a little older than they are.

Heroes All Around You

Kids need heroes to emulate, and the world of sports is a common place to find them. As your children grow up, be sure to guide them in selecting heroes to admire in all areas. If you leave it to chance, the television and mass media will select heroes for them. The outside world will teach your kids to worship people who are famous, notorious, and wealthy. Those characteristics may not exclude someone from being a worthy role model, but they shouldn't be the only standards your kids use to select their heroes.

Make it a policy for your children to spend time around Girl Scouts and Boy Scouts. Go to your local high school and find out from the coaches who are the gymnasts, volleyball players, soccer players, swimmers, and athletes who are really all-around great kids. Find out the names of high school students who have leadership qualities and are involved in music and the arts. Take your kids to practices and introduce them to these high school kids.

Build a picture in your children's heads of what they want to be like as they grow up. Help them to see what makes these older kids worthy role models. When you are recruiting older kids to be babysitters for your own children, do some careful research and pick young people that your children can look up to. Pick carefully because those older kids may become their heroes! Then, when your children get to an age where they are beginning to choose behaviors to use in their own lives, they will have some great models already in their head.

Barbara and I are so thankful to the parents of all of those kids who were our sons' heroes. Probably most of those parents had no idea what a gift they were giving to us, but that certainly does not diminish the value of their gift! My heartfelt thanks also go out to all those students and athletes who played such an important role in shaping the lives of our two sons.

Chapter 16

Peer Pressure

"How can we expect our child to behave if none of his playmates are required to do so?"

This gets at the core of what we are trying to teach young parents: it is much easier to teach a child of any age to exhibit desired behavior if they are in the company of other kids who have been taught similar behavior. The way that parents can create this atmosphere of appropriate behavior is to meet and talk about the standards they expect of their kids. A Parenting with Dignity class is a great way to make this happen!

To build a community to raise your children, start a parenting class and invite all of the parents of children in your sons' and daughters' preschool to attend. Invite the parents of children in Sunday school. Invite the parents of children from the neighborhood. Invite the parents of at-risk families identified by the welfare office. Reach out to the whole community of parents. Remember that from the age of five, your kids will spend more of their waking hours with other people's children than they'll spend with you!

Do not do this with the agenda of straightening out other parents. Do it for the purpose of getting the parents together to discuss what behaviors you collectively want your children to exhibit as they grow up. It takes a village to raise a child: get involved and build that community! I doubt that any of the parents of the kids in the preschool want their kids coming to school and using phrases describing sexual acts in lurid detail! No parents want to see bullying take over the first grade. Parents universally want their children to grow up as law-abiding citizens. As you go through the course, these topics and many more will come up very naturally and you can collectively come up with strategies for teaching the desired behaviors.

Effectively Conducting a Parenting with Dignity Class

Because peer pressure seems to be such a very common concern among parents, it would be a great topic to stimulate interest in a parenting class. I feel compelled to suggest very strongly that you consider using our curriculum titled Parenting with Dignity. It is on videotape or DVD, and it really lends itself well to a small group of parents like you might draw together from a preschool.

First, remember this fact: *You do not have to be a parenting authority to conduct a class!* Our classes don't require leaders or instructors. They're led by what we call *facilitators*. Our experience all across the country has taught us that, without a doubt, the best facilitators for Parenting with Dignity classes are people who are *not* viewed as experts or authorities!

Way too often, authorities and experts scare parents away. If you share our belief that discussions like the ones we are suggesting based upon this curriculum will create a positive community for your children to grow up in, then you, too, can become a facilitator! You need no special training. The curriculum is set up so that the videotapes conduct the class and the discussions are set up by the assignments that the parents work on in their own families. As a facilitator, you need only provide the location for the class and the television for showing the tapes. Beyond that, the facilitator is simply a member of the group.

A good facilitator usually answers questions with questions like, "I don't know, what do you think?" or "That's a great question. Can anyone use one of the principals from this course to come up with an answer?" Good facilitators share their own parenting frustrations and ask for help from the parents attending.

Getting the Families Involved

The basic steps to getting started aren't complicated. Here are some steps to follow that have proven effective in building meaningful parenting classes and provide an ongoing forum for parents to create a positive community in which to raise their children.

The obvious people to get involved first are the parents of your children's playmates. If you can influence them, it will have a profound effect upon your own family. Just think how much more effective your parenting and guidance will be if your children see it practiced in all the homes they visit! It will be much easier to demand good manners from your own children if every other home they visit has similar expectations expressed in similar ways. Kids only know what they experience. If every home enforces the same standards, then those become the ideas that rule your kid's world. When your children get older, the same will hold true for expectations about drug use, study hours, appropriate behavior, acceptable dating behavior, honesty, respect for others, respect for private property, etc.

Here is a formula for filling a class being used by many people around the country. This formula is very simple, and it works! Hold out your right hand. The thumb on that hand represents you. The four fingers represent the four families you selected to invite in the step above and become the Core Families. All it takes is five or six families to begin your community's first highly successful and life-changing Parenting with Dignity class.

Invite those five or six families to an organizational meeting where you introduce the taped curriculum and give them your pitch on why this learning experience will be beneficial. When planning your pitch, think about the things you've learned in this chapter, and about things that are unique to you and your community: problems or concerns you may have that you'd like your core families to work to resolve, as well as strengths and common values that you've seen among the parents you've gathered that you'd like to see acted upon—and you think they'd like to see, too.

Share with them how much easier it would be for each of your families to teach desired behaviors if all homes had similar standards. Ask the parents you have invited to think about how all of you can create positive peer pressure in the circle of all of your kids by teaching them all some common decision-making skills. Share with them some parts of this book that have worked for you, along with your personal experiences with your children.

Then, together, you and your core families can brainstorm and plan: locations, dates, meals, child care, and so on, so that the class schedule meets the needs of everyone as much as possible. (Food will generally increase everyone's enthusiasm. Have a potluck dinner, or coffee and cookies!)

As an assignment for the first class, make each of your core families (including yours) responsible for inviting at least one "reluctant" or "at-risk" family. We all know one family where a parent has been laid off, a child is in trouble, a divorce is pending, or alcohol or drugs have created a problem. Even if we don't know any families in a true crisis, we all can name a family where the parents never attend a PTA meeting, an open house, or any of their children's activities or events. All across the country, people tell us that they don't know how to get those reluctant families involved. It may surprise you, but a face-to-face invitation from someone who knows them personally *really works!*

Getting Started!

What do you need to get started? It's really very simple. You need a room where all attendees can sit comfortably. As I said earlier, this can be a living room, a school classroom, a room at a church, a library, or a break or conference room at your job. Keep in mind that parents whose children are struggling at school may have negative feelings about a school setting. If you use a room at school, move the desks into circles, or push them together to form a tabletop so parents face one another.

You also will need a TV, a VCR, and copies of the handouts for each person attending. All handouts are in the packet that comes with the tapes or are available in color from our website. These are the *only* absolutely necessary essentials. (Watch the Facilitator's Tape for some ideas for getting the copies of the Parent's Workbook copied off for free.)

Tips for Tearing Down Fences

It's important to recognize this common but mistaken idea in the heads of many parents: "Attending a parenting class is an admission that as a parent I have somehow failed or done something wrong." As facilitators we know this isn't true, but if we don't address it head on, this idea can doom our efforts.

Because of this false assumption, parents will, consciously or unconsciously, put up psychological "fences" to keep out any information that might help them be better parents. You may hear, "We've tried everything," or, "We're too busy," or, "Man, you ought to see our schedule," or, "What will we do with the kids while we're in class?" or, "We don't have problems with our kids, it's the kids they play with who have problems, and we can't do anything about them."

To neutralize those psychological fences and false assumptions, you must plan carefully. What follows aren't necessary steps so much as suggestions to help ensure your success in building and conducting your class. If any of these sound like effective solutions to problems you may encounter, plan ahead and include this information on your initial advertising or invitations. Your core group will be of great assistance to you in this planning. The more people you involve in this process the better it will work.

Ask some of the following questions and be prepared with some suggested answers.

"How do we get the kids dinner on class nights?" Suggest going to your local fast food restaurants and asking them if they would be willing to support your efforts by supplying meals for one night of the nine-week class. Avoid using the word "donation." Ask them to "partner with you" in making your community a better place for kids and families. You'll be amazed at the response you receive! Most of these companies are among the most civic- and charity-minded of all American corporations and will be glad to help—especially if you're asking for their product rather than money.

Once you've enjoyed a burger dinner, a chicken dinner, a taco dinner, and a pizza dinner, go to the more formal restaurants and offer them a chance to compete with the fast-food restaurants by putting on a special dinner of their choosing. Many of these restaurants will be willing to host the banquet and awards ceremony at the conclusion of your course. Many will jump at the chance to show off the difference between their food and what is served by their fast-food competitors. In approaching these companies, be sure to point out that all the attendees at your class will be encouraged to frequent the stores supporting the classes with meals. Show the businesses that you can run the handouts from the packet with their logo on it for free advertising.

"What will we do with the kids while we are at class? We can't afford a babysitter or child care." You have lots of options here. First, go to the home and family life teacher at your local high school and see if extra credit might be possible for students who provide toddler care. Or go to local day-care providers and ask if they would be willing to bring some staff members over to provide care in trade for the opportunity to promote their operation. You will also be providing a real service to parents looking for a day-care provider by letting them try out a few for free! As I said earlier, some people actually move their classes from facility to facility so that parents get to visit several during the course of the nine-week class.

"What do we do with our older kids?" Go to your local Boy Scout, Girl Scout, 4-H, FFA, YMCA, YWCA, and other youth activity leaders and offer them the privilege of coming to a class night and showcasing what they have to offer to the older kids of the parents in your class. Ask them to be prompt and to make their presentations fun and energetic. If you get with it here, you can have a really fun program each night of class, and the kids will be dragging their parents to class. Then set up VCRs and movies, music, games, art supplies, video games, or study areas as your space allows for the kids to use while their parents are attending class.

"How do we get dads involved?" The best way to get other men involved is to have one or two involved in the planning of the class! At least have a dad sign all mailings and have a dad listed as a co-facilitator. Each tape begins with a little 20- or 30-second clip of some football action—make sure the men see that. That's why it's there—to entice dads who might think it's okay to come to a class if it involves the NFL. Once you get them there, they'll keep coming back.

"We've run a class for 10 families—but we're just a drop in the bucket. How do we make this an ongoing program and eventually involve every family in the community?" Here is precisely what you do: In the first five or six weeks of class, your job as the facilitator is to select two families from the class to replace yourself in recruiting for and running the next class. (The people you will select will become obvious to you almost immediately. Generally they will be the most energetic and enthusiastic participants.) Then you court and train them to take over when you are finished. Give them the tapes, and promise that you will be available to help them duplicate the process. One class always produces two more and those two produce four and those four produce eight and so on .... *You don't have to do it all!*

"Are there any other helpful hints?" Yes, there are many, but here are a few quick tips to help you get off to a great start:

Print tickets and put a $10.00 or $20.00 price on them. (Free says it has no value; it may seem silly, but charging money establishes value.) Then if someone balks because of price, you can "scholarship" them, but they are still receiving something of value. The money you raise can be used for beverages, food, or more classes.

To get specific help with individual problems or to become connected to other families in similar situations, just e-mail your problem or question to me at mac@drewbledsoe.com. Most of this book is written around the questions and problems that people have had. Your questions will help not only you but also others!

E-mail me also when you come up with a great idea about something that has worked for you in creating a better class. Share it with the world! That is how most of this program came into being. We can collectively learn from our mistakes and successes. As parents we are all in this together.

Trouble in Sunday School

Dear Mac,

Our son, who is only three, has been reprimanded rather severely by his Sunday school teacher for his overly rambunctious behavior. This is quite startling to us, since he is usually a very reserved child. We have talked with the teacher and she says that a group of boys are feeding off of each other. We feel that it is peer pressure from these other boys that is leading our son to misbehave. We teach him our expectations for his behavior, but when he gets around his playmates at Sunday school he follows them and acts out in a way that is not normal for him.

Is it fair to blame those other kids? We feel that the behavior we have taught our son should be enough for him to know how to behave at Sunday school. He should not just follow those other kids. Do you have any suggestions or input for us?

We have read your book, Parenting with Dignity, *and we agree that "the ideas in our son's head will rule his world" so we are feeling pretty helpless. We have placed the ideas about appropriate behavior in his head, but he is letting the behavior of other children override those ideas we have chosen for him.*

Any help will be greatly appreciated.

Respectfully,
Sunday School Parents

Welcome to the world of peer pressure! It will only become more intense as your child grows older, and it will push toward much more damaging behaviors, unless you begin to act now!

These parents are to be commended for recognizing the power of this force while their son is still very young. If they do not act now, peer pressure can become a very damaging force in their family. However, there is good news. Peer pressure does not need to be a negative force! Peer pressure is only negative when it pushes toward unacceptable or wrong behavior. Peer pressure can be one of the strongest allies for effective parenting if you use it to your advantage!

Just think about the situation in this Sunday school for a moment. This child has been taught appropriate behavior, but is being led astray by children who haven't been. What do you think would be the outcome for this child if all of the other children in the class were taught to behave in a similarly appropriate manner? Wouldn't any child who misbehaves feel the peer pressure to match the behavior of all of the other children in the room? These parents' child would almost certainly have behaved appropriately right along with the others in the class!

You say, "We can't raise everyone else's children! What can we do about the behavior of those other children?" The answer is pretty simple really: Get together with other parents and work out some mutually acceptable behaviors for you all to teach your children.

In today's America we seem to have begun to believe that something like this is somehow a violation of personal rights. It is not! We need to reconstruct the town hall meeting! We must reconstruct the concept that "it takes a village to raise a child." We must stop thinking that the walls of our *house* define the walls of our *home*. In order to create the best possible environment for your children, you must get in contact with other parents and expand the walls of your home to include your whole community—and what will be taught in it!

I am not saying that you must all agree on everything. This is America, after all, and it is not *possible* for everyone to agree on everything! But on most of the big issues there will be little trouble in finding agreement. I have traveled all over America and I have discovered something interesting. If I get groups of families together in any part of the country and ask them to brainstorm for half an hour and come up with the 20 biggest problems that their children will face before they are 21, almost every group will form nearly the same list!

Think about this for just a second as it applies to the simple situation regarding Sunday school behavior. Just imagine for a minute that all of the parents of the kids in that class had met and decided upon Sunday school behavior they would all teach their children. Let's imagine they all taught their children that sitting in chairs was acceptable for all kids in Sunday school. Let's also assume they all taught their children to raise their hands and be called on by the teacher before speaking. If those two simple lessons were taught to each child prior to coming to Sunday school, do you think that Sunday school teacher would have had a problem with rambunctious behavior? Probably not. Why? Because all of the kids would have arrived at Sunday school already knowing how to behave appropriately. Peer pressure would have been working in the parents' (and teacher's) favor!

The point is that we may not agree on everything, but we can sure get a handle on some of the critical issues. It does not need to be a big or drawn-out process. Just one or two meetings to agree upon acceptable behaviors—whether it's daycare, preschool, or Sunday school—will put *positive* peer pressure to work for you!

Making the Right Thing "Cool"

Parenting is so much easier to do when raising your children in a community that's teaching its children the same things! Peer pressure can be one of a family's biggest allies if it is pushing in positive directions.

Let me give you a personal experience to reinforce what I am saying about the power of positive peer pressure. When I was in school, I would not have been caught dead letting anyone see my underwear. I am sure the same was true for all but the youngest of you parents. When I think back, the reason I did not show my underwear at school had nothing to do with anything my parents taught me. I don't ever remember my parents needing to tell me, "Do not let others see your underwear!" I didn't show my underwear because it wasn't *cool!* Yet today I visit schools all across America and underwear is showing everyplace. It's become cool to walk around with your underwear showing over the top of your pants! Does this mean we're powerless against the forces of cool? Absolutely not—but we must understand the concept of cool if we are to be effective in raising our children!

Don't get me wrong, I'm not on a campaign to do away with kids showing their underwear. I find it a little offensive, but that's not important at all! I am attempting to help you understand the forces that work on children. What establishes *cool*, what gives peer pressure its leverage in the minds of kids and adults alike, is when a group of respected people do something!

So what we do about this phenomenon as parents is really quite simple. We sit down together and discuss some of the acceptable behaviors that we are going to collectively teach our children. Let's just imagine that, in a given school, 55 percent of the parents had established that they were going to teach their children that showing underwear was unacceptable. Let's imagine that these families were successful, and their children all showed up with pants pulled up. There are going to be lots of kids in that group who are considered cool, and covering underwear has now become cool.

It becomes so much easier for every parent to enforce something as simple as a dress code if lots of other parents are enforcing a similar standard. Kids will choose to dress in a mutually acceptable manner simply because they can be cool *and* comply at the same time.

I know you're reading this book for help with toddlers, but now is the time to begin building that network! Now is the time to lay the groundwork for the future! Start meeting with the parents of the kids your kids spend time with and come to some agreement on the critical issues that you deem to be most important in the raising of your children. Then as we look into the future with these same children 10 years from now, it's a pretty hopeful picture!

It will be so much easier for your son to get out of a car when someone decides to smoke marijuana if four other kids get out with him. It is even easier if those who get out are considered *cool*. You get to that picture if you have laid the groundwork in the years leading up to that event.

By working collectively and cooperatively, parents can build that kind of a community to raise their children.

When Values Differ

I have one final note before leaving this idea of building a community to raise your children. It does work. It works very effectively, but every once in a while you will find your family at odds with something that the rest of the community has chosen to teach. I could use lots of examples here, and you could probably think of some yourself, but there is one that comes directly from my personal experience.

When we lived in Walla Walla, Washington, we ran into a rather unique situation. There was a small suburb of Walla Walla (yes, even Walla Walla has suburbs!) that was actually an incorporated city. The little city was known as College Place. Almost all of the residents of this little town were Seventh Day Adventists. There was no requirement that you profess that faith to live there, but many of their city ordinances reflected their faith. From sundown on Friday until sundown on Saturday, there was to be no loud noise, and the town was "dry," meaning that liquor could not be sold in the city limits.

Now the lesson for me came as I taught at Walla Walla High School, because many of the Seventh Day Adventist students went to the public high school. It is hard to draw generalizations about any group of people, but if you asked just about any teacher, they would tell you that the Adventist students were some of the most respectful and hardworking students at our school. They followed the rules and were nice students to have in class because most had been taught to respect authority and so on.

However, there was one small "problem" with the Adventist students. If they were involved in any activities like sports, music, drama, or others offered at our school, they could not participate in any activity scheduled between sundown on Friday and sundown Saturday. That simple guideline of the church presented some difficult situations for many coaches and advisors to various clubs and activities. What was a coach to do if he or she had an Adventist athlete on the team and there was a game scheduled on Friday? Should the athlete be allowed to participate until sunset and then be replaced? Should the athlete be denied the right to turn out, since the majority of the games were on Friday night? What if the team played on Thursday or Saturday? Should a player who had been starting because the Adventist had been unable to play be pulled from the lineup to let a more talented and skilled Adventist to play?

Here is the lesson for you as a parent. At times your family beliefs might go against the norm for your community. It may not be as graphic as what we experienced, but you will at times find that you have a standard for your family that is different from the community as a whole. That is a good thing. Your children can learn that at times we have higher standards in our family than they do in the rest of the community. In those instances, you must be careful to teach your children the *reason* your family is taking a stand! It can be a great lesson for your children in personal freedom, but choosing to be different and not explaining why will only breed contempt and resentment in your children.

It takes a village to raise a child, but that does not mean that you must be exactly like everyone else. It means that in most cases you will go along with the community standards, and if you as a family choose to be different from the norm, then you must carefully teach your children the reasons why!

Chapter 17
Yelling at Kids

My husband an I have found ourselves caught in the trap of yelling at our kids and now we cannot get them to respond to anything but shouted commands, what can we do?

These parents have taught their kids well! Now they need to teach them something different to replace the negative behavior they taught them.

Without a doubt, yelling does teach kids.

- Yelling at kids teaches them to yell back.
- Yelling at kids teaches them to yell at others.
- Yelling at kids teaches them to ignore adults who speak to them in respectful and dignified tones.
- Yelling at kids teaches them that they are not worthy of being spoken to in civil tones.
- Yelling at kids teaches them that a reasonable way to relieve stress is to yell at others.
- Yelling at kids teaches them that people do not mean what they say until they yell.

The point is, yelling at kids teaches them a great deal, but it rarely, if ever, teaches them anything of much value. I do not think yelling indelibly scars kids or does them irreparable psychological damage, *but it certainly does* not *help them learn productive ways of interacting with the world.* I guess you could say I'm opposed to yelling at kids for the same reason I'm opposed to punishment: *It doesn't work!*

A child who is yelled at on a regular basis simply learns that he doesn't have to listen to instructions delivered in a quiet and dignified voice.

Fact: Teaching Does Not Require Intent!

Remember hearing that? Chapter 2? We adults are teaching children every minute we're with them! Even though we may have no intention to teach nor any idea about what we want to teach, they are learning from us just the same. Kids learn to talk at their own pace and, other than a little vocabulary work, they do so with little intent on our part. They learn verb tenses and sentence construction, usually from parents who couldn't possibly teach an English class! The point is that kids learn many things from us without us intending to teach them.

Kids in France speak French. Kids in Japan speak Japanese. However, take the French girl and raise her in the Japanese home and she would speak Japanese! Raise the Japanese kid in the French home and he would speak French. Raise both kids in my home and they would each speak English. The ability to learn language may be genetic; all normal human beings speak; but the *specific language* they speak is *learned!* Kids learn the language that they are exposed to.

Not only do kids learn the spoken language they are exposed to, they also learn to interpret and use nonverbal communication as well. They learn what a civil tone of voice means. They learn what words like "please" and "thank you" mean. If parents rarely speak in a conversational tone and never enforce anything said in that conversational tone, their children learn that adults rarely mean what they say in a conversational tone.

Kids who hear yelling all the time accept yelling as normal. Think about it, in a kid's life, three-fourths of the words they hear in their first five years are spoken by their parents. If yelled commands are the norm, they'll react just as naturally as kids in France react to French. In time, they'll learn that yelled commands can also be ignored, a dynamic I witness in many homes.

If It Isn't Yelled, It's Ignored

In working on a segment for ABC's *20/20* program, I found a couple with a son who didn't seem to obey commands or requests from his parents. I watched videotapes from a week in their home and noticed an amazing thing. A conversational "young man ..." never got his attention. "Joe!" did little to interrupt his play. "Joseph!" was equally ineffective. But when his parents said "Joseph Alex!" in a loud yell, his head turned, he listened to what they said, and he usually complied!

Why? Because they had taught him that when they shouted his full first and middle name, they finally meant business, and he knew that they would enforce the following command, so he complied. Joseph Alex had learned exactly what his mom and dad had taught him, *even though they did not intend to teach that to him.*

It was pretty simple to restructure effective communication in that family. All the parents had to do was duplicate the actions they had used after their shouted request, only now they had to do it with their *first* request—a civil and polite request for "Joseph Alex" to do something. Say it civilly and politely ... but enforce it.

Parents' Action

What these parents did was first explain to Joe that things had changed in their family. "From now on, Joseph, we will give all of our instructions to you in a conversational tone of voice and we will precede all requests with a 'please.' When we make requests, we will expect you to comply immediately or to ask a question if you do not understand."

Once they had given their instructions to Joseph, they asked him to repeat the instructions back to them. This ensured that he had heard what was said and understood what was being asked of him. Joseph had such a habit of ignoring requests that he actually did not hear them. As a matter of fact, these parents discovered that standing directly in front of Joseph and asking him to look at them was very effective in getting Joseph to listen carefully to what they were saying.

Then the parents would simply say, "Now, I am going to stand here and watch you get started." Over the next week, they were careful not to ask Joseph to do something unless they were willing to stay right there with him to ensure that he did precisely as they asked.

They made no threats about what they would do if Joseph did not immediately comply. They made no statements like, "If you don't get busy, I'm going to send you to your room!" When you make those kinds of threatening statements, you always get caught up in arguments or disputes.

These parents would just stand there until their child started to do what was asked. When he would stall, they would ask him, "Joseph, can you tell us why you are not doing what we asked?"

Normally he could provide no answer, but if he said something like, "I am doing something else," they would simply say, "Joseph, remember what we said. We expect you to do what we ask on the first request, so please get started right now."

It didn't take long before Joseph was willingly obeying dignified and respectful commands. *His parents had taught him a new language!* The first step lay in restructuring their own actions and taking control of what they were teaching their son. Wow! They all felt much more calm and less stressed.

Maintaining Dignity for Both Parent and Child

This brings us to another important reason why yelling at kids is highly ineffective. *Yelling destroys the dignity of both the parent and the child.* Kids can learn to respond to calm directions just as easily as they can learn to respond to yelling. When parents yell at kids, the stress level goes up for everyone, but no one more than the parent. I learned this while teaching.

One day while I was teaching at Walla Walla High School, I had had a particularly tough day. I was being angry and loud with students and was feeling stressed out by my ineffective interaction. The kids were probably okay with it—they had "learned the language" of that guy who yells during third period! My own stress level, however, was near the breaking point.

In my frustration, I sought out the counsel of Lola Whitner, a master teacher who taught in the room next to mine. I said, "Lola, how do you do it? You are 65 years old, a perfect lady, barely five feet tall. You speak to kids in a respectful, conversational tone, and yet the same students I feel compelled to yell at are so quiet and respectful with you. Help me. I must learn what you do!"

Very quietly she replied, "You have quite a temper, Mac." Then she chuckled, "I can hear you through the walls! However, I have one question for you. Can you ever control your temper? Can you ever speak quietly and respectfully to your students?"

"Well, yes, sometimes I can control my temper," I replied. "But often I just blow up."

"Well, Mac," she replied very calmly, "if you control your temper some of the time, then you *can* control it. Now that we've established that you *are capable* of controlling your temper, I'll point out that when you do *not*, it's a choice! *Why don't you choose to control your temper all of the time?*"

Her simple question changed my life. I finally realized that *my* actions were *my* choice! I never again yelled in anger at a class. I chose to be different and I was. The biggest change was my feeling of control and power over my life. From then on, I preserved my dignity and the dignity of my students by choosing not to yell. I chose to speak in a civil, dignified, respectful manner. My students rapidly learned that even though I was not yelling, I still meant what I was saying. My classroom became a respectful, dignified, and relaxed place—just like Lola's!

The Solution!

I was recently asked what would be my short-term solution for parents who found themselves yelling at their kids. I don't have one. I don't put much stock in short-term solutions to life-long problems. Lola did not propose a short-term solution to my problem, and her solution lasted my whole life.

The solution to the problem of yelling at kids lies in changing your manner of speaking to children forever. The long-term, life-changing solution does not involve going into a room and shouting, or hitting a punching bag. The solution does not lie in counting to 10 or leaving the room. The solution lies in deciding to be different—today, tomorrow, and forever.

Decide to be calm, dignified, and respectful, and anticipate the situations or circumstances where you will be tempted to yell. The situations are predictable—I'll bet you can think of five right now that recur regularly! Identify those times and then develop a specific plan of action for those situations. Actually practice the words you will say and the manner in which you will say them.

Commit to a plan of action for how you will act *before* the triggering situation arises. When it does, follow your plan. Feel the calm self-control that wafts over you. This plan will bring dignity and peace to a family.

The Situation

Let's say a recurring situation that causes you to yell is when you ask your kids to help set the table for dinner. It drives you crazy the way they ignore your requests for help! So you resort to yelling. Maybe they help and maybe they don't, but everybody's stressed out again at dinner—and of course, the long-term result is little if any change in their behavior. Dinner will be just the same tomorrow.

Wouldn't you like to create a plan to change this situation forever?

The Plan

Rather than standing in the kitchen and yelling (as you may have previously done), go to where your kids are. Relax, put on a smile, and say respectfully, "I need your help. Would you please get up and come set the table? Look at me kids. I'm smiling, I'm speaking in a polite tone of voice, and I even said 'please,' but I really mean it!"

If they don't immediately move, put yourself squarely in front of them and—again, politely, in the same calm tone—say, "Excuse me, but what did I just ask you to do?" Keep your sense of humor! You may have to point out that you expect an answer because they're in the mode of ignoring you, but stay right in front of them and wait. When they repeat what you said, say, "Okay, you know what to do. I'm just going to wait right here until you start, so, please, let's get going." All of this is said in a pleasant, respectful tone.

Do be patient. It may take weeks for this new approach to take hold if the kids have had years of ignoring your conversational statements and only responding when you yell at them. It will take time to learn the new language you are speaking!

All too often, parents look for quick fixes, gimmicks, or tricks to use with their kids, when what really works is to make simple and fundamental changes in their own ways of thinking and acting.

Some Key Questions

Now before we leave this topic of yelling at kids, I would like to ask the same question I asked about hitting of anyone who is choosing to yell at a child.

On what basis have you decided that you are justified in yelling at your kids?

- Is it justifiable to yell at your kids because you are older?
- Is it justifiable to yell at your kids because you are bigger?
- Is it justifiable to yell at your kids because you are the parent?
- Is it justifiable to yell at your kids because you are more experienced?

Again, it seems to me that all of these would constitute reasons for you to *not* yell at your kids!

Is there any justification for yelling at a child? Yes, I'll grant you that it's justifiable to yell at a kid if he's running toward the street and a truck is coming, or if she's reaching for a boiling pan of water on the stove. Short of an emergency, though, is there any reasonable justification for yelling at children? If not, then why not adopt the previous ideas and learn how to stop it?

Let me just say that I know there are millions of well-adjusted adults that were yelled at as kids. I would simply say that they became well-adjusted adults *in spite of* the yelling, not because of it. Don't ever use the old fallacy, "It was done to me, therefore it's justifiable to do to my kids!"

Do what works. Yelling simply doesn't work very well. Having a plan for dignity and civility works. Use it! You are the first and most influential teacher your toddler will ever have. Take that responsibility and teach!

Chapter 18
Potty Training

"Our daughter is at the age where other people's kids are beginning to use the toilet and she shows little interest in doing likewise. She seems to be aware of her need to go but refuses to use the toilet."

I have a message for *all* parents in a similar situation. *Don't panic!* Unless your child has been diagnosed with a bowel, bladder, or nerve disorder, this will eventually take care of itself.

But let's take a closer look at exactly what we mean by potty training. Simply put, potty training means teaching your toddler to gain control of their bladder and bowel movements, making them in a toilet or small potty. You may choose to teach your children to use a "potty" because it is easier for them to use than a toilet. What you choose is irrelevant. What I am talking about here is simply teaching your child to manage their toilet hygiene independently.

Before we start, it might serve you well to approach potty training the same way you taught eating with a spoon. You put the spoon in front of the child, gave a few pointers, and let it be. Gradually a child will begin to use the spoon. They see you eating with utensils and they imitate. They find that utensils help to eat with a minimum of mess. They learn to do this in a very natural way, free from stress. Make potty training similarly matter of fact and stress-free, and I *guarantee* you'll have success! (I just can't guarantee when.)

What Does Potty Training Involve?

Little kids are used to relieving themselves whenever they feel the urge. Since they were born, they've been breathing, eating, and eliminating waste as naturally and spontaneously as their heart beats. In time, your child becomes aware of the world around him or her, and one change is that they become conscious of these bodily functions.

> Statistics show that girls often are ready to potty train a little before boys, but there is no scientific way to establish when your child will be ready.

The first thing that happens when you begin toilet training involves teaching your child to recognize the feeling of needing to go to the toilet! Of course, children will begin to recognize that feeling on their own. Your job is to help them learn what to *do* about that feeling.

The next step involves teaching them to let you know they have to "go," so that you can help them to remove the clothes and get on the toilet or potty.

Finally, you teach your children to control their functions until they can get to a potty or toilet. Now, let me remind you, this is a *gradual* process. Don't make the mistake of viewing potty training as nothing more than learning bowel and bladder control. You must consider the control of these bodily functions in the context of the child's perception.

I don't wish to make this a bigger topic than it is, but your success in teaching this process will be much more natural if you and your child view it in connection with all of the dynamics surrounding it. For very young children it is rather universally surmised that just "letting go" is pretty rewarding. The urge presents itself as mild tension or discomfort, then after releasing it there is immediate relief. It's understandable that a child might be reluctant to give up that instant gratification. Add the fact that once the diaper is wet or soiled the child gets some very grati-fying one-on-one interaction from Mom or Dad, and it becomes even more understandable that the child will not want to give up that guar-anteed way of getting attention!

Finally, as your child rapidly progresses, you will be teaching them the steps of actually using the toilet by themselves.

There is really very little mystery to this process, and most of the time it progresses rather naturally. The more naturally you handle it, the more naturally your kids will handle it! Believe me when I say that your children sense your attitudes and feelings without you having to tell them!

When Should I Start Potty Training?

Children develop awareness and control over their bodies' functions at different rates. Every child is different, and you should only begin potty training when *your* child is ready.

Just look at the different sizes and shapes of children and realize that no two are alike! There are as many different times for kids to learn to use the toilet as there are different colors of hair. I think this is a great way to visualize this issue. You would never try to change your child's hair color to be like every other child's, and likewise you should only begin potty training when your child is ready, not when the neighbor child or when your nephew began.

Most children are ready to *start* using the toilet some time between eighteen months and two and a half years, but the age when they start and the age when they actually finish can vary widely. One mistake I see young parents make is that they read a parent manual, learn that most kids *begin* toilet training by eighteen to twenty-four months, and jump to the conclusion that their child should *finish* in that time! Toilet training can take weeks for some kids and months for others. There is no right or wrong timeframe. Each child will progress at his or her own pace.

By the age of three, nearly all children are able to control their bladder and bowels during the day. Staying dry at night may come at the same time, but it is common for children to reach the age of six before they are completely dry every night. Some children do not achieve nighttime control until their teen years!

How Will I Know When My Child Is Ready?

It is important not to rush your child. Do not be deluded into thinking you can push them into potty training merely because of their age, or because a playmate is trained, or because your child care agency or Aunt Susie feels the child should be trained by now! Pressure to get trained before the child is ready will often lead to problems later.

Let the child's natural signs guide you. Kids will give you some pretty reliable signs that they're ready! Here are some signs that your child might be getting ready to *begin* to be potty trained:

- Your child begins to mention and use names for bodily functions when they happen, such as, "I peed!" or "I pooped!" (Remember, your children will use whatever words they've heard you using! Pick the terms you want them to use and use them regularly.)

- Your child sometimes "holds" him or herself, indicating that they're aware of something happening. It won't happen every time, but when you see this, make it a point to ask about it, talk about it, and start teaching them to notice those feelings and learn what to do about them.

- Your child indicates the feeling of needing to "go," but when you check the diaper, there is nothing there.

- Your child shows signs of "holding it," at least for a short period. They seem to indicate the need to "go" by moving about, holding themselves, or wiggling, but then they move on to other things and the diaper remains clean.

- Your child begins to complain about dirty or wet diapers. (Not the same as when a three-week-old baby cries when the diaper has been filled.)

- Your child begins to hide behind furniture or go into another room when they feel the urge. Be on the lookout for your child behind a chair with a strained look on his face!

After you start noticing a few of these signals, it's time to actually start the training process!

Basic Training!

Up until now, these body functions have happened spontaneously. Children "go" whenever they feel the need. Now, you are going to teach them to control that urge, then let go as a conscious action.

The first step for potty training lies in selecting your plan of action. The first change regarding your child's potty training behavior, therefore, takes place in you!

It's important to recognize that diaper-changing has been a time of close and happy interaction between you and your child. As you begin to teach your child to control the need to use the toilet, it is important that you insure that your child is getting lots of reassuring one-on-one time at times other than diaper-changing. From my reading and experience with parents during the training process, most children who resist "potty training" feel insecure in their ability to gain attention from their parents at other times. Many of these children will hold onto diapers as a means of commanding attention. It's the one sure way to get Mom or Dad to stop and pay attention to them!

As a parent you can make sure your child doesn't get caught up in this dynamic by providing surefire ways to give your child your one-on-one attention. This is a wonderful time to use Rule #5 and send your child a constant message of love. Go to our list of ways to communicate love to children in Chapter 1, and make sure to send a minimum of two to three of these massages to your young one every day. (I think you ought to be doing this all the time, but this is a critical time to be sure to do it!)

Next, you can make giving up the diaper and using the toilet a more natural transition by gradually making diaper-changing less fun and more matter-of-fact. When children are very young, it is desirable and smart to make diaper-changing a fun time of interaction. Most times parents wisely have toys on the changing table, and they talk and sing to their children during this clean-up process. As your child starts potty training, gradually make diaper-changing an all-business affair, with less and less playing, singing, and conversation. "Slam, bam, you're done!"

Be sure to note that I am *in no way* indicating that you should make changing the diaper into a punishment or a negative experience! All I am saying is to make diaper-changing less social and more matter-of-fact. Think about it: if having a wet diaper ensures that you will sing and play with your child, then it's only natural that the child will not want to give that up. On the other hand, if your child can predictably get your attention in other ways, and diaper-changing has become a quick 1-2-3, it is only natural that your child will be more willing to learn to use the toilet and give up the unpleasant feeling of a messy or wet diaper.

Along the same line of thinking, it will help if using the toilet becomes a fun little celebration. I have come across many parents who made using the toilet or potty a time of battle, anger, and conflict and are shocked that their children didn't seem interested.

Once you see some of the signs mentioned previously, role-play with your child the act of using the toilet or potty. Kids learn many of their behaviors by first observing others, so you may want to have them observe you or their older siblings while they use the toilet. Boys should watch boys and girls should watch girls, for the obvious reason that boys and girls go to the bathroom differently, and kids need the appropriate model for their behavior.

This doesn't have to be completely exclusive, however. As a matter of fact, this is a very natural time to teach your kids that boys and girls are different. If you are a single mom with sons, or a single dad with daughters, don't feel inadequate! Just try to occasionally let your children see someone of their gender going to the bathroom. Ask a grandmother or grandfather, an uncle or an aunt.

If you need to buy a "potty," you may find it helpful to take your toddler with you to choose their favorite one. They come in all shapes and sizes, and it just might make it more fun to use a Nemo or Spider-Man chair. Some people claim more success with a potty that plays music when it gets peed in! I'm not sure I buy that, but do whatever works for you and your child! I don't think that gimmicks like that are necessary, but at times they make things easier. Most of the time, I feel that needing gimmicks might indicate that you're starting too early.

A week or so after noticing some of the signs and consciously beginning the training process, you can start encouraging your toddler to sit on the potty whenever they show signs of wanting to go. Explain to your toddler that the potty is his or her own toilet and keep it within easy access. Over the next few weeks, help your child get comfortable with the potty, for example, by letting them sit on it without their diaper while watching television, looking at books, or hearing a story. Continue to remind them what the chair is for.

Here is a process that has helped some parents. Begin having your child sit on their potty or the toilet about 20 minutes after meals. This is a time when they may naturally feel the urge to go. Take off the diaper and encourage your child to sit on the potty and try to go. If they can't or won't go, occupy them for a short time with a story. If they don't go after about five minutes, have them get up off the potty and watch for signs later. Always give your child lots of praise for their effort in sitting on the potty. (Your child is likely to learn to urinate in the potty first; bowel movements require a little more control.)

Building Good Habits

Once your child is able to communicate when they need to go and has had some success, he can begin to wear training pants, wearing diapers only for sleep. For some kids, wearing "big-boy" or "big-girl" pants can be a significant reward, a rite of passage indicating that they are becoming grown up.

One of the main causes of difficulties in the potty training process is trying to force the training too early. If some of the signs are there, but the child is having no success at all, then it's probably best to stop trying to use the potty for a month or two. There is *no hurry!*

There may be times, even after using the potty successfully for a while, when your toddler may require a diaper. During times of unusual excitement or extended active play, some children will have accidents. Just clean up and move on just like you would have done with a diaper. Spanking and other forms of punishment will just associate the process of controlling their bodily functions with stress and tension. Parents who try to use punishment in the training process most often experience difficulty. Although mistakes may be frustrating, it is vital that you keep praising and encouraging their efforts, helping them to understand that success normally follows practice.

Pressuring your child to go almost never works. It is quite common for a child to become uncooperative or turn using the potty into a battle of wills. This becomes more likely if your child senses that you are anxious or frustrated about the process. If you find yourself in this situation, you need to relax your own tensions before you attempt to teach again.

Potty training can be a very instructive time for you as a parent, because it will affirm very clearly that you ultimately cannot control your children! As I have said many times, children are born with a will! "Teaching them" means teaching them *to choose* to act in a desired manner. Once they start choosing to go in the toilet, it will be liberating and rewarding to the child, but the key word here is *choose!* Do not let it become a battle of wills.

This may take a great deal of patience on your part, and it may seem like your child is getting her way when she defies you by not using the toilet. However, gradually and naturally, your child will become uncomfortable with dirty diapers and will grow to enjoy the freedom and convenience of using the toilet and getting to dress without diapers.

Many times, simply being in the company of playmates who are using the toilet will provide the motivation to use the toilet. When your children are with other kids, it will be totally unnecessary for you to point out what the other children are doing. They're watching each other all the time! You do not need to make comparisons like, "See, Billy and Suzy are using the toilet and are not wearing diapers." If your children are old enough to understand the comparison, they're old enough to make it for themselves. Children are very imitative in their behaviors.

Finally, one of the most important things for children to learn at the time of potty training is hygiene. Washing hands following use of the toilet ought to be the healthy partner of teaching children to wipe themselves. This is critical instruction for health and disease-prevention.

When You Need Extra Help

Patience, understanding, and a lot of positive reinforcement will help you resolve almost all difficulties with potty training. However, if your child is over age three to three and a half and has been trying to use the potty for more than six months without much success, it is advisable to see your pediatrician, to exclude possible medical causes and get further advice. I suggest that you discuss the problem with your doctor first either over the phone or in a separate visit, to appraise the doctor of the difficulty and the techniques that you have used. Be completely honest, because the problem could very well be you. Once you have had this discussion with your doctor, it is probably time to take the child in for an examination to rule out physical or medical problems.

Also see your doctor if your child develops constipation during the training period. In this situation, your doctor will examine your child to rule out medical causes and may then recommend a "regular bowel program" to get the bowels moving again. You should never wait if this type of problem shows up, because it can become chronic.

In summary, the most important part of most successful potty training is the relaxed attitude and well-defined plan of the parents!

Pressure Creates More Problems

Dear Mac,

Our two and a half-year-old son Billy is giving us fits. He seems ready to start using the toilet but he refuses our repeated urgings to do so. We have two older children and they both learned with no hassles, so we don't think the problem is our technique. He is aware of filling or wetting his diaper because he demands to have it changed, but he will go and stand behind a chair and look right at us and then tell us his diaper is wet.

He is openly defying us and he knows it. We have scolded him for doing this but he just keeps on doing it. We have even tried giving him time-out for wetting his diaper but that has only made him more determined to defy us!

We don't want to be the only parents in the preschool next year with a child still in diapers. What are we to do?

Sincerely,
Pottied-out Parents

You wouldn't believe it if you saw how many letters I receive that are almost identical to this one, from parents with similar stories of frustration. If this sounds like you, you have lots of company and your situation is not rare. But that's not much help, is it?

The first part of this situation that needs to change is the attitude of the parents! Potty training is a great learning experience that will teach parents a ton and serve you well in the future of raising your child. Relax, pay attention, and learn from what you are going through.

First, you are being taught, very graphically, that your children will make *all* of the big decisions in their lives. You are not in control, the children are. Children are born with a will—these parents even said it themselves: "That has only seemed to make him more determined to defy us!"

They need to change *their* outlook on teaching *anything* to their child. Ultimately you are teaching your child to make choices. Your child has the power to choose to never use a toilet and you are powerless to make him do anything different! The key is to get him to see that using the toilet is really a benefit to *him*.

Parents' Action

My first advice is to make sure that your child gets sufficient attention at other times during his day. If he has older siblings, he may feel that the one time he gets you to himself is when he has a dirty diaper! Begin the process of potty training by giving him lots of good one-on-one time with each parent. Play with him at a time when his siblings are not involved. No, this isn't bribing him or spoiling him; in fact, you shouldn't consciously connect this attention to using the toilet at all. Just help your child be secure in his ability to get your positive attention. Go to Rule #5 and pick two ways to communicate your love for your son every day. Then do it with a plan.

Next, make diaper-changing a quick process. Do not make it a punishment, but make it something more businesslike, an everyday action to do and be done with.

Next, *relax!* Children can sense when you are tense and uptight with this process. Relax and let them guide you about when they are ready. This young man already knows when he is ready to go—he goes behind the chair and does it. He is pretty obviously sensing his parents' stress, so he, too, is stressed by it.

Most children who have a difficult time potty training are simply mirroring the worry and stress of the parents. Relax and let it happen at its own pace! If you need help putting this in perspective, just ask yourself to name someone you know over age 10 who still has to wear diapers. Can't think of anyone? That ought to reassure you that things will work out.

Index

involvement, 223
materials, 221
psychological fences, 221
starting, 217, 220
tickets, 223
sports, 210
clothes. *See* getting dressed
communities
differing values, 228-229
parenting classes. *See* parenting
classes
positive peer pressure, 226-228
consequences of punishments, 100-101
core families of parenting classes, 219
criticizing
performances, 10, 13
positive statements of expected
behavior, 7, 10
crying at bedtime, 56-60
alerts, 58
flashlights, 62-63
paying attention, 61
physical contact, 60
positive anticipation, 58
routines, 59
cuss words, 136-137

D

defining love, 28
desired behaviors, teaching, 36-37, 50-51
diagnosing learning disabilities, 167-169
differing values, 228-229
dining. *See* mealtimes
disabilities (learning), 157-158
ADD, 159-164
assigning tasks, 170
diagnosis, 167-169
meaningful connections, 166
medication, 165-166
planning, 170-172
turning into strengths, 164-165
dressing. *See* getting dressed

E

eating problems, 79
eating disorders, 91
healthy diets, 80-82
mealtime behaviors, 92-94
picky eaters, 88-91
quantities of food, 82-83, 89-90
undesirable foods, 83-88
elderly people, 150-153
ending criticism with positive statements
of expected behavior, 7, 10
enforcing punishments, 99
equality of siblings, 74-76
exposure
languages, 134-136
sports, 209
extended families, 180-181

F

facial expressions, 138-140
fairness with siblings, 76-77
family interferences, 141
aging grandparents, 150-153
bad habits, 143-144
learning from relatives, 154
pushy parents
independent thinkers, 146-150
screaming, 144-146
fighting with siblings, 72-74
Five Rules for Parents, 5-7
criticizing performances, 10-13
ending criticism with positive statements of expected behavior, 7, 10
repetition, 13-14
self-motivation, 15-17
sending messages of love, 17-18
being positive, 27-28
defining, 28
listening, 25-26
looking, 24
making it, 21-23

M–N–O

P–Q

T–U–V

talent (athletic), 211-213
teaching
appropriate language, 132-133
    exposure, 134-136
    facial expressions, 138-140
    media influences, 130-132
    swearing, 136-137
    tone of voice, 138-140
desired behaviors, 36-37, 50-51
healthy diets, 80-82
love, 29
manners
    appropriate language. *See* appropriate language
    mealtime, 119-123
    funerals/solemn occasions, 123-125
    grandparents, 120-121
    please/thank you, 126-127
respect, 196-197
sex education
    24/7 relationship, 176
    accurate information, 188
    age-appropriate answers, 179-180
    body awareness, 184-188
    extended families, 180-181
    names of body parts, 177
    playgrounds, 181-184
    private conversations, 188
    questions, 177
    relationship education, 178
sharing
    identification, 200-202
    siblings, 202-206
watching parents, 37-43
without intent, 32-35, 232
thank you (teaching), 126-127

tone of voice, 138-140
touching children, 26
transitioning to potty training, 244

undesirable foods, 83-88

values, 228-229

W–X–Y–Z

"What's It Like To Have ADD?," 159-164
"When you thought I wasn't looking" letter, 34-35
wrinkled clothing, 115-117
writing love messages, 19-21

yelling at kids, 231
    destroying dignity, 234-235
    ignoring requests, 233-234
    justification, 238
    self-questions, 237
    solution, 236-237
    teaching without intent, 232